The COUNSELOR and the LAW

A Guide to Legal and Ethical Practice

FIFTH EDITION

Anne Marie "Nancy" Wheeler, JD
and
Burt Bertram, EdD

AMERICAN COUNSELING ASSOCIATION
5999 Stevenson Avenue
Alexandria, VA 22304
www.counseling.org

The COUNSELOR and the LAW
A Guide to Legal and Ethical Practice

FIFTH EDITION

10 9 8 7 6 5 4 3

AMERICAN COUNSELING ASSOCIATION
5999 Stevenson Avenue • Alexandria, VA 22304

DIRECTOR OF PUBLICATIONS • Carolyn C. Baker

PRODUCTION MANAGER • Bonny E. Gaston

COPY EDITOR • Lucy W. Blanton

EDITORIAL ASSISTANT • Catherine A. Brumley

Cover and text design by Bonny E. Gaston.

LIBRARY OF CONGRESS CATALOGING-IN-PUBLICATION DATA
Wheeler, Anne Marie, 1954–
The counselor and the law: a guide to legal and ethical practice/Anne Marie "Nancy" Wheeler and Burt Bertram.—5th ed.
   p. cm.
Rev. ed. of : The counselor and the law/by Barbara S. Anderson. 4th ed. 1996.
   Includes bibliographical references.
   ISBN-13: 978-1-55620-276-6 (alk. paper)
   1. Counseling—Law and legislation—United States.   2. Counselors—Legal status, laws, etc.—United States.   3. Counselors—Malpractice—United States.   I. Bertram, Burt.   II. Anderson, Barbara S., 1952-Counselor and the law.   III. Title.
   KF2910.P75W48   2007
   344.7303´106—dc22   2007014936

DEDICATION

We dedicate this book to our clients and students—teachers each and all.

Contents

Preface   xi
About the Authors   xiii

Chapter 1
THE COUNSELING PROFESSION   1
    Our Perspective   1
    The Counselor   3
        History and Highlights of the Profession   3
        Professional Counselors   4
        Licensed Professional Counselors   4
    The Law   5
    The Practice of Licensed Professional Counseling   6
        Licensing Standards for Counselors   7
            Virginia   7
            Florida   7
            Arizona   8
            Illinois   8
            New York   9
        National Standards for Counselors   9

Chapter 2
THE COUNSELING RELATIONSHIP   11
    Duty and Standard of Care   11
    Who Is a Client?   13
    Informed Consent for Treatment   14
    Fees   18
    Terminating the Counseling Relationship   20
        Client-Initiated Termination   20
        Counselor-Initiated Termination   21

Chapter 3
OVERVIEW OF LAW AND ETHICS   25
    The American Legal Structure   25

Contents

Criminal, Civil, and Administrative Law 26
The Court System 27
    Federal Courts 27
    State Courts 27
    Appellate Process 27
Ethical Standards 28
Ethics and the Law 29

Chapter 4
CIVIL MALPRACTICE LIABILITY AND
LICENSURE BOARD COMPLAINTS **31**
    Competence and Preparation 31
    Duty of Care and Potential Civil Liability/Malpractice 33
        Negligence 33
        Malpractice 34
        Intentional Torts 35
        Criminal Action 36
    Common Complaints Against Counselors 36
        Licensure Board Complaints 37
        Diagnosis and Scope of Treatment 39
        Failure to Treat or Refer 42
        Group Counseling 44
        Crisis Intervention 45
        Repressed or False Memory 46
        Supervision 48
        Birth Control and Abortion Counseling 49
        Sexual Misconduct 50
    Other Civil Actions 51
        Illegal Search and Seizure 51
        Defamation 54
        Invasion of Privacy 56
        Breach of Contract 58
        Copyright Infringement 58
        Insurance Fraud 60
    Other Criminal Actions 61
        Accessory to a Crime 61
        Contributing to the Delinquency of a Minor 62
    Risk Management 63

Chapter 5
CONFIDENTIALITY, PRIVILEGE, AND HIPAA PRIVACY **65**
    Confidentiality 65
    Privileged Communication 66
    Privacy and HIPAA 68
    Specific Concerns Regarding Confidentiality, Privilege,
      and Privacy 71
        Subpoenas 71
        Counseling Minors 72

Confidentiality of Substance Abuse Records 74
Group and Family Counseling 74
Counseling Public Offenders 75
Confidentiality After a Client's Death 75
Confidentiality and Technology 76
Limits of Confidentiality, Privilege, and Privacy 76

Chapter 6
DUTIES TO REPORT, WARN, AND/OR PROTECT 77
Child and Elder/Vulnerable Adult Abuse Reporting 77
Domestic Violence 78
Duty to Report Clients' Past Crimes 79
Duty to Report Unprofessional Conduct of Colleagues 79
Duty to Warn and/or Protect 80
Court Decisions Following *Tarasoff* 81
Law Continues to Evolve 83
Clients With AIDS/HIV+ Status: Duty to Warn or Report? 84
Duty to Warn: Practical Risk Management Guidelines 85

Chapter 7
SUICIDE AND THREATS OF HARM TO SELF 87
Prevalence of Suicide and Threats of Harm to Self 87
Youth and Child Suicide 88
College Student Suicide 88
Elder Person Suicide 89
Male Suicide 89
Other Threats of Self-Harm 89
Ethical Issues of Suicide 90
Legal Issues of Suicide 91
End-of-Life Issues 94
Final Thoughts 94

Chapter 8
PROFESSIONAL BOUNDARIES 97
Role Boundary Issues 97
Dual or Multiple Role Boundaries 100
The Risk of Licensing Board Complaints 102
Reports of State Disciplinary Action 103
Texas 103
Arizona 104
Ohio 105
Maryland 107
The Risk of Malpractice Lawsuits 107
Mishandling of Transference 108
ACA Insurance Trust 109
The Risk of Criminal Prosecution 110
Summary 112

Chapter 9
RECORDS AND DOCUMENTATION   **115**
  Records Are the Standard of Care   115
  The Purpose of Client Records   117
    Client Records Purpose #1: Clinical Management   118
    Client Records Purpose #2: Legal Implications
      for the Client   119
    Client Records Purpose #3: HIPAA Compliance   120
    Client Records Purpose #4: Risk Management
      Strategy   122
  Ownership of Records   123
  Alteration of Records   123
  Financial Records and Financial Relationship   124
  Technology and Client Records/Information   124
  Record Retention   125
  Records Custodian   126
  Summary   127

Chapter 10
MANAGING YOUR COUNSELING PRACTICE   **129**
  Forms of Operation   129
    Nonprofit Organizations   129
    For-Profit Entities   130
      Corporation   130
      S Corporation   131
      Partnership   131
      LLC or LLP   131
    Operating Instruments and Organizational Meetings   132
    Office-Sharing and Informal Group Practices   132
  Business Procedures   133
  Federal and State Taxes, Reporting, and Licensing   134
  Professional Liability Insurance   134
    Considerations When Purchasing Liability Insurance   135
    Do You Need Professional Liability Insurance?   136
  Other Insurance Coverage   137
    General Liability Insurance   137
    Property Insurance   138
    Directors' and Officers' (D&O) Liability Insurance   138
    Fidelity Bonds   138
    Business Overhead Insurance   139
    Employee Benefits Programs   139
    Disability Income Protection   139
    Group Life Insurance   140
  Employment Law Considerations   140
    Employment Discrimination   140
    State Nondiscrimination Statutes   142
    Sexual Harassment   142
    Recruiting, Hiring, and Managing Employees   142
    Employment Contracts   143

Contents

Training and Supervising Employees 145
Hiring Workers as Independent Contractors vs. Employees 147
Billing and Collection Practices 148
Third-Party Payments 149
Access to Facilities: The Americans With Disabilities Act 150
    Who Is Covered? 150
    Public Accommodations 151
    State and Local Government Entities 152
New Counseling Approaches, Techniques, and
   Professional Expressions 153
    Three New Counseling-Related Approaches 154
      Coaching 155
      Technology-Assisted Counseling 155
      Forensic Evaluation 156
  Summary 157

REFERENCES 159

Appendix A
ACA Code of Ethics 165

Appendix B
BUILDING AND MAINTAINING A SUCCESSFUL
SUPERVISION RELATIONSHIP 205

Appendix C
TOP TEN RISK MANAGEMENT STRATEGIES 209

Appendix D
HOW TO ACCESS LAWS AND FIND A LOCAL ATTORNEY 211

PREFACE

This book has an interesting heritage. Originally written by Thomas Burgum and Scott Anderson and published in 1975, *The Counselor and the Law* reflected the counseling profession before state licensure—and before the proliferation of state and federal laws that, over the past 30 years, have shaped the conduct of the practice of counseling. Since the first publication there have been three updates. In 1985, attorneys Bruce Hopkins and Barbara S. Anderson collaborated to update the original manuscript; then in 1990, Hopkins and Anderson released the third edition. Finally in 1996, Barbara Anderson (without Hopkins) completed the fourth edition. We are grateful to all the past authors for providing a foundation upon which we could construct this completely updated and significantly expanded fifth edition of *The Counselor and the Law*. We also want to thank Carolyn Baker, ACA Director of Publications, for her patience and guidance in the development of this manuscript.

The authorship of this new edition of *The Counselor and the Law: A Guide to Legal and Ethical Practice* reflects the collaboration of a practicing counselor and a practicing attorney. We believe the combined perspective of the two of us (the counselor and the lawyer) provides a unique understanding of the law as it relates to the day-to-day practice of counseling. As you read this book, you are likely to hear two distinct voices and perspectives. Nancy Wheeler will offer the lawyer's perspective: She will tell you about the law and how it affects counseling practice. Burt Bertram's voice will reflect an insider's perspective: He will talk about the gray areas of practice that don't always fit neatly in a black and white world. Together we will offer advice and suggestions designed to help practicing counselors and students understand and navigate the complexities of real world practice.

In this book we seek to connect the realities of the practice of counseling with state and federal laws and with the 2005 *ACA Code of Ethics*. It is our hope that this book will serve to provide real answers to practicing counselors who are challenged daily to act in the best interests of their clients and at the same time to be mindful of the legal and ethical duties and responsibilities that govern the profession of counseling. We also hope this book will be a window of understanding for students as they attempt to imagine and prepare for professional practice. Of course we did not, nor could we, address every situation. Laws vary from state to state, and the specifics of any particular situation can influence how state or federal laws or the *ACA Code of Ethics* will apply. Additionally, this book is not intended as a substitute for the considered opinion and advice of your personal lawyer concerning the particular circumstances of a case in the context of local laws and customs.

Anne Marie "Nancy" Wheeler
Silver Spring, MD

Burt Bertram
Orlando, FL

ABOUT THE AUTHORS

Anne Marie "Nancy" Wheeler, JD, is licensed to practice law in Maryland and the District of Columbia; she has extensive knowledge and experience with counselors and the broader field of mental health. For the past 20 years, she has managed the American Counseling Association Insurance Trust Risk Management Helpline. On a daily basis, she helps practicing counselors think through and understand challenging legal and ethical issues. She is the editor of ACA's *Legal and Regulatory Compliance: Updates for Counselors, Mental Health Professionals, and Counselor Educators.* For over 25 years, she has worked with psychiatrists, facilities, and physician associations. This background gives her a unique window of understanding about the multifaceted issues that often confront practicing counselors. She is also an affiliate faculty member of the CACREP-accredited Graduate Pastoral Counseling Program of Loyola College in Maryland. Since the early 1990s, she and coauthor Bertram have together developed and copresented the seminar Legal Aspects of Counseling more than 100 times across the country. They have also produced several tapes and CDs on risk management strategies.

Burt Bertram, EdD, is a Florida Licensed Mental Health Counselor (LMHC) and Licensed Marriage and Family Therapist (LMFT). He has been in practice in the Orlando area for over 30 years. He practices from an interpersonal perspective; therefore, his professional counseling is primarily focused on the resolution of sensitive and complex interpersonal issues. He also has an organization consulting practice focused on group work including the facilitation of group planning, goal setting, and conflict resolution. Additionally, he is an adjunct faculty member in the CACREP-accredited Graduate Studies in Counseling Program at Rollins College in Winter Park, Florida, where he teaches ethics as well as practicum; internship; family, couples, and group counseling; and consultation. Since the early 1990s, he and coauthor Wheeler have together developed and copresented the seminar titled Legal Aspects of Counseling more than 100 times across the country. They have also produced several tapes and CDs on risk management strategies.

Chapter 1

THE
COUNSELING PROFESSION

The practice of counseling and the profession of counseling have evolved into maturity. In this chapter we provide an introduction to some of the legal responsibilities and accountabilities that have come with the maturing of the profession. Most notably we focus on the influence of state counselor licensing laws that have dramatically affected the activities of both licensed and unlicensed professional counselors.

OUR PERSPECTIVE

We understand that, for many practicing mental health professionals and most graduate students, the legal system is a foreign and sometimes frightening place. It is filled with adversarial relationships and governed by rules that are unfamiliar and unfriendly. We want to begin with a word of encouragement. No one knows how often counselors actually engage in unprofessional, unethical, or illegal practice-related behaviors. However, the relative infrequency of censure by ethics committee, licensing board discipline, lawsuit, or criminal arrest when compared to the estimated 250,000-plus practicing counselors in America suggests that formal accusations of questionable behaviors are rare. In our experience, even when there is an accusation against a mental health professional, things often turn out in the favor of the practitioner.

We would be remiss, however, in not stating the obvious: Counselors and other mental health professionals sometimes do engage in behaviors that result in harm to the very people, our clients, we are in practice to serve. Many of these harmful behaviors come down to the counselor's failure to know, understand, or abide by the various state and federal laws that govern the practice of counseling. In this book, we are not recommending a rule-bound defensive practice wherein practitioners are fearful and innovation and creativity are stifled. On the contrary, the core message of this book is simple: We believe that counselors who are mindful and respectful of ethics and the law can develop practices that are creative, thoughtful, passionate, and always in the best interest of the client.

Over the past 20-plus years of working with or following legal cases in which the behavior of a counselor has resulted in harm to a client, we have concluded that offending practitioners seem to fall into one of three broad categories:

- *Intentional disregard:* There are offending practitioners who are intentionally opportunistic, abusive, exploitive, and self-serving in their dealings with their clients. These individuals are not interested in knowing, understanding, or abiding by the law. The best interest of the client is not their primary concern. Such harmful practitioners are not likely to read this book except as it may be required in a graduate course or perhaps as part of a licensing board disciplinary process. We can only hope that all such practitioners will either withdraw from the profession or have a life-altering transformational experience such that they forever leave behind their abusive, self-serving values and behaviors.
- *Careless disregard:* There are offending practitioners who operate along a continuum ranging from innocently unaware to lazy/careless. In their hearts, these practitioners may want to do what is best for their clients. But because they have not taken the time to study and understand the law, it's easy for client interactions to cross legal and ethical boundaries that would have sounded an alarm to a more knowledgeable and mindful practitioner. For these practitioners, the harm done to a client is unintentional, but the damage is real. Reading this book can be an important step toward becoming actively mindful (no longer innocently unaware, lazy, or careless) of the implications for clients of the laws and the ethics that govern our profession.
- *Wrong place, wrong time:* Finally, there are offending practitioners who know and understand legal and ethical mandates and are actively committed to abiding by them, yet still become involved in a client-related situation in which a client is harmed (or alleges harm). As mental health professionals, we sometimes tell our clients that bad things can happen to good people. The same is true for good counselors. Sometimes bad things happen to good counselors—harmful things that simply could not have been foreseen or prevented. It is our hope that this book can help fortify the vast majority of practicing counselors so that if in the unlikely event you are in the wrong place at the wrong time, you will have a depth of knowledge and understanding about the law that will empower you to get help for your client and for yourself before things spin out of control.

It is our hope that this book will serve as a guide to practitioners who are committed to the development of counseling practices that are ethical, legal, and always in the best interest of the client.

The title of this book, *The Counselor and the Law: A Guide to Legal and Ethical Practice,* seems straightforward, but actually the definitions of *counselor* and *law* can be fraught with confusion. Before we move into the specifics, we are first going to define these essential terms so we all know who and what we are talking about.

The Counselor

It seems obvious: counselors provide counseling. And while that's true, it's not that simple. The label *counselor* in our culture is so generic that it almost defies an objective definition in terms of identifying a specific professional endeavor. There are insurance counselors, camp counselors, funeral counselors, and a hundred others, created simply by placing a descriptive noun in front of the word *counselor.* For purposes of this book, the counselor is a practitioner, educated and trained at the graduate level, who is a member of the counseling profession.

History and Highlights of the Profession

What is the profession of counseling? Counseling as a profession, separate and distinct from its sibling and first-cousin professions, is relatively new. The genealogy of counseling is well documented. Gladding (1996), Kottler (2004), Neukrug (2007), and others have ably documented the story of how counseling as a profession has struggled during the past five decades to emerge, separate and distinct from psychiatry, psychology, social work, philosophy, education, and career guidance. Today the counseling field has developed all the characteristics necessary to qualify as a full and mature profession. More than 50 years ago, the American Personnel and Guidance Association (the original name of the American Counseling Association) was established. During the past 50 years, ACA has provided the leadership and the energy to create the profession of counseling. Notable accomplishments include

- *ethics*—creating and regularly updating a *Code of Ethics* (most recently revised in 2005), a process for obtaining opinions on ethical issues, and a process for filing a complaint against a professional member alleging ethical misconduct;
- *interest divisions*—creating and supporting specialized interest areas (divisions) within ACA in which professional members can affiliate, learn, and share ideas with others of similar professional interest;
- *professional development*—convening an annual national professional development convention as well as a host of other regional and state professional development meetings, conferences, publications, and activities;

- *training standards*—sponsoring efforts that resulted in the establishment of the Council for Accreditation of Counseling and Related Educational Programs (CACREP), the organization that defines the standards for training of graduate-level counselors and monitors the implementation of these standards;
- *national certification*—initially sponsoring and advocating the National Board of Certified Counselors, the organization that has established a nationally recognized certification credential that attests to a baseline of general counselor knowledge as well as to specialty credentials in school counseling, mental health counseling, and addictions counseling;
- *state licensing*—together with other professional associations and groups, leading the state-by-state struggle to license professional counselors.

Professional Counselors

The efforts and activities just outlined combined to form the infrastructure of what we now know as the *professional counselor*. It is estimated there are at least 250,000 professional counselors in America, more than 150,000 of whom are unlicensed professional counselors employed in schools, community agencies, and nonprofit organizations as well as health care and treatment facilities. Most professional counselor positions outside of private practice do not require state licensing. Many employed counselors in agencies, schools, government, and nonprofit organizations are licensed and/or are actively seeking licensure. Some professional counselors such as school counselors or addictions counselors may require specialization certification. Most of the information in this book is relevant to all professional counselors (licensed, certified, and unlicensed), to graduate students in counselor educational programs, and to the broader field of counseling-related professionals including counseling psychologists, psychologists, social workers, marriage and family therapists, pastoral counselors, career counselors, psychiatrists, and others. All of these professionals share a common activity: They all engage in a form of the practice of counseling.

Licensed Professional Counselors

The struggle for licensure began in the early 1970s; the first success came in 1976, when the state of Virginia licensed professional counselors. Today 48 states plus the District of Columbia and Puerto Rico have licensed the title and/or practice activities of professional counselors. Efforts continue to secure professional counselor licensing in Nevada and California. (California does have a marriage, family, and child counselor license but not a professional counselor or mental health counselor license.) Nationwide, in 2005, more than 100,000 professional counselors were licensed or were in the process of becoming licensed or registered counselors (ACA , 2007). Typically, a licensed professional counselor is identified as a

- Licensed Professional Counselor (LPC),
- Licensed Clinical Professional Counselor (LCPC),
- Licensed Mental Health Counselor (LMHC),
- Licensed Clinical Mental Health Counselor (LCMHC).

The operative word in each of these titles is *licensed*, and the story of how counselors came to be licensed is largely the story of how the activity of counseling came to be recognized as a separate and distinct professional endeavor.

The Law

We have now arrived at the intersection between the counselor and the law. The purpose of this book is to empower professional counselors (licensed and unlicensed) to understand and thereby respond in a thoughtful and ethical manner to the laws that affect the day-in-and-day-out practice of counseling. In order to do this, two things are necessary. First, we want to be clear what we mean by *law*, and second, we want to provide some detail regarding how state laws/statutes have influenced the legal definition of the practice of professional counseling, regardless of the practice setting.

The word *law*, like the word *counselor*, is also confusing, especially to nonlawyers (and who could be less lawyer-like than many counselors?). For purposes of this book, we define *law* as a set of rules, enacted by a legislative body, that governs a particular activity within society. Laws are everywhere, governing nearly everything. Laws, also called statutes, derive from elected officials who are members of federal, state, or local legislative (lawmaking) bodies. Such bodies include the United States Congress, state legislatures, and municipal (city, town, and county) councils and/or commissions.

As professional counselors and as citizens or residents of the United States, we are all affected by laws that address every aspect of our lives, from whom we can marry, to how we drive our cars, to the proper treatment of children, to the taxes we pay. It's probably safe to say that no one really knows all the laws that affect our every waking moment. However, for counselors, there are some laws that are critical to our functioning. Some of those that directly affect the practice of counseling include

- federal laws that have a direct bearing on counselors and the practice of counseling, such as HIPAA (Health Insurance Portability and Accountability Act of 1996), the Americans With Disabilities Act of 1990, the Family Educational Rights and Privacy Act of 1974 (FERPA, or the Buckley Amendment), and the USA Patriot Act of 2001;

- state laws/statutes, such as counselor licensure laws, the rules developed by state licensing boards to implement the law and regulate the day-to-day practice activities of licensed and nonlicensed professional counselors, and state abuse reporting laws (child and vulnerable adult);
- local laws, including municipal laws that affect when and where counseling can occur, such as zoning and occupational licensing laws.

Additionally, there is a body of law that derives from the common law that has developed over hundreds of years and began in England. Common law emphasizes precedent set by cases in which judges make decisions. This is distinct from statutory law, which is created by a legislature, not a judge (see chapter 3 for a complete discussion). The *Tarasoff* case (noted in chapter 6) is an example of how common law changed clinical counseling and mental health practices across the country to permit or require the therapist to breach confidentiality when a client poses a serious risk of harm to a third party.

THE PRACTICE OF
LICENSED PROFESSIONAL COUNSELING

In many ways, for all the laudable efforts by academics and members of the various professional associations to define and legitimize the practice of counseling, nothing has moved the profession of counseling along faster than the emergence of state licensing of professional counselors. To be fair, it's extremely doubtful that any state would have passed licensing statutes were it not for the relentless efforts of leaders within the professional associations. Yet, only legislative bodies can create laws; and many would argue that laws were what we needed in order to finish the task of defining ourselves and differentiating the work we do from similar services provided by other counseling-related professions.

Much of what we talk about in the pages that follow rests on a clear and operational definition of the practice of counseling. The practice of counseling has been defined and redefined for decades. However, in recent years, as the licensing of professional counselors has spread across the country, the struggle to define the practice of counseling has moved from an academic discussion to a legislative and statutory reality. While academics struggle on, state legislatures have enacted "practice act" counselor licensing statutes that include very specific definitions of the practice of counseling. These state statutory definitions have become the driving force that determines, from a legal perspective, what professional counseling is and what professional counselors can do within the law.

As important as state licensing of counseling has been to the legitimizing of professional counseling, it came with a heavy price. Every state that developed and passed a law regulating the practice of counseling created a unique definition of the practice of counseling. National consensus, supported by law, of the activities associated with professional counseling remains elusive. Therefore, when we talk about the counselor and the law, it is critical for you to keep in mind that definitions vary state by state. We make general statements and give examples, but we always caution you to consult the most recent counselor licensing law and supporting rules applicable in your state.

Licensing Standards for Counselors

To gain an appreciation for the state-by-state journey toward licensing, we are presenting the definitions of professional counseling developed by five different state legislatures. We begin with Virginia (originally licensed in 1976), followed by Florida (licensed in 1981), Arizona (1988), Illinois (1993), and finally New York (2002).

Note that even a casual reading of these five examples clearly illustrates the range of similarities and differences that constitute the practice of counseling as well as the range of definition (content and specificity) of what constitutes the permitted practice activities of the licensed professional. Remember always that the devil is in the details and that licensed practitioners in each state must be careful to determine what is or is not permitted. Is there, for example, language in your state's definition of the practice of counseling that permits the rendering of an independent mental health diagnosis (such that the practitioner can submit an insurance claim on her or his own authority)? Or that permits the professional counselor to conduct psychological tests or assessments?

Virginia. Virginia enacted the first counselor licensure law in 1976. Virginia's current law is a Practice Act. (A Practice Act defines the activities associated with the practice of counseling.) The Virginia law provides the following definition of counseling and the practice of counseling.

> Counseling means the therapeutic process of: (i) conducting assessments and diagnoses for the purpose of establishing treatment goals and objectives and (ii) planning, implementing, and evaluating treatment plans using treatment interventions to facilitate human development and to identify and remediate mental, emotional, or behavioral disorders and associated distresses which interfere with mental health.
>
> Practice of counseling means rendering or offering to render to individuals, groups, organizations, or the general public any service involving the application of principles, methods, or procedures of the counseling profession, which shall include appraisal, counseling, and referral activities. (Va. Code Ann. § 54.1–3500, 2006)

Florida. Florida originally passed a Title Act in 1981. (Title Acts only define the titles practitioners can use to identify themselves.) Several years later the law was amended to become a Practice Act. Florida provides the following definition of the practice of mental health counseling:

The practice of mental health counseling is defined as the use of scientific and applied behavioral science theories, methods, and techniques for the purpose of describing, preventing, and treating undesired behavior and enhancing mental health and human development and is based on the person-in-situation perspectives derived from research and theory in personality, family, group, and organizational dynamics and development, career planning, cultural diversity, human growth and development, human sexuality, normal and abnormal behavior, psychopathology, psychotherapy, and rehabilitation. The practice of mental health counseling includes methods of a psychological nature used to evaluate, assess, diagnose, and treat emotional and mental dysfunctions or disorders (whether cognitive, affective, or behavioral), behavioral disorders, interpersonal relationships, sexual dysfunction, alcoholism, and substance abuse. The practice of mental health counseling includes, but is not limited to, psychotherapy, hypnotherapy, and sex therapy. The practice of mental health counseling also includes counseling, behavior modification, consultation, client-centered advocacy, crisis intervention, and the provision of needed information and education to clients, when using methods of a psychological nature to evaluate, assess, diagnose, treat, and prevent emotional and mental disorders and dysfunctions (whether cognitive, affective, or behavioral), behavioral disorders, sexual dysfunction, alcoholism, or substance abuse. The practice of mental health counseling may also include clinical research into more effective psychotherapeutic modalities for the treatment and prevention of such conditions. (Fla. Stat. § 491.003, 2006)

Arizona. Arizona implemented a Practice Act in 1988, using the title Licensed Professional Counselor. The law provides the following definition of the practice of professional counseling:

Practice of professional counseling means the professional application of mental health, psychological, and human development theories, principles, and techniques to:

(a) Facilitate human development and adjustment throughout the human life span.
(b) Assess and facilitate career development.
(c) Treat interpersonal relationship issues and nervous, mental, and emotional disorders that are cognitive, affective, or behavioral.
(d) Manage symptoms of mental illness.
(e) Assess, appraise, evaluate, diagnose, and treat individuals, couples, families, and groups through the use of psychotherapy.

(Ariz. Rev. Stat. § 32–3251, 2006)

Illinois. Illinois implemented a Practice Act in 1993 defining a two-tiered approach that includes Licensed Clinical Professional Counselor (qualifies for independent private practice) and Licensed Professional Counselor (practitioners not licensed for independent private practice). Illinois defined the practice of clinical professional counseling in the following manner:

Clinical professional counseling means the provision of professional counseling and mental health services, which includes, but is not limited to, the application of clinical counseling theory and techniques to prevent and alleviate mental and emotional disorders and psychopathology and to promote optimal mental health, rehabilitation, treatment, testing, assessment, and evaluation. It also includes clinical counseling and psychotherapy in a professional relationship to assist individuals, couples, families, groups, and organizations to alleviate emotional disorders, to understand conscious and unconscious motivation, to resolve emotional, relationship, and attitudinal conflicts, and to modify behaviors that interfere with effective emotional, social, adaptive, and intellectual functioning. (225 Ill. Comp. Stat. 107/10, 2006)

New York. New York only recently (2002) was successful in obtaining licensure for professional counselors. Professional counselors in New York are titled as Mental Health Counselors. In New York, the practice of mental health counseling is defined as

a. the evaluation, assessment, amelioration, treatment, modification, or adjustment to a disability, problem, or disorder of behavior, character, development, emotion, personality, or relationships by the use of verbal or behavioral methods with individuals, couples, families, or groups in private practice, group, or organized settings; and

b. the use of assessment instruments and mental health counseling and psychotherapy to identify, evaluate, and treat dysfunctions and disorders for purposes of providing appropriate mental health counseling services. (N.Y. Educ. Law § 8402, 2006)

National Standards for Counselors

Currently there are no recognized or accepted national licensing standards for counselors. There are, however, national practitioner certifications, national accreditation standards for graduate programs in counselor education, and momentum toward the creation of a process that will facilitate *licensure portability* (the ability, once licensed by one state, to have that license recognized in another state).

The National Board for Certified Counselors (NBCC) developed the National Counselor Exam (NCE) to

assess knowledge, skills, and abilities viewed as important for providing effective counseling services. The NCE is designed to be general in nature. It is intended to assess cognitive knowledge which should be known by all counselors regardless of their individual professional specialties. Satisfactory performance on the NCE is one of the criteria used by NBCC to identify professionals who may be eligible to become a National Certified Counselor (NCC). (NBCC, 2007a)

NBCC also has developed five specialty credentials:

- Certified Clinical Mental Health Counselor (CCMHC),
- Master Addictions Counselor (MAC),
- National Certified Career Counselor (NCCC),
- National Certified Gerontological Counselor (NCGC),
- National Certified School Counselor (NCSC).

Currently there are over 40,000 NBCC-credentialed counselors (NBCC 2007c). The process of establishing national standards for the accreditation of counselor education programs has been greatly enhanced by the Council for Accreditation of Counseling and Related Educational Programs (CACREP). CACREP is dedicated to (1) encouraging and promoting the continuing development and improvement of preparation programs, and (2) preparing counseling and related professionals to provide service consistent with the ideal of optimal human development (CACREP, 2007b). Currently there are 52 accredited doctoral (PhD or EdD) programs and nearly 500 accredited master's level programs encompassing 10 different programs of study (CACREP, 2007a). Some counselor education departments have several accredited programs of study. Accreditation of graduate counselor education programs has been a significant step toward establishing recognized national standards of scholarship, coursework, practicum, and internship experience for the training of master's and doctoral level counselors. The program accreditation efforts of CACREP have helped the counseling profession address one of the most significant obstacles to counselor licensing portability: agreement on appropriate coursework, length of field experience (practicum and internship), and the minimum number of graduate credits to be recognized as a legitimate program of study. Many counselor education programs are not yet CACREP-accredited; others are somewhere in the accreditation process. National standards for counselor education preparation are a prerequisite for counselor licensing portability.

The issue of the recognition and portability of counselor licensing among states represents a critical next step in the evolution of the counseling profession. The American Association of State Counseling Boards (AASCB) is an alliance of state licensing board agencies throughout the United States that "collects, interprets, and disseminates information on legal and regulatory matters, and works to further cooperation among individuals and associations involved in providing counseling services to the public" (AASCB, 2006). As this book goes to press, AASCB has initiated a collaborative effort with ACA and other leading counseling-related organizations to begin addressing the issue of licensure portability. Counselor license portability rests on reconciling differences in graduate training, postdegree clinical supervision experience, the definition of the practice of counseling, the criteria for independent private practice, and other critical issues.

The good news is that we have come a long way in the past 50 years. We have fought the good fight and as a result have legitimized and codified (by law) our professional activities. We are no longer just well-intentioned people who set out to be helpful. Imbedded in the good news of our professional status is the fact that we are now legally held to defined duties as well as standards of practice. In the pages that follow, we address the laws and statutes that define the practice of counseling as well as discuss the relationship of these laws to the evolving ethics and standards of practice of our profession.

Chapter 2

THE
COUNSELING RELATIONSHIP

It's all about the relationship! For counseling practitioners, nothing is more important than the counseling relationship. Regardless of your preferred theory of counseling, the common denominator that cuts across all perspectives is the primacy of the counseling relationship. The same can be said when we think about the legal implications of the practice of counseling: The counseling relationship remains the central concept. We want to encourage you to combine a legal perspective of the counseling relationship with your existing clinical understanding. Together they form the foundation of competent professional practice. The legal perspective needn't be a burden nor should it invite you to practice defensively or to view the counseling relationship as having an adversarial element. In fact, we hope you will see how knowledge, understanding, and adherence to the law will only serve to support and strengthen the counseling relationship.

DUTY AND STANDARD OF CARE

A legal perspective on the counseling relationship begins with the concept of *duty*. Duty means there is a legal obligation to act in the best interest of the client, to use a *standard of care* that is consistent with the degree of learning, skill, and ethics ordinarily possessed and expected by reputable counselors practicing under similar circumstances. Duty is based on the recognition that as professional counselors, we have a *fiduciary relationship* with our clients. A fiduciary relationship is one in which a person claims to act in the best interests of another, and the other accepts that trust. As counselors, we promise our clients that we will act in their best interests; we ask for their trust, and in so doing we intentionally create the professional relationship that is core to our work. We then have an ethical and legal duty to fulfill that trust. The standard of care is the yardstick against which your profes-

> *Duty* is a legal obligation to act in the best interest of the client.

sional behavior will be evaluated. So you might ask, What exactly is this standard of care and how can I be sure I am fulfilling my duty?

The standard of care is an ever-evolving and ever-rising concept that is formed through a combination of influences:

> *Standard of care* is a level of care that is consistent with the degree of learning, skill, and ethics ordinarily possessed and expected by reputable counselors practicing under similar circumstances.

- *Education:* Graduate-level course work common to all practicing counselors grounds practitioners in theory and basic skills.
- *Ethics:* Ethics codes from the primary professional associations help practitioners determine behaviors and practices that are in the best interest of the client as well as those that are deemed harmful.
- *State laws:* Laws define the practice of counseling (or other mental health disciplines) and further describe specific professional activities that are sanctioned.
- *Credentials:* Specialty credentials provide specific guidance regarding best practices and advanced skills for certain issues.
- *Research:* Clinical research identifies best practices for presenting issues or concerns.
- *Policies:* Institutional, agency, or organizational policies and procedures shape all types of professional conduct.
- *Case law:* Opinions from courts interpret or expand the concept of duty (see chapter 4).
- *Third-party payers:* Increasingly third-party payers (insurance, managed care, etc.) are influencing the standard of care by determining clinical activities that will and will not be reimbursed.
- *Real-world practice:* Actions and behaviors of practicing professionals engaged in the day-to-day practice of counseling in the real world also influence the standard of practice.

As professional counselors we also have *contractual* duties arising from our relationship with clients. A contract is a legal relationship, written or oral, created by an agreement between the parties. In a counseling relationship, this contractual relationship is generally expressly stated; however, the relationship may be implied. Typically, the client completes the informed consent process and documentation and agrees to a fee for the professional service (fee-for-service private practice, insurance/managed care copayment, or agency sliding scale fee) regularly attends sessions in the counselor's office, and pays the agreed-upon fee. It is also possible for a contract to be implied based on the circumstances of the relationship between the parties, even though no fees may be charged.

We need to be mindful of the difference between well-intended helpful and supportive behaviors with another person (acquaintance, friend, or colleague) versus behaviors that cross a boundary and can be misunderstood as providing a professional service. The difficulty arises when the other person believes there is an implied contractual professional relationship (even though the other person may not express it this way), and therefore, the other person comes to expect your behavior to reflect your professional duty. Practitioners are understandably anxious regarding this type of scenario and sometimes overreact and try to avoid any situation in which their caring could be mistaken for a professional relationship.

We are *not* recommending that you stop being a friend or caring for others. Our guidance in this regard is to encourage you to recognize the limits of being helpful and supportive, to be willing to make a referral, and to encourage the other person to act on the referral rather than rely on you. It is important to know at what point the fiduciary and contractual obligations come into existence; that is, simply stated, when does an individual become a client?

WHO IS A CLIENT?

The simple and safe answer to this question is, "Anyone who seeks advice or counseling." It's probably safe to assume that once a person (or family or couple) begins interacting with a mental health professional (in person and in some cases on the phone or electronically over the Internet), a professional relationship has been established. Thoughtful experts often advise practitioners to institute a screening or assessment session before the establishment of a treatment relationship, if possible. We agree. In a perfect world counselors should have the opportunity to determine, through a review of intake information and an initial interview, if they have the requisite competence (education, training, experience, and/or supervision) and legal authority to properly render treatment and, therefore, incur a duty. However, in the real world, unless we clearly inform clients otherwise, they are likely to assume the counseling relationship has begun as soon as there is interaction. Therefore, it is prudent, whenever you are in your professional role, to meet the standards and fulfill your duty whenever you are interacting with a person who is or may become a client. You may, after the initial contact with the client, determine that you do not have the competence or legal authority to provide treatment to that person and therefore want to decline care and provide a referral. You may even decide you do not wish to provide treatment based on other variables (you lack adequate time in your schedule, the presenting problem is outside your scope of practice/interest, or even that you just don't click with the client). Just remember that from the other person's perspective, (s)he is a client until you clearly communicate that you are declining a counseling relationship.

Access the *ACA Code of Ethics* online at http://www.counseling.org or refer to Appendix A in this book.

If you decline to provide care, you have a duty to provide the person with sound information regarding alternatives and referrals.

INFORMED CONSENT FOR TREATMENT

The informed consent for treatment has ethical (ACA, 2005a, Standard A.2.a.), legal, and clinical implications. The intent of an informed consent document is to define the basic counseling relationship between counselor and client. Misunderstanding and disappointment, which are often the genesis of a liability claim and/or licensure board complaint, can be reduced when clients are made knowledgeable of the ground rules of the counseling relationship. The therapeutic relationship is enhanced when clients understand what is expected or required to have a successful counseling relationship. Toward that end, the informed consent for treatment, sometimes referred to as a fact sheet or disclosure statement, is a powerful clinical and legal tool. Typically, the consent for treatment is both verbal and written (ACA, 2005a, Standard A.2.a.), but the underlying assumption is that consent is informed—meaning that the client fully understands the *rules* of the counseling relationship. The quality of the client's understanding can be significantly compromised by many factors including age, education, and physical or developmental capabilities. Cultural differences can also distort the client's understanding. Therefore, although we assume counselors will provide this information in writing, it is important to remain open to alternative means of communication (verbal, interpreter, translator, or some combination). The critical variable is to do everything that is reasonable to ensure that the client really understands what he or she is consenting to for him- or herself or for his or her child. In many states, consent must be obtained from a parent or guardian for a client who is a minor or for an adult who is incompetent to provide consent.

The content of the informed consent form is influenced by agency or institutional policies, state licensing laws and rules, HIPAA requirements, and other binding directives. When developing an informed consent for agency or private practice, the following checklist may be helpful. It is important to keep in mind that not all categories are appropriate for every practice setting.

1. *Voluntary or involuntary client participation:* What is the motivation for the treatment relationship? Are clients voluntarily participating and, therefore, can terminate without external consequences (courts, schools, employers, etc.)? Alternatively, is the treatment required such that failure to participate in or complete the treatment could result in negative consequences for the client? These variables should be fully disclosed in the informed consent.

2. *Client and counselor involvement:* What level of involvement and what type of involvement will be expected from the client? What will the counselor provide? How will this be provided? This information helps the client understand what is expected of him or her.

> The critical variable is to do everything that is reasonable to ensure that the client really understands what she or he is consenting to for her- or himself and/or for her or his child.

3. *Emergencies:* What are the procedures for emergencies, including how the counselor can be reached in the event of an emergency?

4. *No guarantees:* The counselor (agency or organization) cannot guarantee results (i.e., the client(s) will become happier, less tense, less depressed, save the relationship/marriage, stop drug use, obtain a good job, etc.). Only promise what you can be sure to deliver. Generally, such promises (if there are any at all) revolve around the counseling process, not the outcome of the process.

5. *Risks associated with counseling:* Define what, if any, risks are associated with the counselor's particular approach to counseling. We are not talking about physical risks (unless, of course such risks are involved in a given approach); rather, we are talking about the risks associated with change and growth. The client's perspective can change, and as a result, important relationships may be affected and essential life priorities may shift.

6. *Confidentiality, privilege, and privacy:* Be specific about how confidential information will be handled by the counselor and how confidentiality will be addressed in couple counseling, family counseling, child/adolescent counseling, and group counseling situations. How may confidential and privileged information be released? (For a complete discussion of these topics, including HIPAA, see chapter 5.)

7. *Exceptions to confidentiality, privilege, and privacy:* Define specific circumstances in which confidentiality and privilege cannot be maintained (i.e., mandatory abuse reporting) and the range of actions the counselor may consider. (For a complete discussion of these topics, see chapter 5.)

8. *Counseling approach or theory:* What is the counseling orientation or theoretical belief system of the counselor or the agency/organization? How will that affect treatment? This is very important if the counselor or agency subscribes to a particular therapeutic modality that will require the client to work within that model.

9. *Counseling and financial records:* What will they include? How long will they be maintained? How will they be destroyed? State law often impacts the answers to these questions.

10. *Ethics guidelines:* What ethics code defines the counselor's practice? How might a client obtain a copy of these guidelines?

11. *Licensing regulations:* What license does the counselor hold? How may a client check on the status of a licensee?

12. *Credentials:* Beyond licensing, what special/advanced credentials, education, training, and/or experience does the counselor or the agency/organization possess?

13. *Fees and charges:* What are the specific fees and charges? How will fees be collected? How are financial records maintained?

14. *Insurance/managed care:* How do you handle managed care? Are you a provider? What responsibility will you (or your office) take for filing insurance forms? How will copayments be handled?

15. *Responsibility for payment:* Who is responsible for payment of counseling charges? How will delinquent accounts be handled? What charges will be assessed for delinquent accounts?

16. *Disputes and complaints:* How will fee or other disputes be resolved? Provide the address and phone number of the state licensing board for complaints if required by the applicable state licensing statute.

17. *Appointment cancellation policy:* How much notice for cancellation of a scheduled appointment is required? What fees, if any, will be charged for late cancellation?

18. *Affiliation relationship:* Describe independent contractor, partnership, or other relationships with any other practitioners in the office suite. (See chapter 10.)

19. *Supervisory relationship:* Describe any required supervisory relationship along with the reason for the supervision. Provide supervisor's name, contact information, and credentials.

20. *Colleague consultation:* Indicate that, in keeping with generally accepted standards of practice, you frequently consult (on a confidential basis) with other mental health professionals regarding the management of cases. The purpose of the consultation is to assure quality care. Every effort is made to protect the identity of clients.

An important part of the informed consent process includes an honest discussion with your client about the possible implications and consequences of receiving a mental health diagnosis. Of course not every counseling relationship involves the rendering of a diagnosis. This discussion is particularly important in circumstances in which a mental health diagnosis will be made and communicated to a third party (managed care or insurance company, employer, school, etc.). Mental health professionals can never say with certainty how a mental health diagnosis may affect the client in the future. There have been situations in which clients have experienced problems securing life or disability insurance; other clients have encountered problems obtaining a security clearance necessary to qualify for certain types of employment. Sadly, there are people within our culture who make negative judgments about other people with mental health diagnoses. We understand the catch-22 this can create for both the practitioner and the client. Payment to the practitioner or reimbursement to the client for counseling services is frequently dependent on the submission of a claim with an appropriate mental health diagnosis; if there is no mental health diagnosis, there will be no payment. However, in the spirit of informed consent, counselors have a responsibility to talk with clients about the possible future implications and consequences of mental health diagnoses. We also have both a legal and ethical responsibility to render accurate diagnoses—neither to underdiagnose nor to overdiagnose. This is an area filled with potential tension and can be a significant test for the counseling relationship. It is also a prime example of the need to ground the counseling relationship on a firm ethical, legal, and clinical foundation. For additional discussion on the ethical and legal implications of diagnoses, see chapter 10.

Obtaining informed consent from a minor, in addition to consent from a parent or guardian, although not usually legally required (some state counselor licensing laws require obtaining informed consent), is both ethically and clinically in the best interests of the client. We recommend you fully engage minors, to the extent they are developmentally capable, in the informed consent for treatment process. As we said in the beginning of this chapter, it's all about the relationship—which is especially true when working with a child or adolescent.

Counselors have an obligation to monitor the ongoing counseling relationship with each client to determine when or if changes in treatment are warranted and then, if necessary, to obtain an updated informed consent (ACA, 2005a, Standard A.5.e.). Examples of this include (1) a client moving from one modality of treatment (individual, couple, family, or group) to another modality, especially when the new modality involves other people; (2) the relationship shifting from treatment to some form of evaluation (especially when the evaluation has forensic implications); (3) the relationship shifting from treatment to mediation; and (4) the treatment relationship changing to include a research aspect. These and other such eventualities affect the client–counselor relationship and the expectations around confidentiality, privilege, and privacy; it is important that clients are apprised of and consent to these changes.

We want to close this section with a suggestion: Think of informed consent as an ongoing process rather than a single event. It is essential that consent be secured at the outset of counseling, but don't expect that clients will remember everything they read and agreed to many weeks or months earlier. Be prepared to revisit key aspects of the consent. Remember, it's your responsibility to secure and maintain the client's active informed consent for treatment throughout the clinical relationship.

Fees

As a private practitioner, it is reasonable and appropriate to expect to be fairly compensated for providing a competent service. Counselors should not believe or feel, or be encouraged to believe or feel, that there is something wrong about being appropriately compensated for the important work we perform. However, the issue of fees has both ethical (ACA, 2005a, Standard A.10.) and legal implications that can make the provision of quality counseling services more complicated than some other marketplace exchanges.

Under most circumstances, private practitioners are legally entitled to establish any fee for their time and expertise. An exception includes counselors who enter into contractual agreements with third-party payers in which there is an agreed-upon fee for counseling services. Additionally, there is a tradition of service and altruism within the counseling profession that can create tension for some practitioners. Balancing real-world financial needs against this tradition can be challenging. In establishing fees, you are encouraged to be aware of the financial status of clients and the locality in which you practice. Fees vary greatly across the country. Establishing a stated "usual and customary" fee communicates an important message about the value of the counseling service. Ethically, counselors are advised to consider the financial ability of clients, and if the cost of services is beyond the financial ability of a client, the practitioner has an obligation to assist the client, through referral, to obtain alternative services (ACA, 2005a, Standard A.10.b.). However, nothing about setting a usual and customary fee prevents a practitioner from making an adjustment to that fee, on a case-by-case basis, according to financial need or other variable.

An area of both ethical (ACA, 2005a, Standard A.10.a.) and legal jeopardy occurs when a practitioner accepts a client in her or his private practice when the client qualifies for services at the agency in which the counselor is employed. In essence, this amounts to making a referral to the practitioner's own private practice when that counselor or someone else within the agency/organization could have provided the services to the client, likely at a significantly lower cost to the client.

Regardless of the amount of fees charged, counselors should have clear written fee arrangements with clients. These fee arrangements should specify the fees and costs to the client so there is no misunderstanding. We remind you that a solid and trusted counseling relationship is the cornerstone of good clinical practice. Misunderstandings about fees and charges create immediate tension and can quickly undermine the quality of the counseling relationship and can even set into motion an adversarial situation that can lead to accusations of unethical behavior and/or complaints to the licensing board. Therefore, we strongly encourage you, during the informed consent process, to be very clear about fees and charges. Some things to consider when discussing fees with your client are

1. *fees for services*—fees and charges for all counseling services (individual, couple, family, or group);
2. *additional time*—fees and charges for additional time if the session runs late;
3. *telephone consultation*—fees and charges for telephone counseling (other than administrative or counselor-initiated check-in);
4. *other services*—fees and charges for other services (letters, reports, testing, evaluations, phone calls on behalf of the client, coordination of services with other providers, research, etc.);
5. *judicial involvement*—fees and charges for consultation with attorneys, depositions, and court appearances (this may be affected by local laws, rules, or practice);
6. *billing and interest*—the billing/invoicing process and interest charged on overdue accounts;
7. *cancellation/missed appointment*—fees and charges, if any, if a client does not provide 24-hour notice of session cancellation or fails to show for a scheduled appointment.

Counselors put themselves and the counseling relationship at risk when they allow a client to amass a substantial outstanding balance without a clear and honest discussion between the counselor and client that results in a plan for payment—a plan that genuinely meets the needs and ability of both the counselor and the client. In the absence of this discussion, the counselor can be distracted by the outstanding balance. It can become the elephant in the room between you and your client. As we all know, when there is an unspoken meta-issue, it influences or dominates the interaction within a relationship. Have a direct and honest conversation with your client about fees, charges, and payments at the beginning of the relationship and during treatment before it becomes an obstacle to the delivery of quality care. It is the respectful thing to do.

In the case of nonpayment of fees, counselors can pursue legal action against clients in small claims or other courts but should be cautioned that attempting to collect overdue fees can push clients to file claims against the counselor. Probably the best course of action is to meet with the client and openly and honestly discuss the outstanding debt, with a view toward encouraging responsibility and prompt payment. Counselors are not obligated to continue services to a nonpaying client indefinitely but should take steps, absent a crisis, to refer the client to another therapist or counseling service. As with all difficult situations, be sure to thoroughly document information on the past due account, your attempts to invite payment, and your chosen course of action.

TERMINATING THE COUNSELING RELATIONSHIP

In a perfect counseling practice, clients reach an appropriate stopping point at which a debriefing of the experience leads the client and the counselor to a natural point of closure. During this debriefing, you talk with your client about how and when (or if) she or he can return for additional treatment. In the real world of practice, however, debriefing and closure conversations do not generally occur.

Client-Initiated Termination

More often than not, clients terminate the counseling relationship. In many cases, the final session occurs without the counselor realizing it is the final session. This happens in a number of ways. Sometimes clients seem to lose interest in the counseling process, as evidenced by the client's failure to complete homework assignments and/or by presenting for counseling with low energy and minimal investment in the discussion. Other times, clients chronically cancel appointments or fail to return phone calls. There are also times when clients terminate counseling by either leaving a message to that effect or simply not showing for a scheduled appointment.

The ethical and legal tension associated with these no-closure terminations is that, from your point of view, the counseling relationship has ended; however, you don't know how the client views it. Things can get complicated when, months later, you receive a call in the middle of the night from law enforcement or from the hospital advising you that the client has an immediate need and you have been identified as his or her counselor. At that moment you are being asked (sometimes pressured) to immediately accept this client back into your practice. You may or may not want the client back, but there was never a discussion of how/when (or if) the client could return to treatment. There is a lack of clarity. If you don't accept the client, you could risk inviting the client to feel abandoned. If you do accept the client, you have done so without the opportunity to really explore the client's commitment to the counseling relationship. There are some actions you can and should take when clients appear to have initiated termination without explicitly communicating their decision. Clinical documentation is essential. Of course, all along the way, the counselor should be documenting the clinical process. Therefore, if the client begins to demonstrate a reduced commitment to treatment or exhibits ambivalence toward engaging in the counseling relationship, there should be evidence of that in the clinical record. When clients exhibit a pattern of chronic cancellations, no-shows for appointments, or simply drop out of treatment without explanation (and there is no reason to believe the client is in crisis), we suggest you write a letter to the client indicating that you accept his or her apparent decision to terminate treatment. Furthermore, if that was not the client's intention, he or she should contact you within a reasonable time frame. Otherwise, you will close the file and terminate the professional relationship. In the letter, you can indicate how the client can reinitiate a treatment relationship in the future (should that be something you are willing to consider). If you have taken this action and you receive a call in the middle of the night, you are in a much stronger position to either accept or decline a treatment relationship.

Many practitioners, especially those in independent private practice, may want to leave the door open to their clients. Many private practitioners in their statement of office practices and/or informed consent may choose to communicate to their clients the expectation that the counselor and the client are creating an as-needed relationship, very similar to a primary care physician. Under those circumstances, the counselor and the client understand that in the absence of a formal termination, the counselor–client relationship is permanent. The ethical and legal ramification of this office practice is that the counselor retains a duty to the client and may, at any time, be called upon to fulfill that duty.

Counselor-Initiated Termination

Termination of the counselor–client relationship can also occur at the initiation of the counselor. Ethically, you have a responsibility to terminate the counseling relationship if you determine you no longer can be of assistance to the client (e.g., the client has needs beyond your skills and competence), if it is apparent that the client no longer needs or can benefit from your services (you want to avoid creating or maintaining a dependency), or if the client is being harmed in some way through the counseling process (ACA, 2005a, Standards A.11.b., A.11.c.).

Terminating the counseling relationship with a client and making a referral is generally a straightforward activity, assuming the termination is handled appropriately and assuming the motivation for termination is consistent with ethical and legal practice. Serious problems can occur when counselors terminate the counseling relationship during a client emergency or crisis. Ethically, abandonment of the client is prohibited: "Counselors do not abandon or neglect clients in counseling. Counselors assist in making appropriate arrangements for the continuation of treatment" (ACA, 2005a, Standard A.11.a.). Additionally, counselors can legally and ethically terminate the counseling relationship if the client fails to pay the agreed upon fees for service. The core issue here is to do all that is reasonable so the client does not feel abandoned. Client abandonment (real or perceived) often leads to the client initiating an ethics or licensure board complaint, or a malpractice lawsuit.

Counselors often struggle with decisions concerning whether to refer a client when the client poses issues that are beyond the counselor's competence or when the counselor holds values that are at odds with the client's values. If issues of discrimination are involved, the ethical dilemma also quickly becomes a legal problem. *Bruff v. North Mississippi Health Services* (2001) provides case precedent (legally binding only on courts under the federal jurisdiction of the Fifth Circuit Court of Appeals but persuasive authority in other jurisdictions) that may help counselors sort through the difficulties in making such decisions.

In *Bruff*, a hospital-based employee assistance program (EAP) counselor refused to counsel a homosexual client on relationship issues. The counselor was terminated after the hospital offered "reasonable accommodations," and the counselor did not pursue all available job options. The counselor sued the hospital's parent company on the theory that the hospital discriminated against her based on her religious beliefs and thereby violated Title VII of the Civil Rights Act of 1964, as amended by the Civil Rights Act of 1991. Following a substantial jury award against the employer, the appellate court reversed and held that the hospital was not required under Title VII to accommodate the counselor by excusing her from counseling on subjects that conflicted with her religious beliefs. The court indicated that the burden would have fallen on the other two available EAP counselors and would have involved more than *de minimis* cost to the Medical Center.

The court declined to take a position based on evidence produced by both sides about professional standards and ethics codes. In fact, the court specifically stated that its inquiry was strictly limited "to what extent Title VII requires the Medical Center to accommodate Bruff's religious beliefs." However, the case has garnered considerable attention regarding the legal and ethical ramifications of a counselor's refusal to counsel clients on issues pertaining to sexual orientation. Hermann and Herlihy (2006) have cautioned counselors that they must respect clients' values, even if they are different from their own, and that refusal to counsel clients based on, for example, age, culture, ethnicity, or sexual orientation may lead to ethical sanctions, licensure board complaints, and malpractice lawsuits.

The best way to handle counselor-initiated termination is to have solid documentation in the client record that provides evidence of sound clinical decision making. Such documentation will include an awareness of a growing problem (whatever that is), the steps you took to address the problem, and, after careful thought (and possibly, consultation with a colleague or clinical supervision), your conclusion that termination was the appropriate course of action. Of course, providing the client with a referral to another qualified provider or to supportive resources is always an ethical course of action (ACA, 2005a, Standard A.11.c.).

As we said in the opening paragraph of this chapter, it's all about the relationship. We hope you appreciate how important the legal, ethical, and business dimensions of the counseling relationship are to the overall quality of the counseling relationship. When these dimensions are responsibly managed, the counseling relationship is unencumbered, that is, free of unnecessary tension and less likely to lead to ethical or legal problems for the counselor.

Chapter 3

OVERVIEW OF
LAW AND ETHICS

In this 21st century, virtually every aspect of American society is affected by the law. Counselors and other health professionals are subject to a variety of legal and ethical considerations governing their professional practices. It is important that counselors understand the basic concepts of the legal system, the general body of law affecting professional practice, and the impact of professional conduct and ethical standards so they are prepared to address potential problems as they arise in practice.

Legal mandates should be distinguished from ethical codes, which are developed by the profession to guide professional practice. This chapter is designed to help counselors understand and appreciate the differences, similarities, and relationships between the law and ethics.

THE AMERICAN LEGAL STRUCTURE

The American legal system as we know it today evolved from the common law system of England. Rather than codified written laws, the common law was derived from court decisions, which reflected the customs and values of the time. Americans also are governed by the U.S. Constitution, which established our tripartite form of government (legislative, executive, and judicial branches) to initiate, administer, and enforce laws passed by the Congress of the United States (federal laws). Our individual states also have legal systems with legislative, executive, and judicial branches similar to those of our federal government.

Within this structure, laws governing our society originate from two sources: laws (sometimes called *statutes*) passed by governmental bodies such as the Congress or state legislatures; and *rules of law* made by the courts in interpreting the Constitution, federal and state law, and the existing common law. Law made by courts, sometimes called *judge-made law*, takes into account the relevant facts of each particular case, the applicable statutes and administrative regulations governing the situation, and decisions from other court cases (called *precedents*) that might bear on the facts of the case before the court. This all-inclusive approach to interpreting individual cases results in an ever-evolving body of law, within the overall framework of the Constitution, that reflects the changing character of our society.

In appropriate cases, courts also consider standards of conduct relevant to a particular profession. Taking the customary conduct of similarly situated professionals into account when interpreting the particular facts of a case has been an important safeguard for both the public and the affected professionals in many cases. The practice of counseling as well as other mental health professions has been shaped by this activity. Throughout this book, we will highlight several important cases that have served to shape the counseling profession.

This all boils down to a simple but powerful fact: Our body of laws is dynamic and ever-changing. It is not possible to predict accurately the result of any particular case that might be presented in the future, but rules of law guide the analysis of situations that may develop. It is those rules of law that we attempt to present in the remaining chapters, along with practical suggestions for incorporating the law into one's counseling practice.

CRIMINAL, CIVIL, AND ADMINISTRATIVE LAW

There are two major types of law: *criminal law* and *civil law*. Criminal, or penal, law includes acts that are prosecuted by the government, not by private individuals. Crimes are punishable by fine, imprisonment, or death and include offenses such as murder, rape, burglary, robbery, and assault with a deadly weapon. Individuals can also be prosecuted for aiding and abetting someone who has committed such crimes, or for failing to notify proper authorities in some situations (e.g., child abuse) when they have knowledge of such crimes.

Civil law generally includes everything that is not criminal in nature concerning the civil rights of individuals or other bodies. Some of these civil wrongs are called *torts*, which are wrongful actions taken by one private person against another (other than breach of contract). Intentional torts include battery, defamation, and invasion of privacy. Unintentional torts include negligence, which is the basis of most malpractice suits against professionals including counselors. Other types of action that are governed by civil law include contract and property disputes. Violations of civil laws are enforced by private persons bringing suit against the violators in a court of law. The sanctions awarded to successful plaintiffs are usually in the form of monetary damages to compensate the plaintiff for his or her loss.

Beyond civil and criminal law, *administrative law* has assumed new prominence for counselors and other mental health professionals in recent years. Administrative law is created (usually by a process of *rulemaking*) by government administrative agencies charged with the task of developing regulations to help define the laws, or statutes, that are passed by Congress or a state legislative body. For example, pursuant to the federal Health Insurance Portability and Accountability Act of 1996 (usually referred to as HIPAA), the HIPAA Privacy Rule was promulgated by the U.S. Department of Health and Human Services.

THE COURT SYSTEM

Federal Courts

Federal courts were created by Article III, Section 2, of the Constitution of the United States and have the power to hear cases "arising under this Constitution" and the laws of the United States. Federal law provides for several situations in which cases may be brought in federal courts. One is when the case arises under the laws of the United States or presents a question of federal law (federal question jurisdiction, 28 U.S.C. § 1331, 2006). Another is when the case involves citizens of different states and the amount in controversy exceeds $75,000 (diversity jurisdiction, 28 U.S.C. § 1332, 2006). Potential litigants may have the option to bring their claims in either state or federal court if the jurisdictional requirements of the federal system can be met.

State Courts

Most state courts are patterned after the federal system, with trial courts, a middle-level appellate court, and a top-level appellate court (often called a supreme court) as the final arbiter of decisions involving state and federal laws that affect the residents of the state. The names of these courts may vary from state to state, but their function is essentially the same. They can hear both civil and criminal cases arising under either state or federal laws, and their decisions are binding on the residents of the state unless overturned by a higher court within the state or by a federal court.

Appellate Process

In both the state and federal court systems, cases originate in the trial court (called the Federal District Court in the federal system). Both parties put on their case at this level, witnesses are heard, evidence is taken, the relevant law is applied to the facts, and a decision is rendered either by a judge or by a jury. The judge then assigns the appropriate remedies to the parties.

Parties may have the right to appeal decisions of the trial or district court to the intermediate-level appeals court. In the federal system, these 13 courts are called the U.S. Circuit Courts of Appeals. Their function is to review how the law has been applied to the facts of each particular case and to determine whether the trial court made any errors in its decision that should be overturned, reversed, or sent back to the trial court for additional findings of fact. The state appeals courts generally operate in a similar manner.

The losing party can request that his or her case be heard at the third and final level: either the highest court in the state system or, in the federal system, the U.S. Supreme Court. Additionally, cases that have been decided by the highest court of a state may move to the U.S. Supreme Court through the process known as a *petition for certiorari*, or asking the Court to hear the case. The nine justices of the Supreme Court then vote to decide whether to hear the case and, if at least four justices agree, the Court will issue a *writ of certiorari* asking that the case be forwarded to the Supreme Court. Cases accepted by the Supreme Court generally involve issues of federal law in which decisions of circuit courts on similar issues conflict with one another. Very few cases actually end up in the U.S. Supreme Court.

ETHICAL STANDARDS

In addition to the legal considerations that govern the conduct of all citizens, counselors are guided in their professional conduct by the ethical codes promulgated by professional associations, such as the 2005 *ACA Code of Ethics* (see Appendix A). The 2005 version of the *Code*, immediately following its Preamble, specifies that it serves five main purposes:

1. The *Code* enables the association to clarify to current and future members, and to those served by the members, the nature of the ethical responsibilities held in common by its members.
2. The *Code* helps support the mission of the association.
3. The *Code* establishes principles that define ethical behavior and best practices of association members.
4. The *Code* serves as an ethical guide designed to assist members in constructing a professional course of action that best serves those utilizing counseling services and best promotes the values of the counseling profession.
5. The *Code* serves as the basis for processing of ethical complaints and inquiries initiated against members of the association.

In furtherance of the fifth purpose, a complaint procedure has been established and penalties for violations of the standards have been set. These penalties may include a variety of remedial requirements, probation, suspension, or permanent expulsion from the association (ACA, 2005b).

Ethical decisions generally complement the legal parameters but also cover issues that tend to fall into the gray areas (i.e., not expressly prohibited, yet not specifically allowed by the law). They take into account the subtle fact variations in each situation and the reasonable approach to addressing it. The concept of what is ethical also changes with the maturity and perspective of the counseling profession and society at large. For example, as information technology has begun to play a larger role in practice over the past decade, questions regarding its impact on client confidentiality and informed consent have arisen. The most recent version of the *Code* has incorporated new requirements for counselors in this area (ACA, 2005a, Standards A.12.g., A.12.h., B.3.e.). As technological advances become even more widespread in counseling, and as counselors are affected by new laws, such as HIPAA (see chapter 5), future editions of the *ACA Code* are likely to contain even more standards for practicing counselors.

Occasionally, ethical standards and responsibilities conflict with legal standards and requirements. For example, a counselor may wish to preserve a minor's ethical right to confidentiality but may be faced with a parent's demand for information that a particular state law allows. If a conflict between ethics and the law occurs, the *Code* directs that counselors make known their commitment to the *ACA Code of Ethics* and take steps to resolve the conflict. If the conflict cannot be resolved, counselors "may adhere to the requirements of law, regulations, or other governing legal authority" (Standard H.1.b.). ACA has also published a new edition of the *ACA Ethical Standards Casebook* (6th ed.; Herlihy & Corey, 2006a) to provide specific examples that illustrate and clarify the meaning and intent of each major section of the *Code*. The book presents typical situations a counselor may face in practice and analyzes the ethical considerations involved in each situation. Counselors are well advised to study the implications of these analyses carefully and to apply the results to their personal practices.

ETHICS AND THE LAW

The ethical standards of a profession are generally enforced through the internal procedures of the professional association, not specifically by courts of law. However, in the absence of any clear statutory authority or case law precedent to guide a court in a case involving the conduct of an individual counselor, courts may apply the standard of care developed by other similarly situated professionals (in this case, other counselors). Courts may also look to the self-imposed standards of the profession to determine liability. Therefore, counselors should act in accordance with the standards of counselors in their local communities and thoroughly study and follow the *ACA Code of Ethics* as a means of avoiding potential liability. Just as courts have utilized the ethical guidelines and standards of care developed by the legal, accounting, and medical professions, a court could find that a counselor has breached his or her professional duty to a client on the basis of the counseling profession's own internal ethical standards.

Chapter 4

CIVIL MALPRACTICE LIABILITY AND
LICENSURE BOARD COMPLAINTS

Chapter 2 focused on the professional relationships between counselors and their clients and the fiduciary and contractual duties that arise from those relationships. For example, one of those duties, subject to a variety of limitations, is to protect client confidences (see chapter 5). Counselors face a myriad of other professional obligations and must take steps to comply with those duties. This chapter explores these other obligations and the types of complaints, including civil malpractice lawsuits and licensure board complaints, that follow when counselors do not fulfill their duties.

COMPETENCE AND PREPARATION

Perhaps the fundamental goal of professional preparation and competence is to protect clients from harm, just as the fundamental goal of law is to protect society. Exactly what level of professional preparation and competence is required of a counselor obviously varies depending on the type of counseling practice as well as the state in which he or she practices. Corey, Corey, and Callanan (2007, p. 314) aptly stated that competence "is a process rather than something that is achieved once and for all." Competence and preparation include such issues as meeting the required levels of education, training, and skill; knowing when to refer to other professionals or seek consultation or supervision; acquiring expertise in specific practice areas; appropriately representing professional credentials; and enhancing professional growth through continuing education. These areas, among others, may be investigated by state and professional regulatory boards and are supported by the 2005 *ACA Code of Ethics*.

For example, the *ACA Code of Ethics* specifies that counselors "practice only within the boundaries of their competence, based on their education, training, supervised experience, state and national professional credentials, and appropriate professional experience. Counselors gain knowledge, personal awareness, sensitivity, and skills pertinent to working with a diverse client population" (Standard C.2.a.).

Counselors are also admonished to complete "appropriate education, training, and supervised experience" before practicing in a new specialty area to ensure their own competence, and to protect others in the process (Standard C.2.b.). They are also required to "accept employment only for positions for which they are qualified" and to hire only counselors "who are qualified and competent" (Standard C.2.c.). For example, in order to become adept at the skill of diagnosing mental health disorders, counselors cannot just attend a weekend seminar and think that they have mastered the art of diagnosis. Counselors are also expected to engage in continuing education to maintain their skills and are expected to keep current with issues presented by diverse populations (Standard C.2.f.). The Council for Accreditation of Counseling and Related Educational Programs (CACREP) stated the need for continuing education as follows: "no professional preparation program is ever complete, and advances in knowledge, skills, and technology within the profession require lifelong continuing education for counselors as well as monitoring and review of professional standards" (Introduction, *2001 Standards*[1]).

Additionally, counselors may claim or imply only those professional credentials they actually possess and are responsible for correcting "any known misrepresentations of their qualifications by others" (ACA, 2005a, Standard C.4.a.). For example, if a client calls a counselor *doctor* and the counselor does not possess a doctoral degree, the counselor is ethically obliged to bring the error to the client's attention. The majority of states now have licensing statutes that recognize specific credentials for counselors.

Practice within the limits of professional training is more than just an ethical standard; it is also important from a legal standpoint. Because of a counselor's legal duty to a client, the analysis of a claim of negligence or malpractice is greatly affected by professional identity. How the counselor holds himself or herself out to the public will determine the expected practice standards by which he or she may be judged. Counselors who hold themselves out or advertise themselves as specializing in a given area will be judged according to the extraordinary level of skill required of a specialist.

One last area to note in discussing competence is that counselors must be "alert to signs of impairment from their own physical, mental, or emotional problems" and must "refrain from offering or providing professional services when such impairment is likely to harm a client or others" (ACA, 2005a, Standard C.2.g.). This caveat applies to counselors whether the impairment is based on mental or physical health, substance abuse, or adverse prescription medication reactions. It is also important to recognize that impairment can be generated by subtle and nonpathological stressors and life events. The list of stressors and distractions that can impair professional judgment and

---

[1] 2008 Standards are being drafted as of the publication date of this book.

competence includes every imaginable life event, from lack of sleep (caring for a newborn, tending to the needs of an ill family member), to the anticipation of a wedding or vacation, to the mental and emotional preoccupation associated with marital or family problems. Over the course of their careers, counselors will frequently be challenged with a myriad of nonpathological invitations to impairment. Self-monitoring in the form of recognition and appropriate response to impairment of competence is both ethically and legally essential. During times of impairment it may be necessary to limit, suspend, or terminate professional responsibilities altogether.

DUTY OF CARE AND
POTENTIAL CIVIL LIABILITY/MALPRACTICE

Professional counselors must exercise *due care* in their counseling relationships or face potential liability in a civil suit for failing to perform their duties as required by law. Counselors can be sued in a court of law for acting wrongly toward a client or for failing to act when there was a recognized duty to do so, when action or inaction results in injury to another. The end result, or *judicial relief*, is usually in the form of money damages awarded to the injured party to compensate for the injuries inflicted.

Negligence

For counselors, the primary area in which civil liability is found rests in the law of torts (see chapter 3). A *tort is* basically a private injury against the person, property, or reputation of another individual that legal action is designed to set right. Torts can take various forms and fall into two categories. The first, called *negligence*, is the *unintentional* violation of an obligation one person owes to another, such as a counselor's obligation to use all of his or her care and skill in dealing with a client, but it may also include failing to follow all the requirements of a protective statute.

There are four elements to be proven in a negligence action:

1. There must be a *legal duty* arising from a special relationship between the parties that will be determined by the facts of the situation. Whether casual conversation at a cocktail party or giving an informational lecture at a local civic gathering constitutes the existence of a special relationship is questionable, but counselors should be circumspect about giving such advice without adequate disclaimers. A court will then look to the professional identity of the counselor (legally and ethically defined) to determine what skills and experience he or she should be expected to have and by what standards of practice he or she should be bound. In many cases this will be determined by state licensing, certification, or registration statutes.

2. The legal duty arising from that relationship must have been *breached.* That is, the mental health professional failed to uphold the standard of care or practice expected of a counselor in that position or violated some law (e.g., failed to report suspected child abuse or neglect).
3. The plaintiff must prove *causation.* This means that the injuries received would not have occurred but for the counselor's breach of duty. Even though there may have been other contributing causes, if the injury to the client was foreseeable and resulted from the counselor's conduct, the counselor can be held liable for damages.
4. There must have been an *actual injury* to the plaintiff, such as physical harm, emotional distress, or depression, that is evidenced by specific symptoms, worsening of problems, changes in life circumstances, or the like. Generally, some evidence of financial loss also is presented.

This is a very simplified explanation of a complicated analysis that captivates lawyers and law students, but it should raise a variety of questions about the entire picture of professional practice for mental health practitioners, therapists, and counselors.

Malpractice

Malpractice is the term that pertains to most civil suits against professional counselors. As applied to counselors, a malpractice lawsuit is based on negligence in carrying out professional responsibilities or duties. It is important to recognize that professional malpractice is regulated by state law and usually applies only where the professional person is licensed, certified, or otherwise registered according to state statute. However, other counseling professionals can still be held liable for their actions based on a negligence theory (see the preceding section), intentional infliction of emotional distress, or other torts even if the term *malpractice* does not technically apply. Another somewhat broader term that is widely used, especially in conjunction with insurance policies, is *professional liability*. Malpractice is typically found in situations such as the following:

- The procedure utilized by the counselor was not within the realm of accepted professional practice.
- The technique used was one the counselor was not trained to employ (lack of professional competence).
- The counselor failed to follow a procedure that would have been more helpful.
- The counselor failed to warn and/or protect others from a violent client.
- Informed consent to treatment was not obtained.
- The counselor failed to explain the possible consequences of the treatment.

Just as in the analysis for negligence, to establish a case of professional malpractice, the plaintiff must prove the elements of duty, breach, causation, and damages.

The duty owed by the counselor is premised on the existence of a *fiduciary relationship* between the counselor and the client (see chapter 2), one that fosters both trust and confidence. The client has the right to expect due care from the counselor, and the counselor is obligated to provide the standard of care.

The primary problem in a malpractice suit is to determine which standard of care applies to ascertain whether a counselor has breached his or her duty to a client. Professional action or inaction is typically judged by whether a reasonably prudent counselor in the same or similar circumstance would have acted in the same manner as the counselor did. If the answer is Yes, liability usually will not be found. However, when the counselor holds him- or herself out as an expert in a particular discipline, he or she must then meet the standard of care required of an expert in that area. The courts also look to licensing, certification, or registration statutes, as well as professional standards of practice and codes of ethics, to determine the standard of care to apply in each situation. Courts also borrow from case precedents involving other related professions such as psychiatry, psychology, and medicine to measure counselor performance.

Malpractice claims may arise from a variety of issues in the counseling relationship, although all share the common elements of professional duty of care, breach of that duty, causation, and resulting injury. Watch for these elements in the examples discussed in this book.

Intentional Torts

The second category of tort occurs where there has been a direct, intentional abrogation of some person's legal rights, such as the invasion of privacy through an illegal search. Other intentional torts include defamation of character, assault, battery, infliction of emotional distress, or any intentional violation of a protected interest.

A counselor might be held liable for one of the intentional torts, *even though the conduct was unintentional,* if the resulting injury was substantially certain to occur from the counselor's act. This might be more likely in counseling relationships than elsewhere because of the intimate nature of counseling. Counselors should be more aware of the particular vulnerabilities of their clients and may be judged on that basis. An injured client frequently will allege two or more separate causes of action at the same time; for example, the client may claim that an alleged inappropriate touching was an assault that caused emotional distress. The same alleged injury could also form the basis for a claimed breach of fiduciary and contractual duties.

Criminal Action

Certainly few counselors ever anticipate that they might become defendants in a criminal action simply by practicing their profession. But counselors should be aware of certain occupational hazards that could lead to criminal liability. The ideal goal for professional counselors is to maintain appropriate boundaries between themselves and their clients (see chapter 8) so they may interact with clients in a professional, or clinical, manner. Occasionally, however, situations arise that might lead counselors to go much further in protecting their clients or providing emotional support and comfort than the law literally allows. In such cases, a counselor may intentionally or unwittingly risk criminal liability as an accessory to a crime for failing to report child abuse, contributing to the delinquency of a minor, or committing insurance fraud or sexual misconduct.

In addition to the possibility of administrative sanctions and civil or criminal liability, the costs of defending even a baseless allegation can be significant. No professional can totally insulate him- or herself from frivolous claims, but exposure can be limited by careful attention to the duties arising from the counseling relationship. Counselors must have a clear understanding of their professional identity, the nature of the professional relationship, the level of professional preparation and competence necessary, the duty of care expected of a counseling professional, and the standards of practice or code of ethics that establish the permissible boundaries of conduct for the profession.

COMMON COMPLAINTS AGAINST COUNSELORS

Complaints against counselors take a number of forms and are filed in a variety of forums. It's often helpful to look at statistics regarding real-life complaints to see what the most frequent claims are and what types of claims garner the greatest severity of loss (the highest damage amounts). Table 1 represents the

Table 1

ACA INSURANCE TRUST CLAIMS EXPERIENCE (1997–2001)

Type of Claim	% of Cases	% of Dollars
Breach of confidentiality	21	10
Dual relationships	10	5
Suicide	6	55
Failure to provide proper care and counseling	15	5
Touching/physical contact	4	1
Abandonment	6	2
Libel/slander	15	1
Family counseling issues	15	2
Failure to report abuse	8	11

claims experience for participants in the ACA Insurance Trust's sponsored professional liability insurance program as revealed in a study that covered the 4 years between 1997 and 2001 (P. L. Nelson, Executive Director, ACA Insurance Trust, personal communication, January 9, 2006). It includes both civil suits and licensure board proceedings. What's interesting to note is that the greatest frequency of claims or cases is not equivalent to the payout of dollars for that particular category. For example, whereas breaches of confidentiality accounted for 21% of all claims, the overall payout in damages and attorneys' fees represented just 10% of the total; in contrast, suicide claims represented only 6% of claims but a substantial 55% of the total amount of money paid by the insurance carrier.

Licensure Board Complaints

Counselors are often concerned about malpractice suits but do not always realize that many more complaints are filed at the level of their state licensure board. Although many complaints are dismissed, this is often done after considerable time, effort, and expense. Even though an adverse result at the level of the licensure board is not the same as an expensive monetary award in a civil lawsuit, the consequences can range from required continuing education or a reprimand to probation, suspension, or actual revocation of the counselor's license.

If you become the target of a licensure board complaint, it is important to notify your professional liability insurance carrier promptly. A good professional liability policy will provide some payment of attorney's fees so you may receive legal assistance in responding to the complaint. If you are insured through the ACA-sponsored professional liability insurance program, you may be eligible to speak with the Risk Management Helpline and receive preliminary guidance and suggestions for local counsel. Additionally, your professional association staff person responsible for ethics and practice standards may be able to assist you in deciphering the severity of the problem. Attorneys representing disgruntled clients often will use the licensure board complaint process as a springboard for subsequent civil malpractice suits, so it is extremely important that you take board complaints seriously.

What are the typical issues that lead to licensure board complaints against counselors and other mental health providers? Besides the complaints set forth in Table 1 (which comprises both civil suits and licensure board complaints), among the claims often investigated by state boards for counselors, physicians, and other health care providers across the country are

- misrepresentation of credentials (e.g., holding oneself out as a doctor when no doctoral degree has been obtained);
- failure to check credentials of employed therapists;
- failure to make fees and charges clear to clients (including failure to give advance notice of the counselor's practice of charging for missed sessions);

- engaging in behavior in which boundary violations occur (see chapter 8);
- alteration of records;
- making child custody recommendations when appropriate evaluation of all parties has not been conducted;
- violating confidentiality;
- practicing outside of the scope of one's experience, education, training, and licensure;
- submission of insurance claims in the name of a psychologist or psychiatrist without mentioning that the counselor actually performed the work.

In light of these issues, we offer some steps that you can take in your practice to help avoid complaints:

1. Obtain current copies of all licensure board statutes and regulations, as well as the *ACA Code of Ethics* or other ethics codes pertinent to your practice or adopted by your state. Update these documents regularly (perhaps on an annual basis); many are available on the Internet.
2. Always represent your credentials and professional identity accurately and correctly. (Make sure, for example, to enlighten clients who think you are a doctor when you are not, or clients who refer to you as a psychologist or a psychiatrist when you are a mental health counselor). Supervisors should ensure that supervisees accurately portray their own credentials and those of the supervisor.
3. Carefully draft informed consent or professional disclosure statements that may be required by your state. Specify your fees and charges in writing.
4. Obtain continuing education on a regular basis or as required by your state licensure board.
5. Be especially careful to avoid harmful dual relationships and keep up to date on changes in the various ethics codes on this topic (see chapter 8).
6. Develop a resource network of trusted colleagues and an attorney whom you may consult when difficult situations arise.
7. Carefully document actions taken or rejected and your reasons for your decisions (see chapter 9).
8. Obtain legal advice when faced with a licensure board complaint; check your malpractice policy to see if defense costs are covered. Address clients' grievances before they turn into formal complaints.
9. Because monetary disputes often result in complaints, think twice and obtain legal advice before submitting bills to a collection agency.
10. Obtain information about licensure board issues and complaints from your state board's Web site.

Not only will these steps help protect you from a licensure board action; many of these will also help you avoid the slippery slope into a malpractice lawsuit.

Despite the counselor's best intentions, it is not always possible to avoid licensure board complaints. Because clients do not need attorneys to file a board complaint, sometimes there is no rational basis or screening of a complaint before it arrives at the board. Nonetheless, the board may have a legal obligation to investigate the charges. Occasionally, the client's mental health diagnosis (e.g., paranoid personality disorder) actually can fuel a complaint; the client may believe the counselor is conspiring to harm him or her. Additionally, to promote the client's best interests, a counselor may give the client the name and address of the board as part of the informed consent process. This practice is actually required by the counselor licensure laws in some states. Although we concur with this practice, we also suggest that you encourage clients to contact you first to try to resolve any disputes.

One example of a board complaint that was successfully defended is the following. A client suffering from major depression had a history of acting out aggressively when things didn't go his way. He was involved in fights, threatened suicide, engaged in binge drinking, and was accused of arson and property theft. The client filed a licensure board complaint that was rambling and disorganized. Among the allegations in the complaint were that the counselor failed to diagnose the client's symptoms, attributed the client's symptoms to his character, and held herself out as knowing everything. The client further alleged that the counselor told the client he wouldn't need medication if he received counseling from her. The counselor had a very different interpretation of the events. Several items helped in the counselor's defense: (1) the counselor cooperated with the board; (2) the counselor's records were organized and provided good documentation of care and recommendations; (3) referrals were made; and (4) the counselor maintained an accurate accounting of appointments, including the times that the client failed to show (which refuted the client's version of treatment dates). Even though the complaint was eventually dismissed, the insurance company expended significant funds in providing legal assistance (P. L. Nelson, Executive Director, ACA Insurance Trust, personal communication, January 9, 2006).

Diagnosis and Scope of Treatment

The education, training, experience, and other qualifications required for a mental health counselor to render specific mental health diagnoses are typically set forth in state licensing laws. Thus, if counselors render mental health diagnoses, they have a duty to do so with the care and skill expected of other counselors who hold similar qualifying licenses. Obviously, giving a diagnosis you are not qualified or licensed to render could leave you vulnerable to subsequent liability for malpractice. Your determination that a client has a condition requiring medical psychotherapeutic treatment generally also will define the appropriate treatment regimen that is considered the standard of care for that diagnosis. The treatment you provide the client must be consistent with the accepted standard of care for that treatment to avoid potential liability.

The decision to use the *Diagnostic and Statistical Manual of Mental Disorders* (4th ed., text rev.; *DSM-IV-TR*; American Psychiatric Association, 2000) to diagnose mental health disorders and submit diagnoses to insurance companies is complicated by a wide range of legal and ethical issues. These include professional licensing, competence training, economic realities, and reimbursement policies of third-party payers as well as practitioner sociopolitical and cultural perspectives and values. The legal authority to render a mental health diagnosis has long been a major battleground between licensed professional counselors and other mental health providers (e.g., psychologists, social workers, and psychiatrists). Legal authority to render an independent mental health diagnosis must be provided by statute—specifically the state counselor licensing law. Many counselors across the county now have the authority, granted by law, to diagnose mental disorders. Be sure to verify the limits of authority defined in your counselor licensing law.

Having the legal authority, however, does not automatically equate to having the requisite knowledge and skill to render a "proper diagnosis" (ACA, 2005a, Standard E.5.a.). As a counselor, you are ethically charged and legally admonished to practice within the boundaries of your competence. Therefore, establishing competence through education, training, and supervised practice in diagnosing mental disorders is critical. Lacking the ability to demonstrate diagnostic competence can make you vulnerable to an allegation of misdiagnosis (rendering an incorrect diagnosis) or missed diagnosis (failure to recognize and act on clinically relevant client symptoms suggesting a mental health condition that requires attention). Both of these failures could lead to malpractice allegations. Counselors who are diagnostically well-grounded can more accurately provide thoughtful and appropriate diagnoses and, should the situation arise, can more proficiently respond to an allegation of misdiagnosis or missed diagnosis.

In many ways, diagnosis has become entangled with economic realities driven by the reimbursement policies of third-party payers. Third-party payers (HMO, PPO, Medicaid, and other insurance programs) generally will not provide coverage without a mental health diagnosis. Therefore, for private practitioners as well as for agencies, organizations, and treatment facilities that are economically dependent on third-party payers, the rendering of a diagnosis has become the doorway to financial survival. As a result, there can be a temptation, even in the absence of clinical justification, to render a diagnosis on every client who presents for counseling. Too often, economic pressures and agency funding realities have resulted in a skewing of the purpose of diagnosis. Under these conditions, diagnosis, originally conceptualized to be a clinical classification system designed to support treatment and research, has now shifted to become a mandatory box on the claim form that must be completed with an acceptable code in order to receive payment for services. Practitioners engage in all manner of rationalization and justification; but when these mental gymnastics are carried too far, the practitioner can easily cross the line from gray to insurance fraud. Examples of crossing the line include

- *up-coding*—rendering a more serious diagnosis than symptoms call for in an attempt to gain authorization for an increased number of counseling sessions;
- *down-coding*—allowing concerns about possible future implications of a serious mental health diagnosis on the client to convince the practitioner to render a less serious diagnosis;
- *treatment misrepresentation*—providing a modality of treatment that is not authorized by the third-party payer (e.g., couples counseling) while coding the service with an acceptable treatment modality (e.g., individual psychotherapy).

These and other examples can place you at risk of an allegation of insurance fraud. Additionally, if you up-code or down-code a diagnosis, and then, as a result of a client crisis, questions are raised about the level of care you provided, it might be difficult to explain why the level of care did not match the diagnosis.

An additional area of ethical and legal complexity surrounding diagnosis is driven by the sociopolitical and cultural perspectives and values held by individual practitioners. These perspectives and values are best understood by describing two polar-opposite viewpoints. At one end of a continuum are practitioners who subscribe to the medical model. They believe mental health conditions exist in a form that can be objectively assessed and accurately diagnosed. These practitioners believe it is necessary and desirable to conceptualize, diagnose, and treat mental health problems with the precision that other health care professionals apply to the conceptualization, diagnosis, and treatment of physical health concerns. They believe client progress can be behaviorally assessed, resulting in an objective determination when treatment goals have been met. At the other end of the continuum are practitioners who raise serious questions about utilizing a medical model to diagnose and treat mental health problems. These practitioners believe that human beings are far too complex and too culturally and contextually influenced to be conceptualized by a list of behaviors and symptoms as defined in the *DSM-IV-TR*. Furthermore, they contend that documenting progress is not something that necessarily has behavioral dimensions that can be objectively measured. Further, many practitioners point to the cultural insensitivity of many aspects of mental health diagnosis, and they provide historical examples in which mental health diagnoses were used by members of the dominant culture to oppress and pathologize individuals and groups.

In recognition of these differences of opinion, the 2005 *ACA Code of Ethics* has attempted to find a point of compromise on the issue of diagnosis. Counselors are instructed to "take special care to provide proper diagnosis" (Standard E.5.a.) while cautioned that counselors "recognize that culture affects the manner in which clients' problems are defined" (Standard E.5.b.) and that there have been "historical and social prejudices in the misdiagnosis and pathologizing of certain individuals and groups" (Standard E.5.c.). The *Code* concludes by providing counselors with support in refraining "from making and/or reporting a diagnosis if they believe it would cause harm to the client or others" (Standard E.5.d.).

Where does this leave the counseling practitioner? We maintain that, for most counselors, there is a legal and ethical path through these conflicting perspectives. For practitioners who are highly offended by mental health diagnoses, we encourage you to work in settings that do not require the rendering and submission of a mental heath diagnosis. Diagnosis is one thing; client assessment is quite another. On one hand, practitioners who are offended by the *DSM-IV-TR* conceptualizations and classifications still have both an ethical and legal duty to engage in a careful and ongoing assessment of the client in order to provide treatment that addresses the needs of the client. On the other hand, for practitioners who are comfortable with the medical model, the big challenge is to resist manipulating the diagnosis in a manner that will place you at risk. It has been our experience that most counselors find themselves somewhere in the middle between the two perspectives just described. As with many in-the-middle situations, you probably can see truth and wisdom as well as caution and concern in all the positions. As a result, inevitably you will experience some level of cognitive dissonance and discomfort, some of the time, about some circumstances. We encourage you to clarify the limits of your discomfort so you can become very clear about what you will and won't do with regard to the rendering and submission of a mental health diagnosis.

Failure to Treat or Refer

The counselor's primary ethical responsibility is to respect the dignity and promote the welfare of clients. Coupled with the legal duty to render competent diagnoses and provide proper treatment based on training, skill, and experience, these criteria establish the standards of practice each counselor is expected to meet with each client. This may sound fairly simple, but in day-to-day practice myriad complications arise that complicate the counseling relationship and the responsibilities of the counselor.

Generally speaking, courts will not find counselors negligent merely because the client fails to improve during the counseling relationship or the approach the counselor chooses in treatment proves to be erroneous. Courts have ruled that no presumption of negligence arises from a mere mistake in judgment if that mistake is the type that could be made by the most careful and skilled practitioner of that specialty. Again, however, the counselor will be judged according to standards applicable to the counseling profession.

It is important to remember that, at the outset of counseling, you should initiate with your client(s) a discussion of the limits of the proposed course of treatment, as well as the potential risks and benefits. Problems may arise when a counselor determines, or should have determined, that a course of therapy or treatment is not effective for the client, or if the problems presented are beyond the competence of the counselor. In those cases, there is a clear professional ethical duty to seek consultation with another competent professional or to terminate the counseling relationship and refer the client to another qualified professional (ACA, 2005a, Standards A.11.b., A.11.c.). A court could also find that there is a legal duty to consult or refer when the counselor is not competent to meet the client's needs.

Two decisions reflect some confusion in this area about when a counselor or other mental health professional should determine that referral or consultation is necessary. The first involves an industrial psychologist who administered a series of vocational skills tests to a client and met with him four more times in the next year. There was only limited telephone contact with the client after that time, the most recent occurring 7 years after the initial contact. Eight years after the last contact, the psychologist was called to court to defend claims that he had failed to refer the client to a clinical psychologist for treatment of his mental illness, prevented him from seeking appropriate treatment, and aggravated his condition. As it turned out, the court dismissed the client's claim because he did not bring an expert to testify about the psychologist's breach of duty (*Grote v. J. S. Mayer & Co.*, 1990). However, in similar circumstances, it is quite possible that a court could find that a referral should have been made during the initial testing and evaluation.

The other area involves members of the clergy. *Nally v. Grace Community Church* (1984, 1987, 1988, 1989) involved a young man who committed suicide after counseling by a minister in California. Among the issues was whether the client should have been referred to someone more competent to handle his problems. The California Supreme Court refused to hold the pastoral counselor liable for failing either to refer the young man to another professional or to warn the client's parents that their son was on the verge of suicide. We do not advise interpreting this case to mean that professional counselors do not have a duty to refer. It's important to recognize that the *Nally* case involved a nonlicensed person doing pastoral work.

Additionally, state licensure boards could interpret their state laws to require that licensed therapists refer patients/clients to other professionals for services in certain circumstances. For example, the Pennsylvania State Board of Psychology (2000) issued a special notice to its licensees stating that a "psychologist has a duty to refer patients/clients to other providers for services which the psychologist may not legally perform." This duty could be invoked in situations where counselors fail to refer appropriate clients for medication management by a psychiatrist or other physician.

Group Counseling

Group therapy has developed into a widely accepted means of treatment for a variety of counseling needs. It is believed that clients often learn to understand and communicate more effectively with peers and that they may be better able to put their anxieties or fears into perspective than could be achieved through individual counseling. Counselors leading groups must be well trained and skillful in their use of this technique and must be careful to follow accepted standards of practice with groups. As discussed earlier, the concept of privileged communication may not always apply in group settings unless it is expressly granted by state statute. Consequently, the counselor must inform all group participants of the limits of confidentiality within the group setting, including their responsibilities to other group members and, if applicable, the absence of the legal privilege concerning group discussions.

The counselor's duty to each member of a group is the same as in individual counseling sessions: Professional services must be rendered according to the recognized standard of care expected of a competent counselor. Should the counselor fail to bring to that relationship the skill and care of a qualified group counselor practicing within the expert discipline of the profession, the counselor may be liable for breach of professional duty to clients. However, the legal requirement of care is more complicated in the group relationship than in the individual counseling setting for several reasons. First, the counselor may or may not be responsible for forming the group and selecting the members. Once the group is formed, the counselor bears the increased duty of supervising the multiple interactions among the various group members and for protecting each member of the group from physical and/or psychological trauma that may result from the group setting.

Counselors must constantly evaluate the size of the group, its appropriateness for each particular member, whether to refer individual members of the group for special help, and whether to bring in an additional counseling professional to assist in the group sessions. Counselors must also be alert to unanticipated encounters within a group and be prepared to handle potentially explosive situations with a high degree of professional skill to protect each individual member of the group. This requires extensive training and preparation to avoid potential liability.

The *Best Practices* of the Association for Specialists in Group Work (1998)[2] provides an excellent discussion of the responsibilities of the counselor in group work, in terms of providing both adequate information to clients and group counseling services. These guidelines stress the need to screen members before they are admitted to a group, prepare clients adequately before they enter the group so that they are fully informed, set a norm of confidentiality among group members, protect group clients from undue pressure or coercion, treat each member of a group individually and equally, and ensure proper follow-up for group members who choose to leave the group prematurely. The guidelines also emphasize the need for adequate professional preparation before practicing group therapy as well as for ongoing assessment of the group experience. Because a court may take such professional standards into account when judging whether the actions of a group counselor have been negligent, counselors should become familiar with these guidelines and make every effort to provide services accordingly.

One additional note of caution should be sounded. As in all counseling situations, the group counselor has the obligation to remain objective and use good professional judgment with all group members. From time to time, it may be difficult to abide by this dictate with some group members. Consider the situation in which one experienced group leader found himself so angry with one group member's repeated personal and physical attacks that he felt compelled to return the attack physically. Recognizing that these feelings violated his professional responsibility both to the group and to the disruptive client, and catching himself before he acted, the counselor immediately sought the help of a professional colleague to deal with his own anger and frustration. A less experienced counselor might not have acted so responsibly, and a malpractice action could have resulted.

Crisis Intervention

Crisis intervention, or crisis management, is a counseling technique or skill and, of course, generally arises out of an emergency situation. The person who needs assistance may be only a short step from death or serious injury, and the counselor serves as a buffer, hoping to avert tragedy or hold off self-destructive acts or impulses until appropriate medical or mental health treatment can be provided.

The counselor in a crisis intervention situation (assuming a first-time client encounter as opposed to crisis intervention with an existing client)

---

[2]The *Best Practices* are in revision (M. Riva, personal communication, September 12, 2006).

typically has no real control over the person who seeks help. The general legal principle that applies to people in a rescue mode is this: *A person is responsible for harm to another only if the failure to exercise reasonable care increases the risk of harm to another.* The counselor offers to listen to the distressed person, provides words of encouragement or suggestions, and has a duty to use his or her training and skill to assist the distressed individual until therapy or medical treatment can be provided. In this setting, the counselor is not responsible for knowing the history or problems of the person being counseled that are not revealed during the crisis intervention. Consequently, the counselor ordinarily will be subject to a negligence suit *only if* the counselor fails to use reasonable care in counseling *and* that failure increases the risk of harm to the person. Even if the counselor did not use reasonable care, the counselor usually will not be held liable for negligence unless that failure *also* increased the risk of harm or left the person in a worse position than before.

It should be noted that the term *client* has not been used to describe the person being counseled in crisis intervention because that denotes the existence of a relationship between the crisis intervention counselor and the individual in need of assistance. If such a relationship exists, however, the counselor may be held to the same standard of care described previously for the counselor–client relationship. For example, if a Louisiana-based counselor volunteered to do crisis management after Hurricane Katrina, his or her liability risk would be quite small. If he or she provided services to someone who had been an active client before the hurricane, he or she might have a greater duty because the preexisting professional relationship would be presumed to have provided the counselor with sufficient knowledge to render a higher level of assistance.

Repressed or False Memory

In the mid-1990s, the practice of reviving repressed memories of child sexual abuse led to a number of lawsuits against mental health professionals. The concern was that therapists were using hypnosis, guided imagery, or drugs (e.g., sodium amytal) to induce or recover memories of abuse for which there was no corroborating evidence. One jury in Minnesota reportedly awarded more than $2.6 million to a woman who claimed she was injured by false memories of abuse induced after her psychiatrist told her she suffered from multiple personality disorder, probably as the result of repeated sexual abuse by relatives (ACA, 1995). Another jury in California awarded almost $500,000 in damages to a successful winery executive who sued his daughter's therapist and psychiatrist for inducing false memories of abuse in the young woman through suggestion and sodium amytal injections (*Ramona v. Ramona*, 1994). Prior to this lawsuit, Ramona had been sued by his daughter for abuse that she claimed she had repressed for many years.

Concerns about repressed memories stemmed from the increased numbers of reports of cases of child sexual abuse that could not be documented or otherwise corroborated, as well as the increased number of cases that can be verified and the techniques used to reveal these memories. What is known today is that child sexual abuse is a risk factor in a variety of psychiatric disorders. Children who have been abused may try to cope with the trauma in a variety of ways, some of which may lead to a lack of conscious awareness of the abuse for some time. The memories and feelings resulting from the abuse may emerge at a later time. Questioning can influence memories, particularly in young children, and repeated questioning can lead an individual to believe in a memory of an event that did not occur. Further, even without an initial recollection of abuse, a trusted person who suggests past abuse as a possible explanation for problems or symptoms can have significant influence. (American Psychiatric Association, 1993, 2002).

Debate over repressed memory was quite lively in the 1990s. The False Memory Syndrome Foundation was established in Philadelphia and served as a resource and catalyst for litigation. Mental health provider associations responded by trying to help guide their members to navigate the complex practice issues presented by this problem. The Psychiatrists' Purchasing Group (PPG) released an article in April 1994 with suggestions for managing risks when dealing with cases of recovered memories of abuse (PPG, 1994). Some of the recommendations that follow are drawn from this article:

- Be mindful of the kinds of questions you ask (e.g., if the client raises a past history of anorexia, you should avoid a barrage of questions that might indicate you believe the client was abused as a child).
- Remain empathetic and nonjudgmental in your responses and in conversations with the client about possible memories of abuse. If the client has always remembered the abuse, document that. The real problem arises with uncovering repressed memories of abuse.
- Avoid prejudging the truth of the client's reports and statements.
- If a client raises the issue of abuse, talk frankly about the clinical uncertainty of repressed memories at the present time.
- Follow established assessment and treatment techniques.
- Do not pressure the client to believe events that may not have occurred.
- Caution the client not to break off close relationships precipitously unless there is evidence of current danger.
- If you are not specifically trained and competent in this area, consult with a supervisor or more qualified colleague, or refer the client to an experienced therapist.

Additionally, you should avoid accepting, without question, the judgment or diagnosis of a prior therapist (e.g., that the client has dissociative identity disorder). Keep in mind that you may have a duty under state law to report the alleged child sexual abuse if you have a reasonable suspicion that it actually occurred. Finally, carefully document, in the client's files, the alleged facts, the circumstances under which the memory was revealed, the techniques you employed to evaluate and assess the veracity of the memory, and the various treatment options you considered, including consultation or referral to other colleagues.

The issue of recovering repressed memories of abuse is also instructional for counselors in a general sense. Before jumping on the next bandwagon that comes along in the counseling field, make sure there is adequate support in the literature for the techniques you adopt. Be mindful of possible countertransference issues and/or your own unfinished business that may be affecting your response to the client's presenting concerns. Additionally, consultation with colleagues is an invaluable tool in double-checking your own competence and providing evidence, if needed in a subsequent lawsuit, that you took the time to confirm acceptable practice parameters.

Supervision

Supervisors are important resources for handling issues that may arise with a counseling client. However, legal exposure can sometimes result from the supervisory relationship itself. See Appendix B for guidance on establishing an effective supervisor–supervisee relationship. *Supervision* is a formal process whereby a standard of practice is communicated to the counselor being supervised, and the supervising counselor has an obligation to ensure that the supervisee is providing that standard of care to his or her clients. In contrast, although there can be considerable overlap in terms of the interactions, there is one very significant difference between supervision and consultation. *Consultation* is a process whereby one counselor seeks advice from another, but the person seeking consultation is usually free to accept or reject the consultant's advice.

In the context of supervision, a supervisor may be held legally liable for injuries to clients caused by the negligence of a supervisee if those acts occurred in the course and scope of the supervisory relationship. Courts will look to a number of factors to determine whether the supervisor should be held accountable, including the supervisor's control over the supervisee, the location and time at which the act occurred, whether the negligent act was within the supervisee's scope of duty, the supervisee's motivation, and whether the negligent act may have been foreseeable. Depending on the facts, the supervisor may well be found to be vicariously liable for the acts of the supervisee.

Most counselors agree that the process of supervision is critical to the profession's ability to deliver counseling services that meet acceptable standards of care. Nonetheless, supervising counselors need to minimize their exposure to liability as they perform this service to the profession as much as possible. Recognizing that supervisors can be drawn into malpractice cases because of the acts of their supervisees is the first step. Supervisors and supervisees must take other steps to protect themselves and their clients as well. These steps include

- establishing ground rules for the supervisory relationship;
- planning sufficient time for contact and discussion of cases;
- agreeing upon procedures for record keeping;
- documenting any specific instructions/directives provided.

Supervisors should have some mechanism in place for determining that advice is being followed.

There are also ethical requirements regarding supervision, which include appropriate monitoring and regular meetings, ensuring that clients are aware of the supervisee's credentials, education of supervisees regarding client rights, and training in supervisory methods (ACA, 2005a, Standards F.1.a., F.1.b., F.1.c., F.2.a.). The *ACA Code of Ethics* also specifies that counseling supervisors must be aware of and address the role of multiculturalism and diversity in the supervisory relationship (Standard F.2.b.). Additionally, the 2005 *ACA Code* has greatly expanded upon the analysis of establishing boundaries between supervisors and supervisees and permitting certain potentially beneficial nonprofessional relationships with supervisees (Standard F.3.). Responsibilities (e.g., dealing with emergencies and termination of the supervisory relationship) are addressed (Standard F.4.), along with evaluation, remediation, and endorsement (Standard F.5.). Because an increasing number of state licensure boards are also beginning to address the roles and responsibilities of supervisors in their regulations, counselors are advised to review their licensing regulations if they contemplate entering into supervisory relationships.

One last note relates to supervising participants in a peer counseling program in which students are specially trained to offer support and guidance in specific, limited areas to their peers. Just as in other direct supervisory programs, a supervising counselor may be held responsible for the acts of peer counselors. Be certain that all students understand the limits and scope of the program they are working within, including issues relating to confidentiality. If situations arise that are beyond the level of their expertise, be sure they know to report back to the supervisor immediately.

Birth Control and Abortion Counseling

Most counselors who work with minors will be confronted with requests for information and advice concerning birth control and abortion at some point in their careers. Counselors employed by state welfare and family planning agencies certainly deal with such requests on a daily basis. In fact, many state welfare systems include funds for dissemination of family planning information to their clients. Sex and family life education classes are now mandated in many state school systems. Many local jurisdictions have established adolescent health clinics that are empowered to dispense birth control and family planning information to minors who seek their services. Furthermore, because of the widespread nature of AIDS and HIV infection, public service announcements on radio, on television, and in print media openly discuss the use of condoms and advocate safe sex. Minor children are confronted with these messages on a daily basis.

Counselors are generally free to inform clients of the availability of birth control methods without fear of legal liability and to refer clients to family planning or health clinics for more information. In a few states, however, counselors might be held accountable for providing such information to minors without the consent of their parents. Birth control for adolescents remains a highly emotional issue in many communities, and parental consent may be the preferred avenue in some jurisdictions. Referral to a health clinic or physician is always appropriate when minors request contraceptive information or advice. If the counselor decides to provide birth control information, it must be both accurate and complete, and it is important that the client fully understand the information given. Some school boards prescribe that information concerning abstinence also be provided, so it is important that counselors be informed of statutes, local regulations, and school policies in this area.

Advising clients, whether minors or adults, concerning birth control is to be distinguished from counseling such clients about abortion, particularly when the client is already pregnant. Counselors must be cautious not to impose their own views on clients in this highly emotional area and may in fact be restricted from advancing particular positions if they work in certain federally funded clinics. Thus it is critical that counselors become aware of the limits of information that may be provided and exercise great care to provide information that is accurate.

Sexual Misconduct

Despite public condemnation by all the major mental health organizations and considerable publicity about sexual misconduct lawsuits in recent years, a large percentage of all negligence suits brought against psychiatrists, psychologists, and counselors continue to include claims of sexual misconduct (see chapter 8). Clients who have been victims of such relationships have the choice of filing ethical, administrative (licensure board), or legal complaints against their former counselors. Insurance companies now routinely exclude coverage for sexual misconduct, limit the damages that will be paid, or pay only for the legal defense of the counselor and not for any damages that may be awarded (*St. Paul Fire & Marine Ins. Co. v. Love*, 1990).

Standard A.5.a. of the 2005 *ACA Code of Ethics* specifically forbids any type of sexual or romantic relationships or interactions with current clients, their romantic partners, or their family members. Furthermore, the *Code* now restricts counselors from becoming involved sexually or romantically with a former client within a minimum of 5 years following termination of counseling (the former minimum period was 2 years). Even after that time, the counselor still has the obligation to put the best interests of the client first and must ensure that the relationship is not exploitative. (See chapter 8 for a more comprehensive discussion of this issue.)

OTHER CIVIL ACTIONS

Dissatisfied clients may also pursue legal remedies against counselors for a variety of actions outside the traditional negligence or malpractice analysis. Frequently these claims will be coupled with a cause of action for malpractice or negligence, so it is important to understand the elements of each type of action.

Illegal Search and Seizure

The potential for civil liability based on illegal search and seizure usually arises in a school, hospital, or custodial setting and will most likely affect counselors who practice in those types of institutions. Counselors are likely to be involved with disciplinary matters in a school or institutional setting and may be asked to search either a student or resident or his or her room or locker storage areas. In so doing, counselors risk invading the resident's or student's constitutionally protected rights to privacy and to freedom from unreasonable search and seizure as set forth in the Fourth Amendment.

The Fourteenth Amendment extends this constitutional guarantee to searches and seizures by federal and state government officials and is enforced by means of the exclusionary rule, whereby evidence obtained as the result of an illegal search may not be used as evidence in a court of law (*Mapp v. Ohio*, 1961). If a counselor is asked to assist the police in conducting a search, the counselor may request to see a search warrant. A search warrant may not always be required, so it is advisable for counselors to consult with legal counsel and their school administration before acting.

Individuals' privacy rights also are guaranteed by the Constitution, and any "illegal search by a private individual is a trespass in violation of the right of privacy. . . . Any intentional invasion of, or interference with property, property rights, personal rights, or personal liberties causing injury without just cause or excuse is an actionable tort" (*Sutherland v. Kroger Co.*,

1959). As a general rule, teachers or counselors have always been considered private persons in the jargon of search and seizure. The only professional recognized under the law was the law enforcement officer. As any other private person, counselors were not liable for an alleged illegal search of a pupil or resident so long as they were motivated by reasonable cause and acted with reasonable judgment, without malice, and with the best interests of the student or resident in mind. Consequently Fourth Amendment proscriptions generally did not apply to counselors, but they could be sued in tort for invasion of privacy unless these criteria were met.

In *New Jersey v. T. L. O.* (1985), however, the Supreme Court ruled that public school officials, including counselors, are instrumentalities of the state and are subject to the Fourth Amendment commands. As the Court wrote,

> In carrying out searches and other disciplinary functions pursuant to such policies, school officials act as representatives of the State, not merely as surrogates for the parents, and they cannot claim the parents' immunity from the strictures of the Fourth Amendment.

Despite the fact that counselors and other public school and institutional administrators are "representatives of the State" and are therefore bound by the parameters of the Fourth Amendment, this does not mean that all searches are improper. Courts use a balancing of interests test to determine whether a search is reasonable according to the facts presented. As one court concluded, although a student "has a constitutional interest in freedom from governmental intrusion into his privacy . . . the State has an interest in educating children and to do so it is necessary to maintain order in and around the classroom" (*Interest of L. L.*, 1979).

The Supreme Court gave school officials broad powers to search students suspected of carrying weapons, dealing drugs, or violating other laws or school rules in the *New Jersey* case. Although the opinion adopts the position that the Fourth Amendment's prohibition on unreasonable searches and seizures applies to public school officials and that students have legitimate expectations of privacy, the Court also recognized that schools have an equally legitimate need to maintain a learning environment for all students. In order to meet this latter need, the Court ruled that the legality of a student search "should depend simply on the reasonableness, under all the circumstances, of the search." Whether a search is reasonable will depend on whether

> there are reasonable grounds for suspecting that the search will turn up evidence that the student has violated or is violating either the law or the rules of the school. Such a search will be permissible in its scope when the measures adopted are reasonably related to the objectives of the search and not excessively intrusive in light of the age and sex of the student and the nature of the infraction. (*New Jersey v. T. L. O.*, 1985)

School authorities, including counselors, stand in a unique position when it comes to searching school premises. Search warrants are unnecessary to access a student's locker or dormitory room so long as the official has "reasonable suspicion to believe" that illegal substances or items capable of undermining the order and good health of the school environment may be concealed there. Counselors are advised to avoid searches of students to the extent possible (including drug testing), but where this is not possible, counselors must be guided by a standard of reasonableness, as determined by all the facts of the case. A public high school policy requiring all members of the band to submit to a search of their luggage prior to embarking on a concert trip was ruled unconstitutional by the Washington Supreme Court. Although the court recognized a statistical probability that some contraband would be found, because school officials lacked any reasonable information or belief that drugs or alcohol were hidden in the students' luggage, the search was impermissible (*Kuehn v. Renton School Dist. No. 403*, 1985).

In June 1995, the U.S. Supreme Court applied a balancing-of-interests test to uphold a local school board policy involving student searches in *Vernonia School Dist. 47J v. Acton* (1995). This case involved testing all student athletes' urine samples for illegal drugs at the beginning of each sport season and randomly throughout the season. Writing for the majority, Justice Scalia wrote

> Fourth Amendment rights, no less than First and Fourteenth Amendment rights, are different in public schools than elsewhere; the "reasonableness" inquiry cannot disregard the schools' custodial and tutelary responsibility for children. For their own good and that of their classmates, public school children are routinely required to submit to various physical examinations, and to be vaccinated against various diseases. . . . Particularly with regard to medical examinations and procedures, therefore, "students within the school environment have a lesser expectation of privacy than members of the population generally." (*Vernonia School Dist. at 357, quoting New Jersey v. T. L. O, 469 U.S. at 348*)

Justice Scalia went on to explain that privacy expectations of student athletes are even less than those of other students because of the communal showering, dressing, and changing in locker rooms that is required in sports participation. Further, student athletes voluntarily choose to play on a sports team, thus subjecting "themselves to a degree of regulation even higher than that imposed on students generally." Student athletes agree to comply with, for example, rules of conduct, dress, training hours, and minimum grade point averages, so they "have reason to expect intrusions upon normal rights and privileges, including privacy." The court concluded that the drug testing was reasonable, especially in light of these facts: The tests were used to screen only for drugs and not other health conditions; the tests were reliable; results were disclosed only to a limited number of school personnel and parents; and test conditions were similar to those people typically encounter in public restrooms.

The Court further explained that the school board had an important—perhaps compelling—concern for deterring drug use among students of its schools "for whom it has undertaken a special responsibility of care and direction." In view of these circumstances, the policy of the Vernonia, Oregon, school board is reasonable and constitutional, according to the Court. However, Justice Scalia cautioned that not all suspicionless drug testing would be considered appropriate. Each case must meet the test: Is the search one that a reasonable guardian and tutor might undertake?

Counselors working in school settings should be aware that some court cases have not followed the *Vernonia School Dist.* case on state constitutional grounds. For example, an Indiana appellate court refused to uphold suspicionless drug testing based on its reading of the Indiana constitution (*Linke v. Northwestern School Corp.*, 2000). However, in light of the school violence across the country precipitated by the 1999 Littleton, Colorado and 2007 Virginia Tech school tragedies, courts have been more willing in the 21st century to give schools more latitude in conducting searches in order to preserve student safety. Whereas locker searches are generally upheld when there is reasonable suspicion of harmful contraband, strip searches are usually considered highly invasive and may not pass legal scrutiny (Darden, 2006). School counselors should consult local legal counsel if they are asked to participate in any search, seizure, or drug testing activity.

Defamation

A counselor spreads false rumors about the unprofessional conduct of another therapist in the community. A second counselor hears from a third party that her client is abusing drugs, and she calls the client's employer to discuss the situation without first speaking with the client. Both counselors are inviting lawsuits based on the concept of defamation.

The tort action called defamation embodies the public policy that each person should be free to enjoy his or her reputation unimpaired by false attacks, except in certain cases where a paramount public interest dictates that individuals be free to write or speak without fear of civil liability. Violations of this right form the basis for the action, which turns on whether the communication or publication tends, or is reasonably calculated, to cause harm to the reputation of another. In early common law this action was broken down into two separate actions: *slander,* a spoken or uttered word that defames a person; and *libel,* a defamatory writing. For most purposes today, the two forms are treated as one action.

The key elements of a defamation suit brought by a private person are as follows:

1. The information complained of must be defamatory. That means the party must be exposed to hatred, ridicule, contempt, or pecuniary loss.

2. The information must have been communicated to someone other than the defamed person.
3. The defamed person must be alive.
4. The defamed person must have suffered some loss or injury as a result of the defamatory communication.

In addition to obvious injuries such as loss of a job, honor, or award, damages for defamation may also be based on mental suffering and loss of reputation. Some states continue to recognize the common law action for slander in which a communication may be actionable if it

- imputes to another the commission of a serious crime;
- imputes that someone has a loathsome disease;
- imputes a woman is unchaste;
- adversely affects someone's business, trade, or profession.

Counselors may be exposed to liability for defamation in the publication of records, letters of reference or recommendation, or in loose talk that may be untrue or damaging to the client as revealed to a third party. To avoid this, limits must be placed on written or verbal statements about clients. If the client can be identified from information provided in a conversation or in writing, even though the name is carefully withheld, the counselor may become the uncomfortable subject of a lawsuit as a result of that indiscretion.

The major defense to a defamation action is the truth of the statement or information communicated to the third party. In many states this is an absolute defense, just as in common law, although some states also require the statement to have been made in good faith and for a legitimate purpose. Absent some legitimate professional purpose, counselors who make even truthful statements about clients in those states could find themselves subjected to a defamation suit, just as for any other rumors or gossip.

The law also recognizes that in some situations the interests of the immediate participants or of society at large are so great that important, bona fide communications should be permitted freely without fear of resulting lawsuits. Such privileges are granted by statute in almost all states for the proper discharge of official duties and are to be distinguished from the privileged communications discussed in chapter 5 concerning confidentiality. In that discussion, privilege was analyzed as a protection from revealing client confidences should a counselor be called to testify in court. This is a right that belongs to the client and binds the counselor to silence. When the term *privilege* is used in connection with defamation actions, it describes a privilege *to communicate,* which protects the counselor against money-damage defamation suits. The two privileges are not analogous.

Two types of communications are protected from defamation actions: those that are absolutely privileged and those that are qualifiedly privileged. *Absolute privilege* is based on the concept that the public interest in unimpeded communication in certain cases completely outweighs society's concern for an individual's reputation. Thus members of the legislature, judges, jurors, lawyers, and witnesses may speak freely in the exercise of their official functions without fear of civil suit.

Qualified privilege exists in situations where society's interest in unhampered communication is conditionally limited by the general mores as to what is fair and reasonable. Stated another way, based on their positions, certain individuals have a right to receive confidential reports or information that is not appropriate for publication to society at large. Generally, any statement made in a reasonable manner by one who is carrying out duties for a legitimate purpose will be protected by the qualified privilege. Counselors are frequently called upon in the course of their professional duties to make statements concerning clients to other people who have a corresponding duty or interest in receiving that information. For example, a prospective employer may request general information about a client or seek specific information concerning ability or character in the course of conducting a security background investigation. Counselors may need to notify a social service agency of problems in a family to ensure the safety of a client. So long as such communications are made in good faith, with appropriate permissions or releases from the clients where needed; express only facts as known to the counselor; and are made only to persons having a proper interest in receiving the information, they will usually be protected.

Counselors must be cautious whenever they disclose client information to others. If false information is ever transmitted to a third party, corrections should be made as quickly as possible. Counselors who act in a professional manner and are cautious about client information communicated to third parties will generally be protected from defamation actions by the qualified privilege. Here again, it is important to follow the ethical guidelines and obtain clear instructions and releases from clients, preferably in writing, detailing the information to be released. Additionally, this discussion is applicable to counselor's defamatory statements made about colleagues.

Invasion of Privacy

Despite the truthfulness of a defamatory statement and the qualified immunity granted in the counseling situation, a counselor may still be held liable in an action for invasion of privacy if derogatory information is communicated to a third party who has no need or privilege to receive it. The action is based upon undue interference in the affairs of an individual through exposure or communication of his or her private affairs. The injury may result from truthful, but damaging, publications, and the person bringing the suit need not prove he or she has suffered any special injuries. In recent years, concern about dissemination of computer records containing personal and financial information has grown because of the potential for serious harm resulting from erroneous material. The problem is no less severe in the context of educational records and testing or in client records maintained in clinical practice. Counselors working in educational institutions should be thoroughly familiar with the requirements of the Family Educational Rights and Privacy Act (FERPA), or Buckley Amendment, discussed in chapter 5, and take care to protect the student and family rights as set forth in the law.

Counselors employed in all fields are subject to potential liability for invasion of privacy (1) if they administer educational or psychological tests without first fully informing the client of the criteria to be used, what skills or factors the test is designed to measure, and the possible uses of the test results; or (2) if they fail to explain test results. Some state laws now require testing agencies to provide various notices to test subjects and to disclose fully the factors outlined. The 2005 *ACA Code of Ethics* also admonishes counselors to obtain informed consent from clients prior to any assessment and further holds counselors responsible for using and interpreting competently any tests administered, and for releasing information only upon consent of the client, and then only to professionals who can competently interpret the results (Standards E.2., E.3., E.4.). Counselors should keep these criteria in mind when conducting testing and protect the written records of that testing accordingly.

The confidentiality of records also poses a problem for counselors because of concerns about invasion of privacy. The questions as to what should be included in a client or student record, and who might have access to that record, can generally be answered by the rules concerning defamation. First, reasonable care must be taken to ensure that the contents of records are accurate. A counselor who makes an entry designed to injure the client would run a serious risk of liability, even if the information were true. As noted, the reckless disregard of the rights of another can be sufficient to destroy the qualified privilege counselors enjoy in this area. Entering misleading or false information, or failing to make adequate corrections of such information, could meet this lower threshold definition of malice.

Second, the contents of records should be made known only to those who have a legitimate interest in them (for example, parents, professional colleagues, prospective employers) as defined by statute or regulation, or as established by a written authorization to release of information signed by the client or a parent of a minor client. These general rules are, of course, subject to more specific regulations or laws that may govern records in a particular state institution, agency, or school system. Counselors will not generally be held liable in a suit for invasion of privacy if required by law to disclose information or if the disclosure was not malicious and was made to serve certain overriding competing public interests, such as following health regulations, reporting cases of abuse, or protecting a potential victim.

Breach of Contract

Counselors have certain duties arising from either express or implied contracts with clients. Express contracts usually are in writing and signed by the parties, and spell out the rights and responsibilities of each. Express contracts may be made orally and are just as binding on the parties, although proving the specific terms of the agreement may be difficult at some later time.

Implied contracts arise either through the relationship of the parties or as a result of actions of the parties that cause them to respond in a certain way or rely on each other. If a client comes to the counselor's office for a session each week at the same time and is charged a fee for services, which is paid, the parties will be held to have agreed to a contract that includes those terms. All these aspects of the relationship form the basis of the contract with the client, even though it is not expressly written. Should the counselor, absent some justification, fail to uphold his or her end of the bargain under the contract, the client can hold him or her responsible for breaching the contract. Likewise, if a counselor breaches confidentiality, this may be viewed as breaching an implied contract, based on the counselor's professional disclosure statement and ethics code.

Courts also may view professional advertising as terms of an express or implied contract with clients. For example, a firm or practice that advertises in a directory that they are *certified, licensed, registered, bonded,* or the like will be held to fulfill those terms or be found in breach of contract. Similarly, holding oneself out in advertising or client information brochures as an expert in any area also will bring increased responsibilities. Many states regulate the content of professional advertising in their licensing statutes, restricting the use of counseling titles such as professional counselor. Along this line, deceptive or misleading advertising may simultaneously give rise to an action for violation of state deceptive or fraudulent advertising statutes.

Counselors should exercise care in all aspects of a client relationship, but it is especially important to examine critically the whole spectrum of items that may form the basis of any contract with clients, whether express or implied. Written agreements detailing such items as the number and timing of sessions, fees, and payment terms will help to protect counselors (see chapter 2's discussion of informed consent). A counselor should never contract with a client concerning specific results or outcome of treatment, which may prove impossible to achieve.

Copyright Infringement

Original works that are published as articles, books, lectures, curricula, and the like are considered the intellectual property of their creators and are subject to the protection of federal and international copyright laws. This protection gives the copyright holder the exclusive right to print, publish, or otherwise reproduce the work, as well as to display and distribute copies, whether for free or for sale. Using protected material without permission is considered an infringement of the author's or publisher's rights and carries civil and criminal penalties.

Copyrighted material can be used properly by others in their own work as long as the fair use provisions of the Copyright Act of 1976 are followed, or if permission is secured from the copyright holder. The Act sets out four factors to consider in determining *fair use:* (1) whether the material is used for commercial benefit or for nonprofit educational purposes; (2) the medium of the work created; (3) how much of the work is used; and (4) the effect of using the work on the market and salability of the new work. With this in mind, quoting 5 or 10 lines from a research report in support of your findings in a clinical study, with proper attribution to the author, probably falls within the parameters of fair use. Even in that case it is prudent to request permission in advance. However, duplicating copies of an entire course syllabus, research study, or article for distribution to clients or students would infringe on the copyright protection and should not be done.

The widespread use of computers has proved of immeasurable benefit to counselors and administrators worldwide in recent years. Many agencies and institutions now commonly preserve counseling records and data on computer databases and use computers to facilitate client assessment and research. With the efficiency of this wonderful tool, however, a host of concerns have developed of which counselors should be aware. Many of these have been addressed in the 2005 *ACA Code of Ethics* and other professional ethics codes and relate primarily to the misuse of information or assessment tools. Other concerns relate to client misconceptions about computer assessment, counselor competence and training, accuracy of computer-based assessment programs, and the validity of test results.

Another important consideration for counselors who use computers for record keeping and testing is the application of federal copyright laws and licensing agreements. Most adults are aware of the general proscriptions against plagiarism and the protection for written and creative works offered by copyright laws. Such protections also extend to computer operating programs and applications software in word processing, databases, assessment tools, and reporting. Applications software includes testing materials, scoring keys, normative tables, and report forms, according to the Eighth Circuit Court of Appeals. In *Applied Innovations, Inc. v. Regents of the University of Minnesota* (1989) the court ruled that the development, reproduction, marketing, and distribution of software for scoring the Minnesota Multiphasic Personality Inventory (MMPI) infringed the University of Minnesota's copyright of the test because it included copyrighted portions of the instrument. Obviously not all counselors are engaged in developing such scoring software, but this proscription applies to users of such programs as well.

It should be pointed out that borrowing computer programs and using bootlegged computer programs are infringements on the rights of copyright holders and compromise the integrity of testing instruments. Such actions also deprive test and software creators of revenue to which they are legally entitled, and perhaps more important they could lead to the promulgation of defective products that could adversely affect client treatment. Counselors are urged to comply with copyright laws and licensing agreements when they purchase computer software, just as they exercise care to comply with copyright laws in written or other materials.

Insurance Fraud

Insurance fraud is a broad term that involves obtaining money from an insurance company by lying, cheating, or deceit. Although insurance companies may bring civil suits against service providers who misrepresent or misstate services in order to receive insurance reimbursement, insurance fraud may also be pursued by state licensing agencies and through criminal prosecution. All mental health service providers need to understand the specific provisions of insurance programs through which they seek payments and should exercise care in complying with those provisions. Although this is a complex area, there are some specific practice recommendations to minimize the risk of liability for counselors.

First, as a counselor, you must render mental health diagnoses only if you are qualified and competent to render them under state licensing statutes. Report diagnosis codes accurately, and do not be persuaded to use an improper code to gain coverage. Be sure your client understands the full implications of any diagnosis you make and that once it is submitted to an insurance company it will become a part of the client's permanent health record.

Some insurance policies cover only individual psychotherapy sessions or cover individual sessions at a higher copayment rate than conjoint, marital, or family counseling. Be sure to investigate the terms of the particular policy your client is covered under and to use the appropriate codes for third-party billing, even though reimbursement may be limited or denied.

In submitting insurance claims, be careful to state the numbers and length of client visits accurately. Do not assume that two half-hour appointments in 1 week are the same to the insurance company as a single 1-hour appointment, particularly where the insurance company's responsibility for coverage is limited to one visit per week. Keep complete and accurate records of visits, and bill only for those you document.

The person who provides treatment must usually be the one to submit the insurance claim, even though consultants or supervisors may have been involved with the case. It is appropriate to note the names of supervisors or consultants, along with the name of the provider, but these should be clearly identified. This is especially important where an insurance policy covers therapy only when provided by a licensed psychiatrist, psychologist, or mental health counselor. Such services may not be reimbursed if provided by an intern or an unlicensed counselor, even though they may be working under the supervision of a licensed practitioner. Further, charging insurance companies for missed appointments, routinely setting lower fees for clients without insurance coverage, or waiving copayments for those clients may be viewed as insurance fraud.

OTHER CRIMINAL ACTIONS

Accessory to a Crime

Although counselors are honor bound to protect the integrity and promote the welfare of their clients, they also have an obligation to society at large that may override their duty to an individual client. The law makes it clear that any person who advises or encourages the commission of a crime can be charged as an accessory to the crime, even though the person took no active part in its commission. This is called *accessory before the fact*, and an individual convicted of such activity faces criminal penalties. The elements of the offense include the following: (1) evidence exists that the defendant in some way contributed to the crime by aiding or advising the alleged perpetrator; (2) the defendant was not present when the crime was committed; and (3) the alleged perpetrator is convicted of the crime or admits to it (*State v. Woods*, 1982).

However, merely concealing knowledge that a felony (i.e., a serious crime, such as murder, rape, or burglary) is to be committed does not make the party concealing it an accessory before the fact. Thus a counselor who learns from a client during counseling that a crime is to be committed may not always be obligated to reveal that knowledge to authorities, but counselors must be cautious in this gray area. Particularly in view of the *Tarasoff* decision (see chapter 6), counselors must reach a balance between the confidential communications of a client and the need to preserve the safety and well-being of society. Although there is no one hard and fast rule to follow across the country, if you believe a client is about to commit a crime that would threaten the safety, health, or well-being of others, you may have a duty to prevent the act from occurring. This is an active duty that may extend from attempting to discourage your client, to contacting local law enforcement authorities, depending on the circumstances of the case and the law in your state.

A person who assists or aids a felon after a crime has been committed, knowing that the crime has been committed, may be similarly charged as *an accessory after the fact.* Such a person is generally defined as "one who, knowing that a felony has been committed by another, receives, relieves, comforts, or assists the felon, or in any manner aids him [or her] to escape arrest or punishment" (*Criminal Law*, § 174). Three elements must be met:

1. A felony must have already been committed.
2. The person charged as an accessory must have knowledge that the person he or she is assisting committed the felony.
3. The accessory must harbor or assist the felon, intending to shield the felon from the law.

Evidence that a person helped to hide a felon, lent the felon money, gave advice, provided goods, offered transportation, blocked the path of pursuers, or gave false information tending to mislead authorities has been held sufficient to sustain a conviction as an accessory after the fact. It is inaccurate, however, to say that *any* affirmative assistance or relief automatically results in charges that one has been an accessory. Even those acts just enumerated have not always been sufficient to justify conviction when there is no evidence that assistance was provided with the intention of harboring or assisting the felon.

Contributing to the Delinquency of a Minor

Although this topic is of primary concern to school counselors and those who work with families and children, others should be aware of the potential for contributing to the delinquency of minors and of the variety of acts that can trigger the offense. The majority of prosecutions for contributing to the delinquency of minors deal with people who patently attempt to subvert the morals of a juvenile. Even where such acts are unintentional, however, a counselor may not escape liability.

Contributing to the delinquency of a minor is not a common law offense. Unfortunately, not all state legislatures have defined the specific conduct that constitutes the crime, and many jurisdictions leave it to the jury to determine whether a defendant's conduct was criminal.[3] A broad definition of the offense might include any actions that tend to injure the health, morals, or welfare of juveniles or that encourage juveniles to participate in such actions. There is no certainty as to what constitutes this immoral conduct from state to state.

State courts also are divided on the question of intent. The traditional view is that a guilty intent, or *mens rea,* is a necessary element of the offense, but some states do not require mens rea. It is in these latter states

---

[3]See Contributing to Delinquency, *Mens Rea*, 31 A.L.R.3d 848, for an in-depth study of the offense.

that the danger of a counselor's inadvertently crossing the boundary of acceptable conduct is greatest. Most counselors would never deliberately do or encourage any act that would harm a minor. It is the inadvertent act, committed in the mistaken belief that it is legal and, more important, that it is in the best interest of the client, that causes concern. It is not possible in this book to analyze the laws of each state, so to avoid such liability counselors must research the law in the state(s) in which they practice, seek advice from local counsel, and keep abreast of any changes in the statutes or cases that may occur.

RISK MANAGEMENT

It is important that every counselor take active steps to become his or her own risk manager. In short, risk management is a method for identifying potential areas of risk and taking steps to address those areas of vulnerability. In Appendix C, we offer strategies applicable to most counseling practice settings. These strategies are designed to help reduce the risk of a lawsuit, licensure complaint, or ethics investigation, or allow you to respond appropriately in the event of an adverse action.

Chapter 5

CONFIDENTIALITY, PRIVILEGE, AND HIPAA PRIVACY

The effectiveness of the counselor–client relationship depends upon the level of trust between the parties. Therapeutic trust can be established only if the client believes that his or her communications with the counselor will be protected under the doctrines of confidentiality, privilege, and privacy. Although these terms are often used interchangeably, it is helpful to highlight the different nuances of these three terms in order to come to a full understanding of the counselor's obligations to protect client information.

CONFIDENTIALITY

Confidentiality refers to the ethical duty of the counselor to protect his or her client's private communications (ACA, 2005a, Section B.). The term also has legal implications that flow from the counselor's legal duty. A counselor may be sued for failure to protect a client's confidences unless the counselor is acting pursuant to an exception recognized by law (e.g., written authorization by the client, threat of imminent harm by the client against self or others, release of information required by child/elder abuse reporting laws, or as otherwise compelled by law).

As part of the informed consent process, both at the initiation of counseling and throughout the relationship, counselors should inform clients of their right to expect confidentiality and the limits of confidentiality (ACA, 2005a, Standard B.1.d.). Counselors can explain to clients that they are bound by the *ACA Code of Ethics,* which states that "[c]ounselors respect client rights to privacy" (Standard B.1.b.) and "do not share confidential information without client consent or without sound legal or ethical justification" (Standard B.1.c.). Clients should also understand how the counselor will share information with treat-

> *Confidentiality* is the counselor's ethical duty to protect private client communication.

ment team members, subordinates, supervisors, and other professionals (Standards B.3.b., B.3.a., F.1.c., D.1.d.).

Counselors also have an obligation to maintain an awareness and sensitivity regarding different cultural meanings of confidentiality and views on disclosure that may be different from those of the counselor (Standard B.1.a.). This does not mean that counselors should disregard ethical or legal considerations of confidentiality but should, in the spirit of collaborative relationships, have ongoing dialogue with their clients about how, when, and with whom information will be shared.

PRIVILEGED COMMUNICATION

Privilege is a legal term and refers to the protection of confidential communications between two parties. In most states, counselor–client communications are protected from disclosure in the context of certain legal or administrative proceedings, similar to the way in which attorney–client and doctor–patient communications are protected. In other words, the privilege applies when the counselor is called as a witness in a court of law or administrative agency hearing. It is important to note that the privilege usually belongs to the client (who is the holder of the privilege), yet the counselor may be charged with the responsibility of upholding the privilege. The concept of privilege has its roots in English common law. Today, privilege laws protecting counselor–client communications are typically found in evidence codes or counselor licensure laws.

For the privilege to apply, the communication must have been made *in confidence, with the indicated desire that it remain so.* This desire need not be explicitly stated; a simple action such as closing the office door so that a conversation can remain private indicates the desire for privacy. *The communication generally must not be made in the presence or hearing of third persons* or the privilege may be considered waived. In some jurisdictions, the presence of certain third parties does not cause the privilege to be waived. For example, presence of a spouse in marital therapy or presence of a parent, interpreter, or another therapist involved with the client does not always invalidate the privilege.

There are exceptions to the privilege in many states because lawmakers sometimes find that the interests of justice are better served by allowing access to private health information in order to correctly resolve the issues in litigation. For instance, the privilege may be waived when the client puts his or her emotional condition into issue in a lawsuit or when civil commitment proceedings are commenced against a person who is mentally ill and presents a danger to self or others. Additionally, some

> *Privilege* is the protection of confidential communications between two parties in the context of a judicial setting.

courts have interpreted their states' privilege laws to permit otherwise privileged information to be revealed in the context of a child custody suit. This happens because the public policy of protecting children may be deemed greater than the policy reasons for protecting counselor–client communications. Some state courts do not recognize the concept of privilege at all in criminal cases. As in all instances, it is important for practicing counselors to become knowledgeable of the privilege laws in the states in which they practice.

Judges are usually reluctant to expand the privilege in the absence of state legislation. Thus, in states where the counselor–client relationship is not expressly recognized by statute as privileged, a counselor could be required to testify concerning information received from a client. However, it should be noted that the counselor's own thoughts and impressions, or the contents of conversation in a counseling session, may still be protected if they meet the definition of *psychotherapy notes* under HIPAA or *personal notes* under the laws of some states. (See the discussion of HIPAA in the next section.) Federal courts have more flexibility in recognizing privileged communications within the scope of the Federal Rules of Evidence and Criminal Procedure.

The case of *Jaffee v. Redmond* (1996) was the first U.S. Supreme Court case to definitively uphold the concept of a psychotherapist–patient privilege in the federal court system. In this case, a policewoman sought counseling from a licensed clinical social worker after the officer fatally shot a suspect during a stabbing incident at an apartment complex. The family of the deceased suspect sued the police officer, the police department, and the village, alleging use of deadly force in violation of the suspect's civil rights. In the course of discovery before the trial, the plaintiffs (family of the deceased suspect) learned that the policewoman had been in counseling and sought to compel the social worker to testify at the trial and to turn over her notes and records on her sessions with the policewoman.

The trial court ruled that there is no privilege between a social worker and client, but the policewoman refused to grant a waiver of her rights and the social worker refused to reveal the substance of the counseling sessions. As a result, the judge told jurors that they could assume the information withheld would have been unfavorable to the policewoman, and the jury awarded $545,000 to the suspect's family.

The case ultimately was presented before the United States Supreme Court, which carefully looked at the common law principles underlying testimonial privileges and specifically delved into the policy behind Rule 501 of the Federal Rules of Evidence. The Court addressed the question of "whether a privilege protecting confidential communications between a psychotherapist and her patient 'promotes sufficiently important interests to outweigh the need for probative evidence'." The Supreme Court answered this affirmatively, based on both "reason and experience." The resulting decision thus confirmed the existence of a psychotherapist–client privilege in federal court proceedings.

Does *Jaffee* apply to counselors as well as social workers and other mental health professionals? This question was answered by the federal Court of Appeals for the Ninth Circuit in the case of *Oleszko v. State Compensation Insurance Fund* (2001). This court ruled that communications between an unlicensed EAP counselor and a client are protected from compelled disclosure, following the federal psychotherapist–patient privilege established in *Jaffee*.

It is important for counselors to realize that the *Jaffee* and *Oleszko* decisions apply to federal court cases. Most legal disputes are heard in state courts, so the state counselor–client or psychotherapist–patient privilege would apply. As a counselor, what should you do if you are called to testify in court in a state that does not expressly recognize the counselor–client privilege? You should apprise the court of whether you are a licensed professional counselor (or other licensed professional). You should also explain that you are bound by a code of ethics that requires respect for the client's right to privacy, and that testifying would violate professional obligations, if you have not been given a release by your client to testify. Although the decisions in *Jaffee* and *Oleszko* would not necessarily apply in state court, the judge may be willing to look at the policy underpinnings of those cases. You might suggest that your client's attorney attempt to obtain a ruling from the court on the applicability of the privilege; this is usually done in advance by a motion or at trial by a direct request to the judge.

There are numerous situations in which the privilege does not apply to client communications. For example, privilege is considered waived when the client initiates a malpractice action or licensure board proceeding against the counselor. Similarly, a defendant who claims insanity as a defense in a criminal case cannot also claim the physician-patient or counselor–client privilege and withhold evidence of his or her condition, because it is relevant to the defense of insanity. In some states, the privilege may be waived in custody proceedings because of the strong public policy behind protection of children.

PRIVACY AND HIPAA

Privacy refers to the basic right of a person to be left alone and to control his or her personal information. The term *privacy* is the new buzzword in the health care arena in recent years as a result of the enactment of the Health Insurance Portability and Accountability Act of 1996 (commonly referred to as HIPAA). HIPAA called for a variety of standards addressing transactions and code sets, unique identifiers, privacy, and security. The HIPAA Privacy Rule, which is most pertinent to this chapter, was promulgated on the federal level to provide a uniform level of protection that was previously nonexistent because of a patchwork of state laws. This Rule came

> *Privacy* is the basic right of a person to be left alone and to control his or her personal information.

about as a result of concern that transmission of health care information through the Internet and other electronic means could lead to widespread gaps in protection of patient and client confidentiality. The HIPAA Privacy Rule, in its final form, applies to both paper and electronic transmissions of protected health information by *covered entities* (which are explained in this section). The HIPAA Security Rule dovetails with the HIPAA Privacy Rule and requires technical, administrative, and physical safeguards to protect security of protected health information in electronic form.

As a counselor or other health care provider, the first thing that you must determine is whether you are considered a covered entity under HIPAA. The test is whether the provider transmits any protected health information in electronic form in connection with any transactions for which the Secretary of Health and Human Services has adopted a standard. These transactions include such things as health care claims, health plan enrollment and eligibility, and coordination of benefits. For example, if you submit a claim electronically (even if only one time) or use a billing service to do this on your behalf, you are likely to be considered a covered entity who must then comply with all applicable HIPAA regulations. If you do not file for any insurance reimbursement or conduct any electronic transactions, you are probably not a covered entity. However, even if you do not technically fall under HIPAA, you should realize that the privacy standards for maintaining and releasing records and allowing client access to records are likely to be influenced over the next several decades by HIPAA requirements, which are mandatory for most health care providers. In fact, a post-HIPAA decision from a North Carolina appellate court upheld the concept that HIPAA may influence the standard of care in a mental health breach of confidentiality suit, even though HIPAA does not, by itself, create a legal private cause of action against the defendant health care provider (*Acosta v. Byrum*, 2006).

What are some of the things you must do if you are a covered entity under HIPAA? First, you should familiarize yourself with the various HIPAA resources that may be available to help you navigate the HIPAA rules. Next, you must familiarize yourself with the standards and compliance deadlines. The compliance deadline for the HIPAA Privacy Standard was April 14, 2003. If you discover that you are a covered entity but are not yet compliant, you must appoint a privacy officer. This may be you or your office manager if you are a solo practitioner or part of a

> For help in assessing whether you are a covered entity under HIPAA, visit the Web site for the Centers for Medicare and Medicaid Services at http://www.cms.hhs.gov/apps/hipaa2decisionsupport/default.asp

small-group practice. Following this step, you should gather all policies and documents and evaluate them to see if they are HIPAA compliant. Policies regarding client access to records, amendment of records, and accounting of disclosures are mandatory. Authorization forms and informed consent forms may need to be revised. A Notice of Privacy Practices must be developed. Additionally, you will need to revise contracts with your business associates (e.g., billing service, attorney, or accountant with whom you share protected health information). Staff must be trained on your established privacy practices.

Even if you are not technically a covered entity, some of HIPAA's requirements may be good practices for you from a risk management perspective. For example, all counselors should train their office staff, if any, on the rules of confidentiality and should have policies on release of records and clients' rights to access records. It's not advisable to adopt another counselor's Notice of Privacy Practices verbatim if you are not a covered entity. It is better to develop such a notice as part of your informed consent and explain why you are not a covered entity. You should also describe what practices you follow to preserve client confidentiality and what limits of confidentiality the client can expect.

Another issue that requires careful thought is whether to keep separate psychotherapy notes as defined by the HIPAA Privacy Rule:

> notes recorded (in any medium) by a health care provider who is a mental health professional documenting or analyzing the contents of conversation during a private counseling session or a group, joint, or family counseling session and that are separated from the rest of the individual's medical record. (45 C.F.R. § 164.501, 2006)

The definition excludes items such as counseling start and stop times, diagnosis, functional status, treatment plan, symptoms, prognosis, and progress to date. The HIPAA Privacy Rule mandates obtaining a specific authorization to release psychotherapy notes. Although it may take extra work to separate these psychotherapy notes from the official record, counselors should carefully consider whether it may help protect the privacy of their clients. Maintenance of separate psychotherapy notes is not required by the HIPAA Privacy Rule, but some clients may develop an expectation that their records and private communications will be protected to the fullest extent allowed by law. (See chapter 9 for more information.)

Confusing the issue is the fact that some states (e.g., Maryland, the District of Columbia, New York, and Illinois) have mental health laws that create protection for personal notes. These have definitions that differ slightly from the HIPAA definition of psychotherapy notes. Furthermore, whether state or federal law will apply depends on which law is more stringent, or provides greater protection of the client's rights. HIPAA provides what is called a floor level of privacy but does not preempt, or supersede, state laws that provide a greater level of privacy protection to clients. The bottom line is that the decision of whether to keep separate psychotherapy notes or personal notes should be made after carefully consulting with colleagues and possibly local legal counsel.

SPECIFIC CONCERNS REGARDING
CONFIDENTIALITY, PRIVILEGE, AND PRIVACY

Approximately 20% of claims filed against counselors in recent years have arisen from confidentiality and privacy issues. These issues cause a great deal of confusion and concern for many counselors. The ACA Insurance Trust Risk Management Helpline reports that between October 2003 and October 2005, there were 153 inquiries about confidentiality, privilege, and privacy issues, including requests for advice on subpoenas (P. L. Nelson, Executive Director, ACA Insurance Trust, personal communication, November 15, 2005). These 153 questions represented 24% of the total number of inquiries addressed to the Risk Management Helpline. The specific confidentiality, privilege, and privacy concerns that counselors frequently encounter across the country include subpoenas, counseling minors, confidentiality of substance abuse records, group and family counseling, counseling public offenders, confidentiality after a client's death, and confidentiality and technology.

Subpoenas

A subpoena is an official court document that requires the recipient to appear in court to be questioned as a witness, or to be deposed at another location, about facts underlying a lawsuit. A subpoena may also require the production of documents. Subpoenas may come from attorneys representing your client or someone who is proceeding against your client, and you must respond carefully, unless the subpoena is withdrawn or overruled by a judge. Subpoenas are generally drafted broadly to elicit as much information as possible, even though that information may not be relevant or may be protected by a privileged communication statute. Counselors must be careful to protect the privileged communications of their clients to the fullest extent permitted by law. The following steps are designed to help a counselor respond to a subpoena for confidential client information:

1. Consult an experienced health care attorney (see Appendix D). State law or HIPAA may apply, depending upon the circumstances. Remember that state law may outweigh HIPAA if it is more protective of the client's privacy rights. If your attorney agrees, go on to steps 2, 3, and 4.

2. Ascertain whether the client, after advice from his or her attorney, will provide you with written authorization to release information or to testify. If you maintain psychotherapy notes as defined by HIPAA, you must have a specific authorization form in order to release these notes. (If your state has specific protection for personal notes, you might not be required to release them, even with client authorization.)

3. If the client's attorney declines to provide you with signed authorization from the client, request that the client's attorney file a motion to quash the subpoena or a motion for a protective order. The motion should eventually lead to a court order from the judge regarding whether you must testify or turn over information.

4. If the preceding steps do not produce either your client's informed authorization or a court order, send a written notice to the attorney who issued the subpoena. This notice should be customized to the particular facts and may include language similar to the following: "In order to testify or release records or other protected health information pursuant to the subpoena that was served on me in [name of case] on [date], I must receive one of the following: (a) written, informed authorization from [client's name] to release the information requested [and specific authorization to release psychotherapy notes, if applicable]; or (b) a court order [from the judge and qualified to comply with HIPAA, if necessary] to release the information or testify, as commanded by the subpoena." Remember that if you are a HIPAA-covered entity, any protective order you receive must meet all the requirements of 45 C.F.R. § 164.512(e) (2006).

Counseling Minors

Virtually all the standards for protecting client confidences that apply to adults are equally applicable to minors (in most states, minors are people under the age of 18). Certainly some information revealed in counseling sessions would be detrimental to family relationships if divulged to parents or guardians and would destroy the trust between the client and counselor. Nonetheless, parents or guardians, who are legally and financially responsible for the upbringing of their children, have some right to know what is learned in the counseling process. In addition, counselors may feel that sharing certain information with parents or guardians could further the progress of counseling.

The 2005 *ACA Code of Ethics* urges counselors to be sensitive to the cultural diversity of families and to respect the inherent rights and responsibilities of parents/guardians over the welfare of their children/charges according to the applicable law (Standard B.5.b.). The *Code* also recognizes the need for counselors to balance the ethical rights of minor or incompetent clients with the parental rights and responsibilities to protect these clients (Standard A.2.d.). The relevant inquiry often boils down to this: Is the minor client's right to confidentiality outweighed by the need to inform a parent, guardian, or other appropriate adult of information received in the course of counseling? Many factors should be considered in the analysis, including the age, maturity, and educational level of the client; the relationship with parents or guardians; whether disclosure can reasonably be expected to help the situation or could cause harm; and the severity of potential harm or injury that could come if the information is not disclosed (e.g., is the client using crack cocaine?). Counselors should also take into account whether the minor client has been consulted about the disclosure and the position or relationship of the adult who has requested information. State law differs regarding whether the parent controls the ability to access or release information about a minor child. (See Appendix D for information about accessing state laws).

Requests for information about a minor client from nonparents are frequent in school settings. Sharing student information with teachers and administrators is common in schools and is usually considered necessary to the progress of the student but should be limited to the educational-need-to-know situation. Permission from a parent or guardian may be required by law before sensitive confidential information is divulged to a third person.

Counselors in schools that receive federal funding are generally bound by the provisions of the Family Educational Rights and Privacy Act of 1974 (FERPA, or the Buckley Amendment), implementing regulations, and state or local school board policies concerning the disclosure of students' educational records. Although many school counselors have interpreted FERPA to allow them to keep their counseling records as sole possession notes and therefore to keep them from the student's parents, the U.S. Department of Education has stated its opinion that a school counselor's notes are generally part of the education record. According to the Family Policy Compliance Office of the U.S. Department of Education, certain portions may be excepted from the education record if they are memory joggers used only by the counselor (R. Norment, personal communication, May 19, 2006). This may be an issue that will ultimately need to be clarified by future court decisions. Additionally, questions have arisen concerning requests for information from noncustodial parents. FERPA makes it clear that noncustodial parents have the same rights to educational records as custodial parents in the absence of a court order to the contrary. Because of the different interpretations of FERPA, school counselors should seek advice from their school system's attorney or their own attorney when subpoenaed or otherwise requested to reveal confidential information to parents or others.

Confidentiality of Substance Abuse Records

Counselors should be aware of the fact that there are strict confidentiality rules that apply to records of alcohol and drug abuse treatment if the treatment is part of a federally assisted program. The law (Public Health Service Act, 2007) and its implementing regulations (Confidentiality of Alcohol and Drug Abuse Patient Records, 2007) are broadly construed to include providers who receive Medicare or Medicaid funding. Counselors should obtain consultation when they receive third-party requests or subpoenas for records of substance abuse treatment to ensure that both federal and state law requirements are met.

Group and Family Counseling

As already mentioned, privilege is not always recognized in the context of group and family counseling. However, protecting the confidentiality of group participants is an ethical concern, and it is the responsibility of the counselor to address this aspect at the outset of the group relationship. Standard B.4.a. of the 2005 *ACA Code of Ethics* requires counselors to "clearly explain the importance and parameters of confidentiality for the specific group being entered." It is good practice for counselors to clearly communicate to all members of the group that even though the counselor will not reveal client information, he or she cannot guarantee that group members will not do so. It is also advisable to ask group members to sign an agreement that they will honor and protect the confidences of other members of the group and understand the consequences of violating that agreement. (This is actually a legal requirement in the District of Columbia; see D.C. Mental Health Information Act, 2006.) Counselors should also review the confidentiality agreement with group participants periodically.

Counselors working with families or couples face difficult confidentiality issues. For example, what does the state privilege law say, if anything, about whether communications within the family or between the couple will be considered privileged in a court of law? Depending on their theoretical orientation, counselors working with families may not always see the entire family system; as a result, information may be revealed by one family member when another family member is not present. Should those communications be protected? The 2005 *ACA Code of Ethics* states that, in the context of couples and family counseling, counselors "clearly define who is considered 'the client' and discuss expectations and limitations of confidentiality" (Standard B.4.b.). This section of the *Code* further requires counselors to seek agreement and document in writing the understanding among all parties having capacity to give consent regarding confidentiality. In short, it's important to set the ground rules for the family or group counseling and be sure everyone understand the limits of confidentiality. Revealing information about the group, family members, or a family system to individuals outside the counseling relationship should be done only after obtaining a release from all group or family members capable of giving consent, or upon court order.

Counseling Public Offenders

Probably the greatest problem facing counselors in prisons, other adult custodial penal institutions, and juvenile justice facilities and programs is the persistent tension between the ethical guidelines stressing confidentiality and the requirements of sharing information among agencies involved in the correctional process. Clients may wish to discuss particular problems, such as drug use in prison, but failing to reveal that information could cost a counselor his or her job. Clients also know that counselors may be required to report to courts and correctional officials on the progress of their clients, so they might be inclined to present themselves in a more positive light.

Some state statutes may permit access to prison records, beyond the correctional institution, by local parole boards, probation departments, and even community service boards for planning and coordinating postrelease mental health services for offenders. Other than those records restricted by federal law, such as those relating to AIDS or HIV status and substance abuse, counseling records may not be fully protected.

Despite potentially conflicting job requirements and state laws, counselors working with public offender clients still are bound by the ethical duty to maintain client confidences. Client confidences must be protected when possible, but clients should be advised at the outset that the information must be included in periodic court reports (if such reports are required by the state). Clients must also understand that certain criminal activities, including threats of violence that are disclosed in counseling, may need to be reported. Counselors should take extra care in maintaining and documenting prison and other public offender setting counseling records, and information included in periodic reports should be limited to that which is requested.

Confidentiality After a Client's Death

One of the most difficult issues a counselor may face is how to handle requests for information after a client's death. Confidentiality does not automatically die upon a client's death. The 2005 *ACA Code of Ethics* states the following: "Counselors protect the confidentiality of deceased clients, consistent with legal requirements and agency or setting policies" (Standard B.3.f.). From a legal perspective, the issue is often very murky. Some state statutes permit the administrator or executor of the deceased person to access records. Often, that administrator is a spouse or close relative of the client. Would the client want his spouse or significant other to access his private counseling records? Counselors should obtain advice from legal counsel, as well as consult with a trusted colleague, when faced with such requests for access to a deceased client's records.

Confidentiality and Technology

Counselors who are HIPAA-covered entities have obligations to guard the privacy and security of protected health information. However, it's important for all counselors to recognize that their obligations go well beyond protection of the traditional paper record. The 2005 *ACA Code of Ethics* states the following:

> Counselors take precautions to ensure the confidentiality of information transmitted through the use of computers, electronic mail, facsimile machines, telephones, voicemail, answering machines, and other electronic or computer technology. (Standard B.3.e.)

In the past decade or so, counselors and other mental health professionals have had complaints brought against them based on e-mail being sent to the wrong person, voice mail being inappropriately overheard, and computerized records landing in the hands of the wrong party. It's essential in today's world to develop procedures to minimize the risk of such technology-related privacy breaches.

LIMITS OF CONFIDENTIALITY, PRIVILEGE, AND PRIVACY

It is important to remember that one of the primary ethical and legal duties of a professional counselor is to protect the client and others from harm. As a result of that duty, and the competing societal interests in safety and security, there are several counseling situations in which the ethical and legal confidentiality requirements must bend to accommodate public safety interests. In some cases, the counselor has an affirmative obligation to report information learned through the counseling relationship to appropriate authorities. These duties to report or otherwise protect the client are discussed in the next chapter.

Chapter 6

DUTIES TO REPORT, WARN, AND/OR PROTECT

As discussed in the chapter 5, the general rule is that counselor–client communications are confidential and should be protected. However, there are important exceptions to this rule. For example, if you determine that a serious and foreseeable threat of harm exists to a client or some third person, you may have both an *ethical obligation* (ACA, 2005a, Standard B.1.c.) and a *legal duty* to disclose certain information to the proper authorities and/or to notify the potential victim or take other appropriate measures.

CHILD AND ELDER/ VULNERABLE ADULT ABUSE REPORTING

All states now mandate reporting incidents of child abuse, and reporting of elder, disabled, or vulnerable mentally ill adult abuse is permitted or required in virtually all states.[1] In these cases, the counselor–client privilege does not apply, and there may be significant penalties if the counselor fails to report the abuse or neglect. In *Searcy v. Auerbach* (1992), the Ninth Circuit Court of Appeals ruled that a psychologist who did not follow statutory procedures for reporting child abuse was not immune from civil liability; in other words, he could be successfully sued for neglecting to make the required report. The psychologist disclosed his opinion about abuse to the child's father but failed to make the mandated report to the appropriate agency.

These reporting laws came about because the public policy supporting protection of a vulnerable population (e.g., children, people with disabilities, elderly people) was viewed as more important than a client's or patient's right to keep the information confidential. Reporting past incidents of abuse may be required in some states. For example, in the state of Maryland, the Attorney General's Office has issued an opinion stating

---

[1]For more information about each state's adult protective services programs, call the Eldercare Locator of the U.S. Administration on Aging at 1–800–677–1116 or visit the National Center on Elder Abuse at http://www.elderabusecenter.org.

that past child abuse must be reported even in cases where the victim has long passed the age of majority[2] (78 Md. Op. Att'y Gen. 189, 12/3/1993). (A Maryland court could reach a different conclusion, but an opinion of the Attorney General is likely to be given considerable weight in the court's consideration of the issue.)

How should you handle a situation when you are not sure the specific circumstance meets the definition of abuse or neglect? You should consider calling the applicable protective services agency—perhaps requesting to speak to a supervisor —and state the relevant facts without giving names or other identifying information. If the agency representative confirms that it is indeed a reportable incident, then go ahead and relay the names and contact information required by law. The reason we suggest this step is to make sure you are making a good-faith report, which is typically required in order to receive immunity from suit as a result of the report. You should also consider seeking the advice of an attorney in your state if the reporting duty is not clear. Additionally, you may wish to obtain a copy of your state child abuse law, often available online through your state government's Web site.[3]

DOMESTIC VIOLENCE

Most states do not require health professionals to report domestic violence unless it comes under another reporting requirement, such as child or elder/vulnerable adult abuse laws. However, California, Colorado, Kentucky, New Hampshire, New Mexico, and Rhode Island are examples of states with some type of reporting statutes for suspected cases of domestic violence, also frequently called intimate partner violence. In Colorado, the reporting duty applies only to physicians (Colo. Rev. Stat. § 12-36-135, 2006). In Kentucky, domestic violence reporting is a subset of the adult abuse reporting laws, and the reporting duty runs to any person having reasonable cause to suspect that an adult has suffered abuse, neglect, or exploitation (Ky. Rev. Stat. § 209.020–.030, 2006). In New York, there is no mandatory duty to report, but health care staff in hospitals must give suspected victims of domestic violence a victim's rights notice that contains referral information (N.Y. Pub. Health Law § 2803-P and Soc. Serv. Law § 5349-A, 2006).

Additionally, almost all states have some type of reporting requirement for physicians (and other providers, depending on the state) who treat patient

---

[2]The age of majority is the legal age at which a person is considered an adult for purposes of making certain decisions or entering into contracts. In most states, the age of majority is 18.

[3]More information on child abuse reporting laws may be found at the Child Welfare Information Gateway at http://www.childwelfare.gov. This Web site consolidates information from what was formerly known as the National Clearinghouse on Child Abuse and Neglect Information and the National Adoption Information Clearinghouse.

injuries due to guns, knives, or other weapons. This type of reporting duty does not usually involve counselors, especially in the outpatient setting.

How can you decide whether you have a mandatory duty to report in your state? There are useful online resources for accessing state domestic violence reporting requirements.[4] The National Domestic Violence Hotline may also be a helpful tool to have on hand when you are counseling victims of domestic violence.[5] Additionally, the ACA Insurance Trust's Risk Management Helpline may be able to provide assistance or resources to counselors who have their professional liability insurance through that program.[6]

Duty to Report Clients' Past Crimes

There is usually no duty to report past crimes, unless the crime falls under a reporting statute (e.g., child abuse) or unless the client is also threatening future harm against a third party (see this chapter's discussion of Duty to Warn and/or Protect). When in doubt, check with your supervisor, consult with a colleague, or seek legal advice. This does not mean that you should agree to keep a gun or other weapon used in a crime or help to harbor a client who is a fugitive from justice; such an action could lead to a charge against you of aiding and abetting a crime or participating in an obstruction of justice.

Duty to Report Unprofessional Conduct of Colleagues

At some point in your counseling career, you are likely to be faced with a colleague's unprofessional conduct or impairment. According to the 2005 *ACA Code of Ethics*, you should first attempt to resolve the issue informally, provided your action does not violate the client's confidentiality rights (Standard H.2.b.). For example, if you are having lunch in a busy restaurant with some professional colleagues and one of them discusses a client within earshot of other restaurant patrons, your obligation is to remind your colleague that any consultations should be handled in a private environment. If informal resolution is not appropriate, other possible action may include referral to state or national ethics committees, the state licensure board, or other authority. Again, the *ACA Code of Ethics* suggests that action should

---

[4]See the Domestic Violence and Sexual Assault Data Resource Center at http://www.jrsa. org/dvsa-drc/index.html

[5]The National Domestic Violence Hotline number is 800-799-SAFE.

[6]The ACA Insurance Trust may be accessed at 800–347–6647. The toll-free number to the Risk Management Helpline is available to insured counselors who first verify their status with the Trust.

not violate a client's confidentiality (Standard H.2.c.). You should check with your state licensure board to determine whether there is a mandatory duty to report and whether it trumps the duty to preserve confidentiality if you learn of a colleague's unprofessional conduct through a client. Comprehensive information about the various state licensure boards, licensing requirements, and the boards' contact data is available from ACA's *Licensure Requirements for Professional Counselors* (2007).

> The *Tarasoff* case in California ruled that a therapist who knows or should have known that a patient poses a "serious danger of violence to others" and does not exercise reasonable care to protect the intended victim or notify the police can be held liable.

DUTY TO WARN AND/OR PROTECT

The California Supreme Court shocked practicing mental health professionals across the country when it ruled in 1976 that a therapist who knows or should have known that a patient poses a "serious danger of violence to others" and does not exercise reasonable care to protect the intended victim or notify the police can be held liable (*Tarasoff v. Regents of the University of California,* 1976). The case involved a graduate student at the University of California-Berkeley, Prosenjit Poddar, who revealed in counseling that he intended to kill a young woman, Tatiana Tarasoff, because she had refused to continue to date him. The psychologist considered the threat to be serious and called the campus police. The campus police detained the student briefly but released him because he seemed to be rational. They neither notified the city police nor warned Ms. Tarasoff. The psychologist also reported his concerns to his supervisor, a psychiatrist, who directed that no further action be taken because Poddar did not meet the civil commitment criteria in effect at the time. Shortly thereafter, Poddar murdered Tarasoff, whose parents sued the psychologist, the psychiatrist, the outpatient treatment center affiliated with the university, the campus police, and the university's Board of Regents.

The court found that certain duties and obligations arise on the part of a therapist from the special relationship with the client and that this relationship may create affirmative duties for the benefit of third parties. The court specifically stated this ruling:

> [O]nce a therapist does in fact determine, or under applicable professional standards reasonably should have determined, that a patient poses a serious danger of violence to others, he bears a duty to exercise reasonable care to protect the foreseeable victim of that danger. (*Tarasoff* at p. 345)

However, the court also recognized that the confidential character of the therapeutic relationship is critical to its success and ought to be preserved, as is evidenced by the following:

> We realize that the open and confidential character of psychotherapeutic dialogue encourages patients to express threats of violence, few of which are ever executed. Certainly a therapist should not be encouraged routinely to reveal such threats; such disclosures could seriously disrupt the patient's relationship with his therapist and with the persons threatened. To the contrary, the therapist's obligations to his patient require that he not disclose a confidence *unless such disclosure is necessary to avert danger to others,* and even then that he do so discreetly, and in a fashion that would preserve the privacy of his patient to the fullest extent compatible with the prevention of the threatened danger. (*Tarasoff* at p. 347)

Consequently, the court concluded that the psychotherapist–patient privilege ought to be preserved when possible, but not when it conflicts with protection of life. Of course, this poses a difficult call for the counselor who may not be able to truly ascertain whether a client's threats are credible. The counselor might be sued by the client for invasion of privacy or breach of confidentiality. Many states have enacted statutes limiting the liability of the counselor and other mental health professionals when they breach a client's confidentiality in order to protect a third party. To avoid potential liability, it is important to understand the limits of the *Tarasoff* court's opinion and of any subsequent decisions or legislation in the state where you practice.

Tarasoff and a number of cases following it (e.g., *McIntosh v. Milano,* 1979, and *Eckhardt v. Kirts,* 1989) have held that liability applies when the psychotherapist reasonably believed, or should have believed, that the client posed a serious danger to an identifiable potential victim. In the first instance, the counselor must make the judgment that the client poses a serious danger. In the second, there must be an identifiable potential victim. In *Davis v. Lhim* (1988), the Michigan Supreme Court enumerated factors a mental health professional should consider when deciding whether a client might act upon a threat to a third person. These factors include the clinical diagnosis of the patient, the context and manner in which the threat is made, the patient's opportunity to act on the threat, the patient's history of violence, the factors that provoked the threat, whether the threats are likely to continue, the patient's response to treatment, and the patient's relationship with the potential victim.

Court Decisions Following *Tarasoff*

In several cases, courts have declined to impose liability in the absence of a readily identifiable victim. Other courts have held that the duty to warn is broad and extends to foreseeable victims of the client who may not be specifically identifiable but nonetheless would be likely targets if the client were to become violent or carry through on threats (*Hedlund v. Superior Court,* 1983; *Jablonski v. United States,* 1983). The Arizona Supreme Court also used this standard and found a psychiatrist liable for failing to protect a foreseeable victim within the "zone of danger," that is, probably at risk of harm from the patient's violent conduct (*Hamman v. County of Maricopa*, 1989).

Another court rejected the foreseeable-victim analysis altogether, holding that there is a duty to exercise due care in determining whether a patient poses an unreasonable risk of serious bodily harm to others (*Perreira v. Colorado*, 1989). Interestingly, the Florida appeals court declined to follow *Tarasoff* in 1991, ruling that imposing a duty to warn third parties would require a psychiatrist to foresee a patient's dangerousness, which is virtually impossible, and would undermine psychiatrist–patient confidentiality and trust. The court realized the difficulty of predicting dangerousness, comparing it to a therapist using a crystal ball (*Boynton v. Burglass*, 1991). Florida has a statute permitting psychiatrists to warn third parties, but reporting is not mandatory according to case law (*Boynton v. Burglass*, 1991; Fla. Stat. § 491.0147, 2006). The *Boynton* court specified that the ruling also applied to psychologists, psychotherapists, and other mental health professionals. Therefore, in Florida, counselors may breach confidentiality to prevent clear and imminent physical harm to a person, but there is no mandatory duty as exists in California under *Tarasoff*. However, counselors in Florida should be mindful of any new case law that may further define the duty to warn/protect; they should also be aware of any duty imposed by their licensure laws.

Texas is also among the few states that have expressly decided not to adopt the *Tarasoff* ruling. In 1999, the Texas Supreme Court held that mental health professionals have no common law duty to warn readily identifiable third persons of a patient's threats against them (*Thapar v. Zezulka*, 1999). However, by statute in Texas, counselors are permitted to make certain disclosures to law enforcement or medical personnel in situations in which there is a risk of imminent physical injury to a third party. However, there is no specific grant of immunity built into the statute, which could create a decision-making challenge for the therapist (Tex. Health & Safety Code § 611.004, 2006).

Two related cases from the State of California, where *Tarasoff* was decided, appear to expand the meaning and intent of the California immunity statute: *Ewing v. Goldstein*, 2004, and *Ewing v. Northridge Hosp. Med. Ctr.*, 2004. In those cases, a California appeals court decided that psychotherapists who predicted or actually believed that a patient posed a threat of serious bodily injury or death to a third person have a duty to warn, even though the threat was relayed to the therapist by a family member of the patient, not the actual patient. This ruling could raise serious questions for counselors and other mental health professionals if courts interpret the immunity laws in such a broad fashion. For example, who should be considered a family member for purposes of deciding whether there is a duty to warn/protect?

Most cases impose liability on a therapist for failing to warn/protect only when there is resulting personal injury. However, the Vermont Supreme Court ruled that the duty to warn and protect applied in a property damage case. In *Peck v. Counseling Service of Addison County, Inc.*, 1985, a counselor was told by her client that he wanted to burn down his father's barn. Unfortunately, after promising his therapist that he would not carry out that threat, he did set fire to the barn. The court was quite concerned that arson posed a grave danger to human life and was unwilling to limit the duty owed by the therapist.

Law Continues to Evolve

These cases demonstrate that the courts around the country continue to grapple with the issues of confidentiality and the competing duty to warn potential victims of violent patients or clients. In the 1980s and 1990s, a majority of state legislatures passed laws providing immunity for mental health professionals who take action to protect potential third-party victims from the dangerous behavior and threats of patients and clients. However, there are many differences among these state laws as to what actions trigger a duty, what actions of the mental health professional will fulfill that duty, and whether counselors are among those covered by the statutory protection.

In Virginia, there is an immunity law that clearly applies to professional counselors as well as other mental health professionals. It specifies that mental health service providers have a duty to take precautions to protect identified or readily identifiable third parties from violent behavior or serious harm when the client has communicated to the counselor, orally, in writing, or by sign language, a specific and immediate threat to cause serious bodily injury or death. The counselor may seek involuntary admission to the hospital (civil commitment), make reasonable attempts to warn the potential victim, notify the appropriate law enforcement authority, or provide counseling in the session in which the threat was communicated until the provider reasonably believes the client no longer has the intent or ability to carry out the threat (Va. Code Ann., §54.1-2400.1, 2006). The law also makes health care providers immune from civil suit for breaching confidentiality in communicating such threats, failing to predict harm in the absence of a threat, or for failing to take precautions other than those specified in the law.

As the law in this area continues to evolve, it is important to keep informed of judicial and legislative actions in your state that affect your practice area. You may wish to subscribe to one of the many mental health law bulletins available through commercial publishers. These tools can help keep you apprised of legal developments that you might otherwise miss.

CLIENTS WITH AIDS/HIV+ STATUS:
DUTY TO WARN OR REPORT?

Another dilemma that arises for counselors is whether to warn partners of human immunodeficiency virus-positive (HIV-positive) clients or those with acquired immune deficiency syndrome (AIDS), or report to a public health agency when the clients are not exercising safe sex practices. Knowing the potential for transmission of HIV and the potentially deadly nature of the resulting AIDS infection, society certainly has an interest in protecting unsuspecting partners of clients who may be HIV-positive. However, there is a strong reason to protect the confidentiality of clients who are HIV-positive. Virtually all states now have statutes governing reporting of HIV and AIDS cases to public health authorities and corresponding confidentiality duties, but many of the laws that either permit or require reports are limited to reporting by physicians.

The *ACA Code of Ethics* provides an ethical perspective in Standard B.2.b.:

> When clients disclose that they have a disease commonly known to be both communicable and life threatening, counselors may be justified in disclosing information to identifiable third parties, if they are known to be at demonstrable and high risk of contracting the disease. Prior to making a disclosure, counselors confirm that there is such a diagnosis and assess the intent of clients to inform the third parties about their disease or to engage in any behaviors that may be harmful to an identifiable third party.

As a counselor, if you practice in a jurisdiction where statutes clearly define the actions you should take regarding reporting of AIDS/HIV, you should follow the statutory mandate. Your state public health department may be able to help you ascertain what your obligations are under state law. What should you do if you practice in a state in which the obligations are not clear for counselors or in which you're not certain whether the law is consistent with your ethics code? First, make sure that you remain current about appropriate ways to protect against transmission of AIDS/HIV. Next, you might consider speaking with your client and educating him or her about safe sex practices and seeing then if the client is willing to make responsible decisions. If the client refuses to inform his or her partner(s), one option might be to call the appropriate public health agency without giving a name and find out what it is able to do without compromising the client's confidentiality. Another possibility is to refer the client for a medical evaluation by a physician, who may be able to make a report to the appropriate public health authorities without facing liability for breach of confidentiality. The health agency may be able to do contact tracing or take other action to protect third parties at risk. Another option is to see if the client is willing to speak directly to the public health agency in your presence. In any event, if your duty is unclear, you should consider obtaining consultation from the public health agency, an attorney, and a colleague well versed in ethics.

Duty to Warn:
Practical Risk Management Guidelines

In the absence of explicit state laws, counselors still may have an ethical duty to disclose information when required to prevent clear and imminent danger to the client or others. The real question for the counselor is, How can I fulfill my legal and ethical duties to protect human life, act in the best interest of the client, and remain protected from potential liability? The following guidelines are suggested to help protect human life, afford maximum privacy protection for the client, and help keep you from being a defendant in a malpractice case:

- *Apprise clients of the limits of confidentiality* at the outset of counseling and give periodic reminders.
- *Consult* with a trusted colleague and/or supervisor.
- *Know the law* in your state and whether it requires a communicated threat against a specifically identifiable victim or if it encompasses a broader duty. If there is a statute that provides immunity for good faith acts on your part, know what it says about actions you must take. Your state counseling association or your local attorney may be able to help you understand your legal obligations.
- *Review the 2005 ACA Code of Ethics* or other ethics codes applicable to your practice.
- *Consult with your attorney* if you are concerned about your exposure or if your legal duty is unclear.
- *Make referrals* where appropriate.
- *Obtain prior history* (medical/behavioral). Has the client acted out violently in the past? What were the circumstances? Was it premeditated? Does the client frequently make impulsive decisions? Is substance abuse an issue? Is the client delusional? Is there reason to believe the client is only discussing a fantasy, not a real threat?
- *Inquire* about the client's access to weapons, homicidal ideation, and current plans.
- *Consider all appropriate clinical responses and the consequences* of each (warning the potential victim(s); calling the police; involving a psychiatrist to do a medication evaluation; changing treatment plans; hospitalizing the client). If clinically appropriate, involve the client in your decision making. Do not reveal confidential information that is not necessary to protect potential victim(s).

- *Know and follow applicable institutional policy.*
- *Document* all actions you take, those you reject, and the rationale behind each decision (see chapter 9).

Following these steps cannot totally protect a potential victim or erase a counselor's liability when a client harms another person. However, they can go a long way toward establishing that a counselor is acting within the standard of care expected of practicing counselors today.

Chapter 7

SUICIDE AND THREATS
OF HARM TO SELF

A ny threat of harm to self, especially threats of suicide or a completed suicide by a client, are stressful and disturbing issues in any counseling practice. In this chapter we (1) outline some of the ethical and legal issues surrounding the response to threats of suicide and harm to self; (2) offer some practical strategies for managing the ethical and legal risks associated with client threats; and (3) address some of the moral, ethical, and legal complexities associated with assisted suicide. But before beginning these discussions we want to provide a brief overview of the prevalence of suicide, threat of suicide, and threats of harm to self.

PREVALENCE OF SUICIDE AND
THREATS OF HARM TO SELF

Suicide, threats of suicide, and other threats of harm to self are a chilling reality for practicing counselors and other mental health professionals. Depending on the practice setting, many counselors regularly face the clinical complexities and ethical and legal implications of responding to clients who threaten harm to self. The American Association of Suicidology (2006) reported that in 2003, in the United States, 31,484 people committed suicide, making suicide the 11th leading cause of death. Of those 31,484 deaths, 12% (3,988) were youth (ages 15 to 24) and 14.6% (5,248) were elder persons (ages 65 and older). Males in general have the highest suicide rate (69%), resulting in the death of 22,830 men. The national suicide rate in 2003 was 10.8 per 100,000. Wyoming (21.8), Montana (19.6), Nevada (19.4), and Alaska (19.1) had the highest rates of suicide per 100,000 people. New York (6.1), the District of Columbia (6.4), Massachusetts (6.7), and New Jersey (6.8) had the lowest rates of suicide. The American Association of Suicidology estimates that there are 25 suicide attempts for every one completed suicide (100 to 200 attempts for youth and 4 attempts for elder persons). Using the 25 to 1 ratio, there were 787,000 attempts in the United

States during 2003. The frequency of suicide and suicide attempts makes it almost inevitable that most practicing mental health professionals will be involved with these clinical challenges.

Youth and Child Suicide

School counselors, marriage and family therapists, child psychologists/therapists, and other child-based practitioners are confronted with students and clients who threaten suicide. In 2003, across the nation, 3,988 youth (ages 15 to 24) and 244 children (ages 10 to 14) completed suicide. Suicide was the third leading cause of death for youth in 2003 (American Association of Suicidology, 2006). Suicide rates for children (ages 10 to 14) have increased 99% between 1980 and 1997. For every completed suicide by youth, it is estimated that 100 to 200 attempts are made. Based on the 2005 Youth Risk Behavior Surveillance Survey (Centers for Disease Control and Prevention, 2005), 8.4% of students in grades 9 through 12 reported making an attempt at suicide in the previous 12 months (10.5% female and 6.0% male). A prior suicide attempt is an important risk factor when evaluating the potential lethality of suicidal ideations from students and clients.

College Student Suicide

The overall rate of completed suicide among college students is roughly 7.5 per 100,000, making it the second leading cause of death among college students. Four male students complete suicide for every female student; however, at least twice as many females as males attempt suicide (Jed Foundation, 2006). Research estimates project 1,100 suicides to occur on college campuses each year (Jed Foundation, 2006). The American College Health Association surveyed more than 190,000 students at 324 colleges and universities (spring 2000–fall 2004) about various aspects of student health, including suicidal thoughts. Data from this survey indicated that 9.5% of the students surveyed had seriously contemplated suicide (American College Health Association, 2006). According to the Jed Foundation (2006), risk factors for college age students include

- mental illness: 90% of adolescent suicide victims have at least one diagnosable, active psychiatric illness at the time of death, most often depression, substance abuse, and conduct disorders. Only 15% of suicide victims were in treatment at the time of death.
- previous attempts: 26 to 33% of adolescent suicide victims have made a previous suicide attempt.
- stressors: Suicide in youth often follows a time when the youth has been in trouble or has experienced a disappointment or rejection.
- firearms: 64% of suicide victims ages 10 to 24 take their lives with a firearm.

For college and university counselors, suicide assessment and appropriate intervention constitutes a daunting clinical challenge and poses a significant risk of liability to institutions of higher learning.

Elder Person Suicide

Older Americans are disproportionately more likely to die by suicide. Comprising only 13% of the U.S. population, individuals age 65 and older accounted for 18% of all suicide deaths in 2000. Among the highest rates (when categorized by gender and race) were White men ages 85 and older. The suicide rate in 2000 for this group of White males was 59 deaths per 100,000, more than five times the national rate of 10.6 per 100,000 (National Institute of Mental Health, 2006). Risk factors for suicide among older persons differ from those among the young. In addition to a higher prevalence of depression, older persons are more socially isolated and more frequently use highly lethal methods. They also make fewer attempts per completed suicide, have a higher male-to-female ratio than other groups, have often visited a health care provider before their suicide, and have more physical illnesses. Suicide rates among elder persons are highest for those who are divorced or widowed. In 1998, among males ages 75 and older, the rate for divorced men was 3.4 times and for widowed men was 2.6 times that for married men. In the same age group, the suicide rate for divorced women was 2.8 times and for widowed women was 1.9 times the rate among married women (National Strategy for Suicide Prevention, 2006).

Male Suicide

No demographic group is more at risk of completing suicide than males; overall, males are four times more likely to complete suicide than females (males 17.6 per 100,000 vs. females 4.3 per 100,000). Of all demographic categories, White males have the highest incidence of suicide (19.5 per 100,000). Additionally, with males the ratio of suicide attempts to suicide completions is far smaller than the ratio of attempts to completions with females. When males talk about taking their lives, generally they are more serious and more likely to follow through on threats. Firearms are currently the most often utilized method of suicide by essentially all groups, but males in particular tend to utilize methods that are the most lethal (American Association of Suicidology, 2006).

Other Threats of Self-Harm

Threats of suicide are not the only threats of harm to self that present clinical, ethical, and legal complications for counselors. Threats of self-inflicted injury occur among youth and college-age clients as well as among mentally and emotionally disturbed populations. These behaviors, although generally not intended as suicide threats, often result in harm, sometimes serious self-inflicted harm. The American Self-Harm Information Clearinghouse (2006) estimated that approximately 1% of the population have, at one time or another, used self-inflicted physical injury as a means of coping with an overwhelming situation or feeling. The most common form of self-inflicted injury is cutting and self-mutilation, but other forms include burning, head banging, biting, skin picking, hair pulling, hitting the body with objects, or hitting objects with the body. Whitlock, Eckenrode, and Silverman (2006) investigated self-injurious behaviors in college students and reported that both males and females self-reported scratching or pinching with fingernails or other objects to the point that bleeding occurred or marks remained as the most common method of self-harm (51.6%). Other forms included banging or punching objects to the point of bruising or bleeding (37.6%), cutting (33.7%), and punching or banging oneself to the point of bruising or bleeding (24.5%). Self-harm is generally understood to be a female phenomenon, and although there is some disputed support to this claim, the authors of the study believed that the public perception of self-harm with cutting may account for this belief.

In addition to these types of intentional self-harming behaviors, counselors must also respond to a nearly endless list of client at-risk and danger-courting behaviors, everything from driving while under the influence of alcohol or drugs and engaging in unprotected sex and/or substance abuse, to minors who provide personal information while chatting online. The theme of self-harming behavior, in all its endless permutations, is the prime turf of the clinical work done by many counselors.

ETHICAL ISSUES OF SUICIDE

When clients present with issues of threatened harm to self, we are thrust into a complex and critically important decision-making process. The issue of a mental health professional's response to a client's intention to harm or kill himself or herself brings into sharp focus a collision between two deeply held moral principles: autonomy (the client's right of self-determination) versus beneficence (promoting good for the client). The 2005 *ACA Code of Ethics* (Standard A.1.a.) advises us that "[t]he primary responsibility of counselors is to respect the dignity and to promote the welfare of clients." We can generally assume that preventing the client from self-inflicted harm or death is promoting the welfare of the client (beneficence). There may be special circumstances in which a client can make a compelling case for suicide as an expression of dignity and welfare (autonomy and beneficence). We address these special circumstances later in this chapter. However, under most circumstances, in order to respect the dignity and promote the welfare of the client it may be necessary for the counselor to take some action—action that could involve breaching the confidentiality of the client (not respecting autonomy). Ethically, we are supported by the *ACA Code of Ethics*, which states, "The general requirement that counselors keep information confidential does not apply when disclosure is required to protect clients or identified others from serious and foreseeable harm" (Standard B.2.a.). In other words, under certain circumstances, beneficence trumps autonomy. This gives us the ethical latitude to take action, including disclosing confidential information if, after thoroughly assessing the "client's *ideation, plan,* and *means*" (Herlihy & Corey, 2006a, p. 224), we conclude the client is at a level of risk such that he or she must be protected from him- or herself. It is important to note that protecting the client from harm can be accomplished in many forms, not all of which involve breaching confidentiality.

Two other ethical considerations affect our professional practice when dealing with clients at risk of harm to self. In keeping with the moral principle of autonomy, we are ethically instructed to provide our clients, during the informed consent process, with an explanation of the ground rules and expectations of the counseling relationship, including the limits and exceptions to confidentiality. We are further admonished that informed consent is an ongoing process; it is our responsibility to keep our clients informed of any changes in the counseling relationship as time and circumstances change (ACA, 2005a, Standards A.2.a., A.2.b.).

Ultimately, ethics serve to guide effective clinical decision making. When faced with a suicidal client, practitioners must initiate action that is based on conclusions drawn from the assessment of the client's likelihood of danger to self. When possible, an important ethical, legal, and clinical strategy is to consult with other practitioners to help ensure that all options have been identified. In some cases, responding to the clinical needs of a suicidal client might be beyond the boundaries of competence for a counselor. Although the ethical principal of not practicing beyond the boundaries of competence might be relevant (Standard C.2.a.), an inexperienced practitioner should not use this ethical guideline as justification to abandon the client while in the middle of a suicidal crisis. The counselor should immediately obtain consultation or supervision and remain an active agent until the client has stabilized.

Legal Issues of Suicide

In recent years, suicide cases have led to a large percentage of the malpractice claims against mental health professionals. As discussed in chapter 4, liability will ultimately be determined on the basis of whether a legal duty exists to protect the client from self-inflicted harm and whether the counselor's conduct violated that duty and led to the harm. In many instances involving mental health professionals, the duty is the most clear when the client is hospitalized or under some type of custodial care. However, even in the outpatient or school settings, liability can occur.

One element that sometimes leads to a malpractice claim is the failure to conduct an adequate evaluation of the client. If a client denies suicidal intent but evidences signs of serious depression, the counselor should conduct further inquiry and possibly refer to a psychiatrist or psychologist for further evaluation. Another factor that often leads to liability is the failure to obtain information about past treatment. As mentioned earlier, the statistics clarify that a past serious suicide attempt is a likely indicator of future suicidal behavior. Failure to follow institutional policies, client abandonment, and failure to follow up with a client recently discharged from the hospital are other ways to invite a lawsuit when dealing with an at-risk client. Yet another factor that increases potential liability is the failure to keep adequate records (see chapter 9).

The case of *Stepakoff v. Kantar* (1985) illustrated the problem with inadequate record keeping and suicide. In that case, the patient had been treated for bipolar disorder for over a year. Several days before his death, the patient's wife left town, with the expectation that the patient would leave the house before she returned. The defendant psychiatrist planned to go away for the weekend but developed a plan for the weekend, including coverage. He met with the patient and decided against involuntary hospitalization. Over the weekend, the patient was found by the police, having killed himself by carbon monoxide poisoning.

At the subsequent malpractice trial, there was much attention focused on a note written by the defendant psychiatrist after he last met with the patient. The note included this sentence, "There is a question of whether he will make it over the weekend." Although the doctor said he meant that he wasn't sure the patient would be able to carry out planned activities, the note was susceptible to different interpretations. The jury eventually sided with the defendant, but the result could have been different. The lesson learned from this case is that taking the time to fully document one's thoughts—especially when the client is at risk of harming himself—can help to reduce the likelihood that the counselor will be held liable for a mere mistake in predicting harm.

Prior to the 1990s, it was rare for counselors, especially school counselors, to be held liable for a client's suicide. In *Bogust v. Iverson* (1960), a college professor/counselor was found not responsible for the suicide of a student that occurred some 6 weeks after the counselor terminated counseling sessions with the student. The court ruled the counselor had no duty to commit, seek treatment for, or warn the parents of the student because there was no evidence that he was aware of the student's suicidal tendencies. In recent years, counselors are discovering that they may have a duty to protect clients from harming themselves, if such harm is foreseeable. In 1991, the Maryland Court of Appeals ruled in *Eisel v. Board of Education of Montgomery County* that summary judgment (i.e., the court's dismissal of the case without a full trial) was not appropriate in a case in which two school counselors failed to warn the father of suicidal statements made by his child.

In this case, a middle-school counselor was informed that a student, Nicole Eisel, had told other children of her plans to kill herself. That counselor involved the counselor assigned to Nicole, and the two counselors interviewed Nicole. She denied making such statements. Neither of the counselors notified Nicole's parents or school administrators. Nicole joined with a friend from another school in a murder/suicide pact, which was carried out on a school holiday, away from school grounds. Nicole's father brought suit against the counselors, alleging breach of their duty to intervene to attempt to prevent the suicide. The circuit court granted summary judgment in favor of the counselors, finding an absence of any such duty.

The Court of Appeals ruled that the summary judgment was erroneous, and distinguished the facts in this case from previous case law finding that therapists could rarely be held liable for outpatient suicides. The negligence complained of in *Eisel* was not failure to prevent the suicide by exercising control or custody over Nicole, but failure to communicate to Nicole's parent information possessed by the counselors. The plaintiff parent argued that had he been warned of the contemplated suicide, he might have been able to intervene. An argument also was made that the school stands in loco parentis in its relationship with students, and that results in "a special duty to exercise reasonable care to protect a pupil from harm" (pp. 451–452). Further, Nicole's counselor was specially trained in crisis intervention techniques, suicide warnings, and crisis psychiatric services.

The court went on to analyze that Nicole's suicide was foreseeable because the counselors had direct knowledge of Nicole's intent to commit suicide. The State of Maryland and Nicole's school have suicide prevention programs aimed at responding to communicated threats of suicide to intervene, including the recommendation in a policy memorandum to "share your knowledge with parents, friends, teachers, or other people who might be able to help. Don't worry about breaking a confidence if someone reveals suicidal plans to you. You may have to betray a secret to save a life" (p. 454). The court went on to discuss whether the breach of the counselors' alleged duty to notify the parents was the proximate cause of the suicide, the concept of moral blame, and the scope of the burden on the counselors to have notified the parents, as measured against the risk of death to a child. Once the facts were fully developed in all these areas, the court concluded, "a jury could find that there is indeed a duty imposed on counselors to notify parents" in the event they receive information about such potential harm.

The upshot of the *Eisel* case is that all counselors are vulnerable to lawsuits based on client suicide and other attempted self-harm. Counselors should be very careful to follow school or other institutional policy and carefully document all actions. Other professionals should be involved where appropriate.

End-of-Life Issues

End-of-life issues present complicated moral, ethical, and legal questions. In an earlier section of this chapter we introduced the idea that there may be situations in which respecting the dignity and welfare of a client might mean that a counselor chooses not to intervene when a client confides his or her intention to commit suicide. We are reminded of the language from the Purpose Statement in the 2005 *ACA Code of Ethics* concerning reasonable differences of opinion: "Reasonable differences of opinion can and do exist among counselors with respect to the ways in which values, ethical principles, and ethical standards would be applied when they conflict." End-of-life issues are likely to present one of the most conspicuous examples of reasonable differences. In the *Code* an entire Standard (A.9.) is devoted to this issue. Of particular relevance is Standard A.9.c., which acknowledges the special circumstances surrounding providing "services to terminally ill individuals who are considering hastening their own deaths" and provides counselors with "the option of breaking or not breaking confidentiality, depending on applicable laws and the specific circumstances of the situation and after seeking consultation or supervision from appropriate professional and legal parties."

The ethical and legal jeopardy for counselors is clouded by several complicated issues including (1) who is the client (the terminally ill patient or the family members); (2) who has legal competence to determine what course of action is in the best interest of the patient (the terminally ill patient or a health care guardian); (3) the strongly held views by everyone involved concerning the proper (moral, ethical, and legal) course of action; (4) state laws that may be more or less prescriptive in terms of the duties and responsibilities of health and mental health professionals; and, last but not least, (5) the values of the counselor who is providing services. It is easy for the counselor to get caught in the cross fire of these many conflicting perspectives. We want to emphasize that the *Code* provides the "option of breaking or not breaking confidentiality" (in recognition of the differences in values of counselors) but only in the context of applicable laws and only after seeking consultation or supervision. Because of the intensity of emotion and the conflicting moral, ethical, and legal perspectives, we can't emphasize enough the critical importance of obtaining knowledgeable and competent consultation throughout the decision-making process.

Final Thoughts

Each suicide intimately affects at least six other people. The lives and well-being of survivors of suicide are deeply affected, sometimes impacting a person for a lifetime. From 1979 to 2003, there were 749,337 suicides in the United States, resulting in over 4.5 million survivors of suicide. The implications of suicide, suicide attempts, threats of suicide, and the impact on survivors of suicide remain one of the most complicated and ethically and legally challenging issues faced by professional counselors in every setting. When faced with these complexities, responsible counselors should not go it alone. Obtaining competent colleague consultation and/or clinical supervision is absolutely essential.

Chapter 8

PROFESSIONAL BOUNDARIES

It's all about the relationship; and central to the counseling relationship is the practitioner's ability to actively define, respect, and manage professional boundaries. Mental health professionals have a unique responsibility, defined both ethically and legally, to manage the boundary between the role of professional counselor and client, including any other co-occurring roles that connect the counselor and client. The complexity, the power differential, and, in some cases, the vulnerability of counseling clients demand that we exercise extraordinary care to ensure that we are taking steps to define and respect the boundary between ourselves and our clients. For counselors and other mental health professionals, role boundary blurring and violation in the form of inappropriate or mismanaged dual or multiple relationships and sexual misconduct are the royal road to ethical and legal jeopardy. When role boundaries are blurred or violated, clients are often put at risk or harmed, which can quickly lead to ethical complaints, licensing board disciplinary proceedings, malpractice lawsuits, and even felony charges against the practitioner. Role boundary issues for professional counselors also have a bearing on the relationship between graduate faculty and students, between clinical supervisors and students/interns, and between counselor–researchers and research subjects.

ROLE BOUNDARY ISSUES

Role boundary issues cover a wide range of circumstances from egregious and harmful situations that result in harm to the client and the destruction of the counseling relationship, to benign situations that result in a ripple of misunderstanding that generally can be successfully worked through, to situations in which the client clearly benefits from the existence of multiple roles. In almost all cases that result in harm to the client, boundary issues are driven by inappropriate or mismanaged dual/multiple relationships. Dual relationships are the common denominator of boundary violations. Many authors have explored the intricacies of dual relationships; Herlihy and Corey (2006b) provided an exhaustive and balanced discussion on the topic. For our purposes, dual relationships occur when

- a practitioner has a nonprofessional relationship with a person (no matter how casual or intimate) and then a professional counseling relationship is initiated; or
- a professional counseling relationship exists and either the counselor or the client initiates a nonprofessional relationship (no matter how casual or intimate). In fairness, sometimes nonprofessional relationships are not initiated by either the counselor or the client; sometimes these other relationships emerge from familial, social, community, school, or work-related connections that were unknown to either the counselor or client prior to initiating the professional relationship. Sometimes the other relationship is an inherent and unavoidable aspect of the counseling environment.

Dual or multiple relationships can also include situations in which one relationship (either the professional relationship or the nonprofessional relationship) has ended (very recently or even years ago) and another relationship (nonprofessional or professional) is initiated. Of course, there are legally and ethically forbidden dual relationships (more about that later). Romantic and sexual relationships are obviously problematic, but other examples include counseling family members, workplace supervisors and subordinates, and family members of work associates as well as people who have a significant connection to a family member or who are intimates of the counselor. The core concern is not the type of the co-occurring dual role or the length of time that has passed since the professional or nonprofessional relationship has ended but rather the potential for and/or the actual damage that is done to the client as a result of the blurring or violating of boundaries associated with the dual relationship. The damage typically presents in the following five broad categories:

1. *Loss of objectivity/clarity.* Dual relationships can add an additional layer of distraction to a professional relationship that inherently includes challenges to objectivity and clarity. Most mental health professionals recognize that counseling and psychotherapy are subjective endeavors. Objectivity is not really possible: Perception is influenced by a host of

> The core concern is not the type of the co-occurring dual relationship or the length of time that has passed since the professional or nonprofessional relationship has ended but rather the potential for and/or the actual damage that is done to the client as a result of the blurring or violating of boundaries associated with the dual (professional and nonprofessional) relationship.

conscious/unconscious, social, cultural, political, and life experience variables. During graduate training, postdegree supervision, and ongoing colleague consultation, counselors are constantly striving to maintain as much clarity in interacting with clients as possible. The loss of objectivity/clarity may be consciously recognized by the counselor or it can occur below the counselor's awareness. In any event, loss of objectivity and clarity represents a dynamic in the counseling office that prevents the counselor from being fully present for the client and challenges the ethically mandated primary responsibility of the counselor "to respect the dignity and to promote the welfare of clients" (ACA, 2005a, Standard A.1.a.). Dual relationships represent another layer of distraction that a counselor must sort through in order to maintain an acceptable level of objectivity and clarity.

2. *Potential for misunderstanding.* Misunderstanding between human beings is natural and inevitable. Under normal circumstances, misunderstandings that occur within a counseling relationship can be worked through and often can become important diagnostic and therapeutic opportunities. When a counseling relationship is intertwined within a dual relationship, there is increased opportunity for misunderstanding. Interactions that occur in the nonclinical relationship can create misunderstanding within the counseling relationship and vice versa. In human interaction, misunderstandings can quickly multiply, with one misunderstanding feeding on another until there is a breakdown of the counseling relationship. We are ethically charged to do no harm and whenever possible "to minimize or to remedy unavoidable or unanticipated harm" (ACA, 2005a, Standard A.4.a.); misunderstanding fueled by a dual relationship can be a frequent doorway leading to client harm.

3. *Conflict of interest.* Co-occurring or sequential dual roles can create a conflict of interest—a situation in which a counselor (or someone or something important to the counselor) can be affected by decisions or behaviors the client is contemplating. A conflict of interest can tempt a counselor to use the power of the counseling relationship to sway the client in a direction preferred by the counselor. Such inappropriate influence can easily result in harm or loss to the client. Even if the counselor resists the temptation to influence the client in the counselor's preferred direction, there can be doubt and suspicion. Further, if the counselor is successful in not imposing her- or himself on the client, the counselor must make peace with sacrificing his or her preferences or best interests. No matter which decision the counselor makes, there will always be suspicion about whose interest the counselor was serving.

4. *Breach of confidentiality and privacy.* When clinical and nonclinical roles get intertwined, it becomes difficult for the counselor to remember what

information can be discussed where and when. When noncounseling roles are informal or intense (friendships, social groups, business/work associates, etc.), the likelihood of a breach of confidentiality and a violation of the client's right of privacy dramatically increase. These circumstances again challenge the counselor's commitment to ethical practice (ACA, 2005, Standards B.1.a., B.1.b., B.1.c.) and can risk a complaint to the state licensing board.

5. *Exploitation.* Mental health professionals who intentionally misuse the power differential inherent within the counseling relationship to take advantage of a client or former client are behaving in an abusive and exploitive manner. These situations tend to be the most ethically and legally egregious and often involve sexual or financial exploitation. These dual relationships are not innocent; they are not just a momentary lapse in judgment. They are the basis for real harm to a client as well as ethical and legal consequences to the counselor, including ethical complaints, licensing board discipline, malpractice lawsuits, and possibly felony imprisonment.

When any of these occur it can easily be argued that the counselor breached her or his professional duty and that the breach resulted in damage (loss or pain) to the client or destruction of the counseling relationship.

Counselor–client relationships are not the only type of dual or multiple relationships that can lead to ethical and legal problems for counselors. Other examples include

- the relationship between a faculty member and a student;
- the relationship between a clinical supervisor and a supervisee, trainee, or intern;
- the relationship between a counselor researcher and a research subject.

In some cases, the circumstances will play out a little differently, but the results are similar: The person in the one-down power position—the vulnerable person—will be harmed either because the professional allowed another relationship to emerge or because once the other relationship presented, the counselor failed to properly manage the complexity of the dual roles.

DUAL OR MULTIPLE ROLE BOUNDARIES

Of all the aspects associated with the professional functioning of counselors, nothing creates more controversy, confusion, and risk than the issue of professional boundaries and boundary violations. What constitutes the proper management of the boundary between the counselor and the client is the subject of continued professional debate. Thoughtful experts disagree as to how casually or strictly the boundary should be enforced, but there is no disagreement that clients can be harmed when we fail to effectively manage boundaries or when professional boundaries are violated.

The 2005 *ACA Code of Ethics* no longer contains the term *dual relationship*; instead, the new *Code*, in Standard A.5.c., addresses "Nonprofessional Interactions or Relationships." Practitioners are advised that "[c]ounselor–client nonprofessional relationships with clients, former clients, their romantic partners, or their family members should be avoided, except when the interaction is potentially beneficial to the client." Standard A.5.d. of the new *Code* provides specific guidance that outlines the responsibilities of the counselor when initiating nonprofessional interaction with a client:

> When a counselor–client nonprofessional interaction with a client or former client may be potentially beneficial to the client or former client, the counselor must document in case records, prior to the interaction (when feasible), the rationale for such an interaction, the potential benefit, and anticipated consequences for the client and former client and other individuals significantly involved with the client or former client. Such interactions should be initiated with appropriate client consent. Where unintentional harm occurs to the client or former client, or to an individual significantly involved with the client or former client, due to the nonprofessional interaction, the counselor must show evidence of an attempt to remedy such harm.

In this book we utilize a wide range of terms for what the 2005 *ACA Code of Ethics* refers to as *nonprofessional interactions or relationships*. Our use of the terms *dual relationships*, *multiple relationships*, and *co-occurring relationships* is intentional. Throughout the discussion that follows we attempt to utilize the language of the new *Code of Ethics* while at the same time utilizing terminology found in disciplinary sections of many, if not most, state counselor licensing laws and supporting rules. State counselor licensing boards across the county typically approach the topic of dual or multiple relationships with current or former clients in ways that are consistent with the 2005 *ACA Code of Ethics*. Generally, state licensing boards caution against dual relationships. Practitioners are urged to avoid co-occurring relationships whenever possible, and when or if they are initiated, the practitioner is admonished to ensure that the dual relationship (the nonprofessional relationship) is intended to be beneficial to the client.

We want to offer a note of prudence. Licensing board members around the country continue to wrestle with this topic: state laws and rules are constantly under review. Some states seem to be considering narrowing the circumstances under which any form of co-occurring professional and nonprofessional relationship between counselor and client would be considered appropriate. We are mindful that when it comes to disciplinary decisions, the language in the state law or rule is open to some degree of interpretation by individual board members. We urge you to consult the most recent version of the statute and rules that govern the practice of counseling in your state. Carefully read the language in the statute and rules and consult with knowledgeable colleagues to ensure you fully understand the limitations and prohibitions as defined in the statute. For more detailed information we suggest you consult the ACA publication, *Licensure Requirements for Professional Counselors* (ACA, 2007), which is a complete guide to state licensing laws. Additionally, we encourage you to carefully review disciplinary decisions made by your licensing board; it is important to understand how the law and rules are being interpreted by the board members. Most licensing boards publish disciplinary decisions; they can be obtained either through the licensing board Web site and/or through board-published newsletters or reports. Furthermore, Corey, Corey, and Callanan (2007) and Herlihy and Corey (2006b) offer a comprehensive discussion of the topic of dual relationships. We strongly encourage you to refresh your perspective by reviewing the discussions in these two publications and the references cited therein.

There is, however, little or no disagreement regarding the issue of sexual misconduct. The 2005 *ACA Code of Ethics* prohibits sexual or romantic "interactions or relationships with current clients, their romantic partners, or their family members" (Standard A.5.a.). The language in this latest update expands this prohibition to include sexual or romantic "client interactions or relationships with former clients, their romantic partners, or their family members . . . for a period of 5 years following the last professional contact" (Standard A.5.b.). The language also expands on the ethical responsibilities of a practitioner who might want to become romantically or sexually involved after 5 years by cautioning that the practitioner must "demonstrate forethought and document (in written form) whether the interactions or relationship can be viewed as exploitive in some way and/or whether there is still potential to harm the former client; in cases of potential exploitation and/or harm, the counselor avoids entering such an interaction or relationship" (Standard A.5.b.).

THE RISK OF LICENSING BOARD COMPLAINTS

Typically state counselor licensing boards have the authority to impose a wide range of disciplinary consequences on licensees or professionals in the process of becoming licensed. Each state board delineates violations and a disciplinary due process that is involved in determining whether a complaint against a counselor is accurate. Once due process has been fully exercised and a determination has been made, disciplinary consequences can be imposed. Terminology defining disciplinary consequences varies from state to state but is likely to include disciplinary actions ranging from very severe (permanent revocation or permanent denial) to least severe (reprimand or fines). It is not uncommon for discipline to involve more than one consequence. Often there are fines in addition to whatever other discipline is imposed. The typical range of disciplinary consequences includes

- *permanent revocation of license:* The person is permanently prohibited from the practice of counseling in that state.
- *permanent denial:* The person is permanently denied the opportunity to apply for a license to practice counseling in that state.
- *surrender:* The person voluntarily agrees to surrender his or her license and no longer practice counseling in that state.
- *suspension:* The person is suspended from practice for a period of time.
- *suspension with stipulations:* The person may continue to practice but has agreed to abide by certain conditions that may include supervised practice, restricted practice, additional continuing education, or other requirements.
- *reprimand:* The person may continue to practice but receives a formal letter of reprimand.
- *administrative penalty (fines):* The person may continue to practice but a monetary fine is assessed against the counselor.

Reports of State Disciplinary Action

To put the risk of mismanaged dual relationships and boundary violations into perspective, we offer some compelling data as reported from several counselor licensing boards around the country. To date there is not a central repository for collecting the specific circumstances and/or types of disciplinary actions imposed by licensing boards against licensed and prelicensed counselors. However, a sampling of representative data from several states provides compelling enough evidence that mismanaged dual/multiple relationships and sexual misconduct boundary violations are likely to be the basis for 25 to 50% of substantiated complaints against licensed counselors, at least as reported by the following four representative states.

Note that these are but four examples of boundary blurring or boundary violations. Each case is more complicated and more human than a public record summary can communicate; but what is absolutely safe to assume is that these four examples, and a hundred other similar cases across the country each year, result in harm to a client, damage to our profession, and significant loss to the practitioner involved. Damage to the practitioner includes personal stress and trauma, loss of professional esteem, and real economic costs (e.g., loss of employment, lost billable hours, attorney fees, imposed fines, cost of supervision, and expenses associated with ethics training).

Texas

Texas Board of Examiners of Professional Counselors (ACA, 2007)

- Practice and Title Act—passed 1981
- Licensed Professional Counselor (LPC): 12,800 licensees

The Texas Board of Examiners publishes an annual summary of disciplinary violations (see Table 2) for Licensed Professional Counselors, Licensed Marriage and Family Therapists, and Licensed Social

> Texas Board of Examiners of Professional Counselors: http://www.dshs.state.tx.us/counselor/default.shtm

Workers. The categories of violations among the three mental health-related professions are different, but the message in Texas is clear: Mismanaged dual relationships, boundary violations, and sexual misconduct make up a significant percentage of the total violations reported for 2004 and 2003 (Texas Board of Examiners of Professional Counselors, 2007).

It is important to note that the overall number of individuals included in Table 2's percentages is small. The best that could be determined from the available data on the Web site is that during 2004, eight or nine Licensed Professional Counselors and nine Licensed Marriage and Family Counselors were found in violation of the law and/or codes of ethics.

Arizona

Board of Behavioral Health Examiners (ACA, 2007)

- Practice Act—passed 1988
- Licensed Professional Counselor (LPC): 2,200 licensees
- Licensed Associate Counselor (LAC): 383 licensees

> Arizona Board of Behavioral Health Examiners: http://www.bbhe.state.az.us/complaints.htm

The Arizona Board of Behavioral Health Examiners is charged with enforcing adherence to a very de-

Table 2

TEXAS LICENSING BOARD DISCIPLINE VIOLATIONS: PERCENTAGES OF COMPLAINTS INVOLVING BOUNDARY VIOLATIONS 2004 AND 2003

Complaint	% Professional Counselor		% Marriage and Family Therapist		% Social Worker	
	2004	2003	2004	2003	2004	2003
Sexual misconduct	42.9	30.0		66.0		14.25
Maintaining professional boundaries			28.6		7.1	
Dual relationship				17.0	28.6	
Total	42.9	30.0	28.6	83.0	35.7	14.25

tailed list of prohibited behaviors. Two of these behaviors directly address dual relationships and sexual misconduct:

> *32-3251(12)(v)* Any sexual conduct between a licensee and a client or former client.
>
> *32-3251(12)(y)* Engaging in a dual relationship with a client that could impair the licensee's objectivity or professional judgment or create risk of harm to the client.
>
> For purposes of this subdivision, "dual relationship" means a licensee simultaneously engages in both a professional and nonprofessional relationship with a client that is avoidable and not incidental. (Ariz. Rev. Stat. § 32-3251, 2006)

The Arizona Board provides an annual detailed summary of the disciplinary violations including a brief description of each violation and the sanctions imposed. For the years 2000 to 2006 (July), the board reported that 139 adverse actions (board disciplinary sanctions) were levied against licensees. The 139 actions did not include another 61 actions involving persons applying for licensure. Of the 139 actions, 25% (34 actions) involved dual relationships or sexual misconduct (Arizona Board of Behavioral Health Examiners, 2006).

Ohio

Counselor, Social Worker, and Marriage and Family Therapist Board (ACA, 2007)

- Practice and Title Act—passed 1984
- Licensed Professional Clinical Counselor (LPCC): 3,496 licensees
- Licensed Professional Counselor (LPC): 3,751 licensees

Ohio Counselor, Social Worker, and Marriage and Family Therapist Board: http://cswmft.ohio.gov

Data provided by the board, from public disciplinary records for the period 1986 through January 2006, indicated that during the period 1998 to 2004, 55 counselors licensed under this law were found to be in violation of the law. Of those 55 violations, 23 (42%) involved mismanaged dual relationships and/or sexual misconduct boundary violations. In an effort to make these data more human, several descriptions of dual role complications are offered from public records obtained from the board. None of the descriptions involve sexual misconduct as there seems little point in recounting behavior that is so obviously inappropriate and totally preventable.

- *Boundary violation/dual relationship:* In 2004, a licensed professional clinical counselor (LPCC) was disciplined for multiple boundary violations with a client. This case provides an example of the slippery slope of dual relationships. It appears that the counselor did not intend to do harm; in fact, one could argue that in the beginning the counselor was motivated by an exaggerated need to be helpful. The counselor went to church with the client, allowed the client to stay in the counselor's home and do housework in lieu of rent, went out to eat and shopped for alcohol with the client, attended family social functions with the client, and then when all perspective was lost, the counselor hired the client to work in an administrative capacity with clients. The counselor was reprimanded, suspended from practicing for 1 month, ordered to attend ethics training, and after the month's suspension, the counselor was required to receive a year of supervised practice.
- *Blurred boundary/dual roles:* In 2003, a licensed professional clinical counselor (LPCC), who is also a member of the clergy, was disciplined for blurring the boundary of the role of professional counselor. The individual's actions with a client were consistent with the role of clergy, but were deemed inappropriate in the role of professional counselor. The counselor was suspended from practice for 3 months.
- *Boundary violation/dual roles:* In 2003, a licensed professional clinical counselor (LPCC) engaged in a boundary violation by inappropriately mixing the role of treating counselor with the role and responsibilities of a forensic evaluator. The counselor agreed to provide a court-ordered forensic evaluation for a person who was a former client (in violation of the terms of the court-ordered evaluation) and then offered to provide counseling based on the findings from that evaluation. The counselor's license to practice was suspended for 3 months, and the counselor was ordered to receive face-to-face supervision once per week for 3 years. (The supervisor will report in writing to the board as outlined in the consent agreement.)
- *Blurred boundary/multiple relationships:* In 2003, a licensed professional counselor (LPC) employed by a college entered into multiple relationships (none seemingly inappropriate) with a student whom the counselor was seeing for individual counseling. The other roles were consistent with the counselor's duties and responsibilities at the college, but as reported in the public documents, these multiple roles confused both individuals to the detriment of the client. The counselor also failed to properly document the intake and counseling relationship. The counselor was reprimanded and was ordered to receive 1 hour of supervision per week for 2 years and complete and pass an ethics course.

Maryland

Board of Professional Counselors and Therapists (ACA, 2007)

- Practice and Title Act—passed 1985
- Licensed Clinical Professional Counselor (LCPC): 1,578 licensees
- Certified Professional Counselor (CPC): 103 licensees
- Licensed Graduate Professional Counselor: 30 licensees

> Maryland Board of Professional
> Counselors and Therapists:
> http://www.dhmh.state.md.us/bopc/

The numbers of counselors disciplined in Maryland are few, but data provided by the Board of Professional Counselors and Therapists are consistent with other states we are highlighting. From October 2001 to January 2006, 17 practitioners in Maryland were disciplined; of those, nine cases (53%) involved mismanaged dual relationships and/or boundary blurring, confusion, or crossing. Specifically, six practitioners were disciplined for sexual misconduct and three for other dual relationship violations (Maryland Board of Professional Counselors and Therapists, 2006).

THE RISK OF MALPRACTICE LAWSUITS

In the 30 years that the ACA Insurance Trust has been tracking claims against counselors, allegations of sexual activity involving counselors and their clients, or the spouse of a client, continue to create the largest claim costs in the professional liability insurance program. These allegations are the most frequent causes of lawsuits and result in the highest expenditure of funds. Many lawsuits allege malpractice, or failure to treat the problem that brought the client to counseling. Yet, in most cases, the underlying cause for a claim is an ill-advised dual role relationship. In one study of cases involving the ACA Insurance Trust professional liability program, 35% of the claims involve allegations of sexual advances by the counselor or inappropriate touching of clients (P. L. Nelson, Executive Director, ACA Insurance Trust, personal communication, August 24, 2006).

Most insurance carriers will not defend or pay any judgment in which there is an admission or proof of sexual misconduct. An attorney who is experienced in lawsuits against professionals will immediately realize that a complaint couched simply in terms of intentional sexual misconduct will lead to a denial of insurance coverage. This means that the claim will have less economic possibility, because the deep pockets of the insurance company are not likely to be involved. Therefore, most claims and lawsuits involving allegations of sexual misconduct will include other allegations of malpractice. As a result, the insurance carrier usually has to expend funds to provide a legal defense for the professional. Another common tactic among plaintiffs' attorneys is to claim negligent hiring, training, or supervision of the primary counselor. That brings more defendants into the picture.

Sexual intimacy with a client is a serious breach of trust and objectivity, a statement affirmed by the courts. If an attorney representing a plaintiff can convince the court that sexual intimacy occurred, the likelihood of a large negligence award is high. In many cases, allegations involve less than actual intercourse. Nevertheless, the possibility of a large settlement or verdict remains. Almost all legal defenses fail, even those claiming client consent, no harm to the client, denial of sexual contact altogether, or relationship begun after treatment ended (P. L. Nelson, Executive Director, ACA Insurance Trust, personal communication, August 24, 2006).

Mishandling of Transference

Claims of sexual misconduct by therapists have been based largely on the mishandling of the transference phenomenon and the countertransference that occurs when the therapists experience reactions similar to those of their clients. Courts have found that the mishandling of this transference, resulting in sexual contact or touching, constitutes negligence or gross negligence for which damages can be awarded. Clients alleging sexual misconduct generally must prove in court that there was a counseling relationship, that sexual contact occurred between the counselor and the client, and that the client suffered some emotional injury as a result of the contact. In some states, clients also must prove that the contact occurred under the guise of treatment. In several states, however, a sexual relationship between a counselor and a client is sufficient grounds for a claim of negligence, whether it occurred under the guise of treatment or not. The spouse or companion of a client who has engaged in sexual relations with a counselor also may bring a malpractice action and recover actual damages.[1] Attorneys who represent victims of alleged sexual misconduct now have a wealth of case law to guide them in securing damages for their clients, and there are few defenses available to the counselor who initiates or permits sexual contact in a therapeutic relationship.[2]

A case in the state of Washington (*Doe v. Wood*, 1994) illustrates the danger to unwary counselors. A certified mental health counselor provided

---

[1]See, for example, *Horak v. Biris*, 130 Ill. App. 3d 140, 85 Ill. Dec. 599, 474 N.E.2d 13 (1985); *Rowe v. Bennett*, 514 A.2d 802 (Me. 1986); and *Figueiredo-Torres v. Nickel*, 584 A.2d 69 (Md. Ct. App. 1991).

[2]The only defense that has consistently been effective once the act of sexual contact has been proved is that the suit is time-barred by the statute of limitations. Whether the client was competent to bring the action and the actual final date of treatment or sexual activity also are important in this determination.

therapy to a couple and also socialized with them during the treatment period. The wife told her husband she had developed romantic feelings for the counselor, who later acknowledged the feelings were reciprocal. The counselor terminated the therapy. The husband later discovered letters from the counselor to the wife expressing his desire for a relationship with her. The couple separated, and the husband experienced a variety of symptoms of depression and emotional distress, and had difficulty working, resulting in a loss of income. He sued the counselor for professional negligence, intentional infliction of emotional distress, and outrage, claiming the counselor violated the standard of care by having a social relationship with the couple, pursuing a romantic relationship with the wife, betraying the patient's trust, and terminating the counseling relationship abruptly. The court awarded $525,000 on the professional negligence issue.

Another important reported decision is *Simmons v. United States* (1986). The facts of that case were that a client who had emotional problems sought the assistance of a social worker employed by a federal agency. After seeing this client for 5 years, the therapist initiated a sexual relationship with the client. The following year, a third party notified the therapist's supervisor, who allegedly did nothing to remedy the problem or discipline the social worker. The client's mental status declined; she was hospitalized and attempted suicide. Two years after therapy ended, the client was informed by her new therapist that her problems were due to the social worker's mishandling of the transference phenomenon.

The client sued the federal government under the Federal Tort Claims act, and the appellate court upheld the award granted at the trial court level. The social worker was found to be negligent by mishandling the transference phenomenon, and the supervisor was also found negligent.

ACA Insurance Trust

This section lists several other examples of inappropriate or mismanaged dual relationships involving counselors. These cases are reported by P. L. Nelson, Executive Director, ACA Insurance Trust (personal communication, August 24, 2006).

- A counselor worked with a couple on marital problems. The couple eventually separated and later divorced. Five months after the last session, the husband asked the counselor to go out to dinner. A relationship developed, and the ex-wife brought a lawsuit against the counselor.
- A client in treatment for PTSD and dissociative identity disorder brought on by sexual abuse at the hands of her father as a child was in treatment for an extended period of time. A lawsuit was filed when the client became dissatisfied with her progress. The suit alleged

among other things that the counselor breached ethical standards by getting involved in a dual relationship by asking the client to clean his garage and include him in her will.

- A client told her counselor she was going to be laid off from her job. The counselor allegedly told the client that he would buy a piece of property and set her up in a business that they would jointly own. Counseling sessions then allegedly shifted to business planning, but insurance was being charged for psychotherapy. When the counselor eventually backed out of the deal, the client was left with no job and no future. She then filed a lawsuit alleging breach of ethics by engaging in a dual relationship, which caused her harm.
- It was alleged that a counselor treating a survivor of severe sexual trauma made sexual advances to the client. The client subsequently committed suicide, and the family sued the counselor. In this case, the counselor was exonerated, because it could not be proven that sexual contact ever occurred.

It is important to note, even in cases where the eventual outcome of a malpractice lawsuit is in the favor of the counselor, that there are still real consequences to the practitioner. These include emotional consequences (fear, anxiety, anger, and stress), economic consequences (loss of revenue while preparing a defense, including depositions and court appearances), and professional esteem consequences (embarrassment and damage to the counselor's reputation from reports in the media and/or professional publications).

The scenarios just listed represent only a few of the cases filed against practicing counselors insured through the ACA Insurance Trust. Many cases that involve a wide range of malpractice allegations (in which a mismanaged dual relationship or sexual misconduct was involved) have been settled out of court; still others have resulted in jury damage awards.

Counselors should keep in mind that they may also be held liable for the sexual misconduct of their business partners or supervisees if they knew or should have known that such activity was occurring and failed to take steps to stop it. Is a practice partner seeing a client at unusually late hours or away from the office? Does your supervisee lock his or her office door during sessions? Have any clients or coworkers complained or made remarks about the behavior of a supervisee? If so, as the employer or supervisor, you must take immediate steps to ensure compliance with the standards of care and protect the client(s) involved.

THE RISK OF CRIMINAL PROSECUTION

Several states now have provisions in laws that govern mental health professionals that provide for criminal prosecution against mental health professionals who engage in certain forms of sexual misconduct. Florida is an example of a state with criminal prosecution for psychotherapist sexual misconduct. Florida law provides the following language:

Sexual misconduct by a psychotherapist; penalties.
(1) Any psychotherapist who commits sexual misconduct with a client, or former client when the professional relationship was terminated primarily for the purpose of engaging in sexual contact, commits a felony of the third degree, punishable as provided in s. 775.082 or s. 775.083; however, a second or subsequent offense is a felony of the second degree, punishable as provided in s. 775.082, s. 775.083, or s. 775.084.
(2) Any psychotherapist who violates subsection (1) by means of therapeutic deception commits a felony of the second degree punishable as provided in s. 775.082, s. 775.083, or s. 775.084.
(3) The giving of consent by the client to any such act shall not be a defense to these offenses.
(4) For the purposes of this section:
  (a) The term "psychotherapist" means any person licensed pursuant to chapter 458, chapter 459, chapter 464, chapter 490, or chapter 491, or any other person who provides or purports to provide treatment, diagnosis, assessment, evaluation, or counseling of mental or emotional illness, symptom, or condition.
  (b) "Therapeutic deception" means a representation to the client that sexual contact by the psychotherapist is consistent with or part of the treatment of the client.
  (c) "Sexual misconduct" means the oral, anal, or vaginal penetration of another by, or contact with, the sexual organ of another or the anal or vaginal penetration of another by any object.
  (d) "Client" means a person to whom the services of a psychotherapist are provided. (Fla. Stat. § 491.0112)

Similarly, Minnesota makes psychotherapist–patient sex a criminal offense (Minn. Stat. § 609.345). The Minnesota Court of Appeals (*State v. Ohrtman*, 1991) has recognized that it is a fourth-degree criminal offense for a psychotherapist to engage in sexual contact with a patient during a psychotherapy session. Further, the patient's consent does not constitute a defense to the action, and the definition of psychotherapist includes the clergy, and psychotherapy by definition includes counseling. However, the court was unwilling to rule that a hug between a psychotherapist and patient was unlawful touching under the statute.

The bottom line is that sexual contact between counselors and clients is ethically wrong, constitutes a breach of the standard of professional practice owed the client, causes actual harm to the client, and may violate criminal statutes as well. If you find yourself being drawn into a situation that could lead to such contact, you must keep the best interests of your client as your first priority. Refer the client to another counselor if appropriate. Terminate your relationship with the client in a timely manner but be mindful to avoid abandoning the client. Do not assume that termination allows you to then take up a romantic or sexual relationship with the client. Seek consultation or supervision to ensure that the relationship remains open and professional, and secure the professional assistance you need to avoid mishandling the relationship with your client.

SUMMARY

We have devoted a significant amount of time to a description of the legal and criminal consequences that can come from mismanaged dual relationship and boundary violations in the form of sexual misconduct. We did so because, despite how easy it is to manage and/or eliminate these areas of risk, these are still the issues that most frequently ensnare counselors and mental health professionals. We don't want to leave the impression that all dual (co-occurring professional and nonprofessional) relationships are inherently bad, because they are not. Clients, students, and supervisees can greatly benefit from a well-conceived and well-executed dual relationship. Additionally, in the real world sometimes circumstances make it very difficult not to be involved in dual relationships. When faced with the opportunity to initiate a dual relationship, stop and carefully evaluate the unique circumstances that are being presented. Don't depend on your own assessment; consider the input from a trusted colleague or supervisor.

Many authors, including Herlihy and Corey (2006b), have provided suggestions that can help you sort through the complexities so you can make a decision and then document your thinking. The process begins by asking, Is the dual relationship avoidable? In other words, can someone else competently provide the professional service or can some other arrangement be made to eliminate or distance the nonprofessional relationship? If after careful and honest reflection, the answer is that the dual relationship is avoidable, then steer clear of it! If it's not avoidable,

- assess the potential risks and benefits to the client;
- check to make sure your proposed action does not run afoul of your state licensure law;
- discuss with the client the potential problems and benefits.

If the risks outweigh the benefits, decline to enter the relationship (and also, of course, provide your rationale, document your thinking, and refer as needed).

If the benefits outweigh the risks,

- secure informed consent;
- seek consultation;
- engage in ongoing discussion with the client to ensure the relationships are being managed properly;

- document and self-monitor;
- obtain supervision.

If you follow this decision-making process, including the requirements for ongoing discussion with your client, self-monitoring, and supervision, you have a better chance of not sliding down the slippery slope into behaviors that place the client at risk of harm and you at risk of ethical or legal complications. Ultimately, our role in this book is not to tell you whether you should or shouldn't enter into dual relationships but rather to help practitioners in the real word and students preparing for the real world to be aware of the controversy, confusion, and risks surrounding the dual relationships and boundary violations so they—and you—can better manage the ethical, regulatory, and legal risks that saturate this topic.

Chapter 9

RECORDS AND
DOCUMENTATION

Well-organized and well-documented client counseling records are the most effective tool counselors have for establishing client treatment plans, ensuring continuity of care in the event of absence, and proving that quality care was provided. Good records also provide reliable information for decision making in court cases in which difficult issues are presented, and they help the counselor avoid or effectively respond to licensing board complaints and malpractice liability. Additionally, with the growth of managed care, counselors must carefully document their services to ensure reimbursement.

RECORDS ARE THE STANDARD OF CARE

There was a time, many years ago, when it was common practice for counselors and some other mental health professionals to refrain intentionally from keeping client records. Some vestiges of this counselors-don't-keep-records thinking still exist today. We want to begin this chapter by stating very clearly the current standard of professional counseling practice. Counselors have an explicitly stated legal and ethical duty to create and maintain client records on every client. Over the last two decades, the standard of care regarding client records and many aspects of the contents therein has been made quite clear. In fact, failure to maintain adequate client records could form the basis of a claim of professional malpractice because it breaches the standard of care expected of a practicing mental health professional. We acknowledge that record-keeping requirements for K–12 school counselors are not as clear. The U.S. Department of Education, equivalent state agencies, school systems, administrative districts, and individual schools often develop record-keeping policies that may or may not coincide with the standards for clinical counseling. For that reason, most of our comments in this chapter will pertain primarily to counselors practicing in clinical settings.

The 2005 *ACA Code of Ethics* unambiguously requires counselors to maintain client records: "Counselors maintain records necessary for rendering professional services to their clients and as required by laws, regulations, or agency or institution procedures" (Standard A.1.b.). HIPAA (see chapter 5) has introduced a language defining much of the contents of client records and psychotherapy notes. State counselor licensing laws often incorporate the *ACA Code of Ethics* as the standard of practice and may have other requirements regarding record keeping. It is, therefore, essential that you remain mindful of the applicable laws in your state.

In some respects the standard of practice for records and documentation remains an uneven field. Some state counselor licensure laws provide few details on the specifics of what must be included in a client record. Other state laws and supporting rules more clearly prescribe the contents of a counseling record. Arizona is an example of a state that carefully defines the contents of counseling records. The Arizona Board of Behavioral Health Examiners has developed very detailed standard of practice rules pertaining to client records and treatment plans. The details in the treatment plan rule exceed ethical requirements. In Arizona, a licensee shall

1. Work jointly with each client served or a client's legal representative to prepare an integrated, individualized, written treatment plan, based on the licensee's diagnosis and assessment of behavior and the treatment needs, abilities, resources, and circumstances of the client, including:
   a. One or more treatment goals;
   b. One or more treatment methods;
   c. The date when the client's treatment plan shall be reviewed;
   d. If a discharge date has been determined, the aftercare needed after discharge;
   e. The signature and date signed by the client or the client's legal representative; and
   f. The signature and date signed by the licensee.
2. At a minimum, review and reassess the treatment plan according to the review date specified in the treatment plan and at least annually with each client or the client's legal representative to ensure the continued viability and effectiveness of the treatment plan and, where appropriate, a description of the services the client may need after terminating treatment with the licensee.
3. Ensure that all treatment plan updates and revisions include the signature and date signed by the client or the client's legal representative and the signature and date signed by the licensee.
4. Upon written request, provide a client or a client's legal representative an explanation of all aspects of the client's condition and treatment.
5. Ensure that a client's treatment is in accordance with the client's treatment plan. (Ariz. Rev. Stat. § 32-3251, 2006)

The standard of practice regarding records and the documentation of counseling and psychotherapy services is an area of continued professional evolution. The full impact and implication of the HIPAA privacy regulations have yet to be tested in court. Inevitably, courts will rule on various aspects of federal and state laws; these rulings will further clarify practitioner duties regarding records and documentation standards. As you read this chapter, please keep in mind that there are some questions we can't answer. In some cases there is no standard answer; in other cases, the diversity of practice is so great that all we can say is, "It depends." Therefore, our purpose in this chapter is to define the minimum ethical and legal expectations (as we understand them today) and to offer specific direction for documenting client interactions and situations that could lead to licensure board complaints and/or accusations of malpractice.

THE PURPOSE OF CLIENT RECORDS

From our perspective, the purpose of client records and documentation of counseling services can be divided into four broad and overlapping categories: (1) clinical management—how records and documentation serve to assist the practitioner in providing quality care for the client; (2) legal implications for the client—how records and documentation can serve the client who is involved or becomes involved in a judicial proceeding (e.g., court mandated treatment, divorce proceedings, and child custody); (3) protection of health information—how HIPAA regulations have defined record keeping and appropriate use and disclosure of information; and (4) risk management for counselors—how records and clinical documentation can serve as a risk management strategy to help protect counselors from licensure board complaints and lawsuits. Before discussing each of these four categories, we need to define, for purposes of our discussion, two important terms:

1. *Client record*—the physical and/or electronic folder(s) or file(s) sometimes referred to as the *chart* or the *general treatment record* in which protected health information pertaining to the care of the client is maintained. Specific content within the client record will be influenced by the treatment setting (private practice or agency/organization policies), the client's presenting concerns, and relevant state and federal laws. Typically, the contents include the following:
   - client contact information
   - dates of service (including start/stop times)
   - participants (who attended counseling sessions)
   - informed consent (signed and dated)
   - financial charges and payments (may be stored separately)
   - clinical assessment and/or diagnosis
   - authorizations to release confidential information;
   - collateral information (testing results, letters, reports, e-mails, court/legal documents, information obtained about the client from others including past clinical records and communication from third parties)
   - treatment plan

- prognosis and progress tracking
- session notes (chart notes, progress notes, process notes)
- psychotherapy notes (see the Purpose #3 discussion)

2. *Clinical documentation*—the act of recording, in any form, relevant information gained during the course of the counseling/treatment relationship.

Client Records Purpose #1: Clinical Management

On the most obvious level, well-organized and well-documented client counseling records assist practitioners in providing quality care to clients. Unlike medicine or other professional services, counseling and psychotherapy rarely unfold in an objective and linear manner. The twists and turns inherent in the counseling process require constant attention and thoughtful reflection. The intellectual and physical processes associated with documenting counseling sessions provide practitioners with an opportunity to reflect and gain perspective on the evolving dynamics of the case. Although there are some client stories and situations that vividly remain in the mind of a practitioner throughout the course of treatment, most client situations can easily become mixed with other current or past client circumstances. Quality care is enhanced when counselors are fully present in the session, empowered with the client's story, and mindful of the treatment plan. Being present and prepared is facilitated by the timely and careful documentation of the previous session. Regular review of the client's record in preparation for the session is responsible practice that reflects an ethical commitment to providing the client with the best possible care.

There is probably no more critical moment in any counseling relationship than when the counselor and client are working through threats of harm to self or others. When clients disclose thoughts, feeling, or intentions that place the client or others at risk, we are duty bound to assess the potential threat and to take appropriate action. Responding appropriately and then fully documenting the at-risk situation and your response to it is essential, both from a quality of care perspective and from a risk management perspective (more about that later in this chapter). A habit of competent documentation of at-risk situations can actually support the care you give to your client. When faced with an at-risk situation you can almost see the documentation that will be needed. Seeing the documentation makes it easier to engage in the careful decision making and clinical interventions that will result in quality care. The connection between quality care and good documentation is that each supports and promotes the other. Thorough documentation facilitates good preparation that enhances quality care that invites thorough documentation—all of which supports a practice that is ethically, legally, and clinically sound.

Quality documentation also facilitates continuity of care from one practitioner to another, which is an essential element of clinical management. Sometimes another practitioner must temporarily step in when the treating counselor is not available; at other times the treating counselor must transfer or refer the client to a new counselor. In these instances, good records provide a means of communicating valuable information to the covering or new practitioner.

Client Records Purpose #2: Legal Implications for the Client

Counseling and psychotherapy records often become relevant when clients are involved in a legal proceeding. Honest and nonjudgmental clinical documentation of client issues and progress in addressing issues can serve the client's legal needs in a variety of ways. Clients reasonably expect that issues discussed and progress achieved will be documented and available should the information be needed in a judicial proceeding. The specific legal proceeding can range from civil matters (divorce and child custody) to workplace injury and workman's compensation lawsuits to criminal proceedings. Sometimes counseling is initiated at the behest or encouragement of the attorneys or judge involved in a legal proceeding. Clients are often court ordered into counseling and/or attorneys may encourage clients to seek treatment in anticipation of a court order or to demonstrate responsible action on the part of their clients. At other times, counseling is initiated without any judicial involvement or anticipated involvement, but unforeseen circumstances occur that place the client into a judicial context. When that occurs, counseling records often become relevant to the judicial proceeding.

We encourage you to assume that any client record could end up being read in open court. Therefore, professional and thorough documentation should be the standard so that if release of client records is authorized by your client or legally obtained by the court, the record will accurately and professionally reflect the clinical experience. To that end, practitioners are encouraged not to include names or identifying information about third parties (particularly the names of extramarital lovers and/or business partners that may be involved with your client). This is not to say that the names of family members and/or significant others relevant to issues in the counseling need to be excluded from records.

Further, client records do not always reflect favorably on the client and actually may be detrimental to the client in a judicial proceeding. The clinical record should honestly reflect the reality of the counseling experience and should never be constructed or altered to artificially reflect favorably on the client or the counselor. If, at the outset of the counseling relationship, it is likely or even possible that client records or a report of client issues and progress will become involved in a judicial process, you are encouraged during the informed consent process to clearly define the ground rules of your involvement and the nature and type of records that will be maintained.

Client Records Purpose #3: HIPAA Compliance

We recognize that not every counseling practitioner or practice setting is a HIPAA-covered entity (see chapter 5), and therefore HIPAA requirements do not pertain to every mental health practice. However, we believe that, over time, HIPAA requirements will continue to influence and may ultimately come to define the standard of practice with regard to records and documentation. Therefore, we have included HIPAA compliance as one of the reasons for record keeping. A major purpose of the Health Insurance Portability and Accountability Act of 1996 (HIPAA) was to address concerns that the transmission of health care information through the Internet and other electronic means could lead to widespread gaps in protection of patient and client confidentiality (see chapter 5 for a complete discussion). In the process of developing HIPAA-compliant rules and procedures, the standard of practice regarding client records and documentation was affected. During the past several years, practitioners have adopted HIPAA language and practices, and some state laws have been developed or modified to provide consistency with HIPAA requirements. All is far from settled; there are significant unanswered and untested questions that await court rulings or rulemaking that will bring further clarity.

From a HIPAA perspective, counseling records include two broad sections of individually identifiable information defined by HIPAA as *protected health information.* The protected health information includes client demographic information (e.g., name, date of birth, address, telephone number, e-mail). It also includes (if appropriate) diagnosis (see chapter 10), prognosis, treatment plan, progress to date, dates of service (including start/stop times of sessions), participants in the session, and financial data (charges, payments, balance). This type of protected health information is confidential but, under appropriate circumstances, may be accessed by third-party payers.

Psychotherapy notes, also commonly referred to as *process notes*, are given an added level of protection by HIPAA if they are maintained in a separate physical or electronic file. The added level of protection means that disclosure of psychotherapy notes requires a separately executed client authorization (assuming the notes are maintained in a separate file). Practitioners can, of course, integrate psychotherapy

> *Psychotherapy notes* are "notes recorded in any medium by a mental heath professional documenting or analyzing the contents of conversation during a private counseling session that are separated from the rest of the individual's record."
> (45 C.F.R. § 164.501)

notes within a single file that includes all client protected health information, but if handled in this manner, psychotherapy notes are then covered under the general rules governing the disclosure of protected health information.

> HIPAA-Compliant Software Notes 444:
> http://www.notes444.com/

A decision must be made: Should the mental health practitioner create one file containing all protected health information, including psychotherapy notes, or should the practitioner create two files, one for the regular protected health information (as just outlined) and one for psychotherapy notes? Maintaining two separate records on each client can be taxing and complicated, but with certain client populations or treatment settings, it may be in the best interests of the clients to do so. Agency policy, state statutes, and the unique practice habits of a counselor may dictate or influence this decision. We are aware of at least one clinical documentation software program (Notes 444)[1] that purports to automatically create two separate electronic files. When a practitioner records session data, psychotherapy notes (process notes) are entered into a separate field and automatically filed in a separate psychotherapy notes file.

Whereas HIPAA has provided a definition of psychotherapy notes, relevant questions remain. Would some or all information contained in a traditional SOAP Note (Subjective, Objective, Assessment, and Plan) or a DAP Note (Data, Assessment, and Plan) be considered a psychotherapy note? What about practitioners who document in a free-form narrative manner? What portion of the narrative information would be considered to fall within the purview of a psychotherapy note? What about the relationship or family-systems-based counselor who views the relationship (couple, family, or group) as the client and documents accordingly? Or the practitioner who has ethical questions about the legitimacy of mental health diagnoses—and therefore organizes and describes treatment in ways that are different from the medical model around which HIPAA is constituted? To our knowledge, these important questions remain as yet untested and unanswered. In many ways the answers to these and other documentation questions represent the frontier of the continued evolution of the standard of practice for mental health professionals. You are encouraged to be ever mindful of the evolving standard of care regarding documentation. Expect continued change—and keep current!

---

[1] We are not endorsing any particular product for HIPAA compliance; it is up to the reader to ascertain the effectiveness of any software program.

Client Records Purpose #4: Risk Management Strategy

The final reason for keeping records is very simple. Well-organized and well-documented client counseling records are the most effective tool counselors have for successfully responding to licensing board complaints or threats of a malpractice lawsuit. If there is a question about what you did or failed to do, and there is no documentation in the client record that reflects what the client said/did or documentation that describes your clinical decision making, it can be argued that it never happened. It will be your word against your client's word. We are trusting people. It is hard for us to think that a client might intentionally accuse us of something inappropriate or suggest that we failed in our duty to serve the client's best interests. Sadly, counselors are sometimes falsely accused of wrongdoing. Sometimes clients legitimately misunderstand our words and intentions, misquote our comments, or misinterpret our actions. When the counseling relationship breaks down—and the client feels stressed, betrayed, and abandoned—anything is possible. Documentation is your first and best line of defense.

This is particularly true when dealing with high-risk issues in the counseling process. High-risk issues include threats of harm to self or others, transference and countertransference issues, and complicated legal and ethical issues that can be open to interpretation. Examples of such issues include (but are not limited to) pregnancy, abortion, sexual activities and drug abuse of minors, allegations of child abuse and elder or disabled adult abuse, illegal client actions, and infidelity. When these issues present, it is important to carefully document your clinical decision making and your professional actions. Threats of harm to self or others are common and always potentially explosive clinical issues. From a risk management documentation perspective, we recommend that each at-risk situation be fully documented in the client record to include

- *at-risk situation:* Document what the client did or said that suggested she or he was considering engaging in or was actively engaging in a high-risk activity.
- *assessment:* Based on your clinical experience and knowledge of the client, document the severity level of this threat.
- *options:* List the options you considered as appropriate responses based on your assessment. Listing options demonstrates that you were thinking broadly and that you considered a range of alternatives before reaching a decision.
- *rule out:* Describe what options you ruled out and why each was determined to be inappropriate. These descriptions clarify your clinical decision making.
- *consultation and/or supervision:* If there is time, obtain and document any colleague consultation or supervision you received in order to evaluate options and clarify a course of action.

- *actions taken:* Describe the options you chose, including what you said or did. This helps clarify how you implemented the options you determined to be appropriate.
- *follow-up:* Document what happened—what you did—and how things progressed until there was resolution.

Nothing about this process assures that you will make all the right choices and that every at-risk client situation will have a positive outcome. Unanticipated and tragic things do happen: Clients commit suicide or murder and harm others or themselves. The standard is not that you ascertain the unknown. The standard is that you conduct a careful assessment of the situation, consider a range of options, make a thoughtful clinical decision, competently implement your decision, and remain mindful and vigilant (if necessary) until there is resolution. The end result may not be positive; sometimes it is tragic. From a risk management perspective we want you to have carefully documented what you did and why so that others can see that you brought your best professional judgment and skill to the situation.

OWNERSHIP OF RECORDS

Under most circumstances in a private practice setting, counseling records (the physical or electronic record) belong to you. In a school, agency, or other treatment facility, counseling records are the property of the organization. However, the information contained in those records belongs to the client. You have an obligation to protect the confidentiality of client records, as discussed in chapter 5, but you should always operate under the assumption that a variety of individuals may at some time have access to your records, including professional colleagues, insurance and managed care companies, attorneys, courts, employers, schools, and even your client.

ALTERATION OF RECORDS

Evidence of altering client records can lead to serious consequences. Erasures, whiteouts, crossed-out and blacked-out notes, and notes out of sequence in a paper record suggest that changes and alterations may have been made to the original record. Someone reading the record might conclude that you are disorganized or perhaps less than honest. Additionally, electronic documentation that was created at a time other than when services were provided can cast suspicion on the accuracy of the record. Notwithstanding ethical confidentiality concerns, the contents of counseling records may be discoverable by a court of law, inspected by insurance companies, and released to others upon waiver by your client, so you must ensure that your record keeping is complete, accurate, and free of any extraneous materials that could prove embarrassing at some later time. Notes in the margins, telephone numbers casually jotted down on the back of a record, and doodles have no place in client records. Personal criticism of your client in progress notes could be extremely embarrassing or harmful to the client if disclosed at some later date.

All client record documentation should be made contemporaneously, not constructed after the fact, and particularly not after receiving a subpoena. It is also important never to change or alter records so they look better before you release them. If you determine, for whatever reason, that you need to add and/or clarify information in the client record, you can do so by making a currently dated entry in the record. This entry can be appropriately titled to reflect the nature of the addition to the record. Examples include Progress Summary, Progress Update, and Clarification; the point is to date the entry with the current date and then provide the relevant information. Although there still may be criticism of the timeliness of your documentation, there can be no valid accusation that you attempted to alter the original record. Of course, the best practice is to keep client records current so you are never in a position to address deficiencies in the record.

FINANCIAL RECORDS AND FINANCIAL RELATIONSHIP

Financial records should also be maintained on all clients to accurately document the financial relationship. This is true for fee-for-service, third-party payers, copayment relationships, and services provided by grants or purchase of service arrangements. Whether these records should be kept with counseling records is a matter for individual consideration. Many practices have separate billing departments that handle financial matters, and counselors have limited, if any, contact with fees and collections. There should be some mechanism, even in larger practices, to inform a counselor if a client is delinquent in paying for services. Too often, counselors do not discuss a growing unpaid balance with their clients. At some point the delinquent account becomes a problem between the counselor and the client or the agency and the client—a problem that threatens the counseling relationship. Unpaid counseling fees may also reflect other underlying problems of which the counselor should be aware. Counselors are encouraged to maintain accurate financial records, keep clients apprised of any outstanding balances, and proactively address financial delinquency so that mutually agreeable payment plans can be established that do not threaten the counseling relationship.

TECHNOLOGY AND CLIENT RECORDS/INFORMATION

Many counseling agencies and private practitioners now maintain client records, schedules, and financial information on computers. This medium certainly helps to reduce paperwork and saves time, but there are some potential problems. First and foremost, authenticating the content and dates of records may be difficult with electronic media designed to be flexible and maneuverable. Be sure to include dates of entries in computer records, and establish procedures to ensure security of access to computer files. You should also implement a plan for frequent backup of information to avoid losing files if a computer crashes (or

Examples of software programs:
Psych Advantage:
    http://www.advantagesoftware.com/
TheraScribe:
    http://www.helper.com/
Therapist Helper:
    http://www.vantagemed.com/
    behavioral_health_practices/behavior_
    health_practice_management.htm

the computer operator accidentally erases information). There are several software programs on the market specifically designed for mental health professionals. These programs[2] can assist practitioners in the creation of the entire client record (all protected health information) including scheduling, financial and billing information, treatment planning, counseling session notes, and even reports on client progress.

RECORD RETENTION

Records should be retained for at least the minimum period of time set by state law, if any. Federal tax policy, state records or licensure statutes, agency policy, and/or other administrative requirements may influence the specific amount of time that client counseling and financial records are maintained. As already discussed, client records serve many purposes and should be available for a reasonable amount of time. Years after treatment has concluded, clients may need to access their records as evidence of their state of mind during a particularly difficult time of life. Counselors may need to refer to client records to competently respond to allegations of ethical violations, negligence, or malpractice. Therefore, we encourage the establishment of a records retention policy for your firm, agency, or practice. Develop the records retention policy in keeping with your state licensing statute, HIPAA requirements, and the statute of limitations in your state (the number of years after an allegation of malpractice that a client has in which to bring suit). All client records should be kept, not just some of the records. The record retention policy should specify how records will be maintained in storage (microfilm, microfiche, computer PDF files, boxed paper files, etc.). Finally, the policy should define where records will be stored to keep them safe and secure, and how and when they will be destroyed.

---

[2]We are not endorsing any particular product for HIPAA compliance; it is up to the reader to ascertain the effectiveness of any software program.

If there is no set minimum period of time for record retention in your state, you may wish to retain records for a minimum of 7 years. If you see Medicaid clients or others under a federally funded program, you may wish to keep the records for at least 10 years (the longest period of time in which a false claims action could be brought against you). If you counsel children, you may wish to keep them for a set period of time after the client reaches the age of majority.

RECORDS CUSTODIAN

Last, but not least, you should appoint a records custodian to take custody of counseling records in the event of your death or disability. The concept of a records custodian is one that we have been suggesting for a number of years. The 2005 *ACA Code of Ethics* also calls for appointment of a records custodian in the case of a counselor's incapacitation, death, or termination of practice (Standard B.6.h.). The appointment of a records custodian will be of little concern to counselors who work in large practices or agencies; the agency is automatically the custodian of the records. But for small practices, especially sole practitioners, it is important that a trusted professional colleague be appointed the caretaker of your client records. The records custodian has two primary responsibilities: (1) to notify and provide referral assistance to your clients in the event of your sudden death or disability and (2) to take custody of your client records to ensure their continued security (both for the benefit and protection of the client and for protection of you or your estate in the event of a malpractice lawsuit). Obviously, it is important to appoint a records custodian who is a credentialed mental health professional and someone for whom you have professional regard. However, you should not appoint someone who will be too distressed in the event of your sudden death or disability to competently support your clients and provide for appropriate referral. Frequently, counselors practicing in the same community will agree to a reciprocal records custodial arrangement. You might want to consider including this information in your will.

In the event you decide to close your practice, whether to relocate, change professional direction, or retire, clients should be provided with information about how to access copies of records. Some state counseling laws define a process for client notification; in some cases a notice must be placed in a local newspaper. The point is to ensure that records continue to be maintained after relocation, cessation of practice, or retirement for the time specified in your records retention policy and/or as defined by law, and that a process be established and communicated whereby clients can gain access to records.

SUMMARY

Accurate, timely, and thoughtful client records are not only the prevailing standard of care for practicing professional counselors but also a risk management strategy that is completely under the control of the counselor. Competent record keeping serves both client and counselor. Counselors are strongly encouraged to adopt and maintain a system of record keeping that is consistent with federal laws, prevailing state counselor licensing board laws and rules, institutional policies, and the unique needs of a given client population.

Chapter 10

MANAGING YOUR COUNSELING PRACTICE

As a professional, you must determine whether to practice as an employee of an agency, corporation, or other entity; establish your own solo private practice; or join with colleagues. This decision will be guided by a variety of factors, including the extent to which you are willing to take both financial and emotional risks, your security and predictability needs, and your professional preparation and experience. For some counselors, the steady income and security resulting from being employed by another is of paramount importance. For others, the freedom to be one's own boss is the overriding factor. In the end, it is your choice (assuming there are not licensure restrictions).

Based on your choice, you will face an array of restrictions and possibilities determined by federal, state, and local laws and regulations. If you choose to practice as an employee of an institution or counseling agency, you may be spared from complying with some of the governmental requirements for employers. The purpose of this chapter is to provide some guidance about the business aspects of both private and public professional counseling practices. Please keep in mind that the material that follows is, by necessity, very general. It is intended to raise issues and questions for you to consider. It is not designed as a substitute for good legal, business, and financial planning. You are encouraged to consult with relevant professionals before making crucial decisions about your professional practice.

FORMS OF OPERATION

Nonprofit Organizations

One of the threshold decisions in establishing a private counseling practice is whether to operate as a for-profit or nonprofit entity. Many services provided by the counseling profession are housed in nonprofit organizations. This approach can offer a host of advantages, not the least of which is tax-exempt status and the resulting ability to attract charitable gifts and donations and send mail at discounted rates.

To qualify for this preferential treatment, the organization's programs must be within the bounds of what are considered charitable, educational, or scientific activities within the scope of section 501(c)(3) or 501(c)(4) of the Internal Revenue Code (2006). This form is probably most appropriate if the counselor is motivated less by the objective of building a business and deriving profit and more by the prospect of operating a program that emphasizes research, publications, seminars, or the provision of certain types of counseling services. A counselor may own a nonprofit entity in the sense of controlling its board of directors. Furthermore, a counselor who is an employee may receive a reasonable salary, and an independent contractor may also receive reasonable payments for services rendered to a nonprofit organization.

Generally speaking, a nonprofit entity must qualify for tax-exempt status under federal tax law. Once that is accomplished, there is probably a similar exemption under state law as well. However, the privileges of tax exemption come at a price, including limitations on lobbying and political activities and the filing of annual informational returns required by the Internal Revenue Service for most exempt organizations.

For-Profit Entities

Although many practices are incorporated, this is by no means mandatory. For many years, small businesses have operated successfully as unincorporated, sole proprietorships. Whether a counselor practices alone or as part of a group is a matter that involves personality and economic circumstances rather than simply considerations of law. However, the form of the business is very much dictated by legal considerations, a chief determinant of which is the avoidance of personal liability.

Corporation. Forming a corporation generally shields the individual owners, directors, officers, or employees of the corporation from personal liability for acts arising out of its business operations because it is a separate legal entity. If creditors initiate lawsuits against the corporation, the private assets of the individual officers, directors, or employees will usually be immune from their reach. This would include claims for uncollected debts, false or misleading advertising, nonpayment of taxes, accidents that occur on the premises, and other similar situations. It is important to stress that incorporation is not advisable in all situations. Professional corporations (those available to counselors, psychologists, physicians, etc., under most state laws) typically do not shield counselor shareholders from their own malpractice liability. They usually do protect counselor shareholders from the negligent acts and omissions of their shareholder colleagues. Therefore, professional corporation status may not be the accepted mode of operating for many solo practitioners.

Additionally, the initial costs of incorporation and attendant filing fees are not substantial, but the continuing formalities necessary to maintain the corporation may prove onerous. These may include separating the financial records of shareholders and the corporation, holding regular meetings of shareholders and directors, issuing stock and maintaining stock transfer records, and filing annual reports. Furthermore, the limited-liability advantage available to corporations only applies so long as the corporate formalities are preserved. Failure to adhere to these formalities, particularly regarding commingling of funds and filing required reports, can lead to loss of corporate status and its attendant liability limitations.

S Corporation. Another possibility to consider is the subchapter S corporation. Under federal tax law option, the S corporation allows an enterprise to be created as a corporation under state law, thereby preserving the shield against personal liability, yet be treated as a partnership for federal tax law purposes. This means that the tax deductions and tax credits experienced by corporations are not frozen at the corporate level but are passed along to the stockholders in their personal capacities. You should speak to your accountant before electing subchapter S status.

Partnership. Where two or more counselors are in the same practice, one alternative to incorporating may be to form a partnership. Sometimes, this form of operation is more tax advantageous than the corporate form. With the usual partnership form, liabilities as well as assets are shared among partners. The downside to this is that you might be liable for the acts and omissions of your partner.

LLC or LLP. In recent years, some counselors and other professionals have chosen to set up a similar entity in the form of either a limited liability company (LLC) or a limited liability partnership (LLP). The details are governed by state law. Like the subchapter S corporation, the LLC achieves a limited liability for owners similar to that of a stockholder of a corporation while permitting partnership-style pass-through treatment of income for tax purposes. There are usually no particular limitations set on who may be a member of an LLC. Additionally, flexibility of allocating income, losses, and cash flow is permitted, and the strict qualification rules of the subchapter S corporations do not apply. There are, however, some disadvantages to this entity, mostly arising from the uncertainty about how jurisdictions that do not recognize LLCs deal with them and the expense that may be incurred by a small counseling practice. With the LLP form, a partner may not be shielded from the general debts and liabilities of the partnership (such as leases).

There is no one-size-fits-all business operational form that suits all counselors in all jurisdictions. Any counselor thinking of starting a private practice or agency should engage the help of qualified professionals, such as a certified public accountant (CPA) and attorney who specializes in business formation issues (see Appendix D for further information on finding such professionals).

Operating Instruments and Organizational Meetings

Regardless of which organizational form is chosen, business entities are governed by the operating instruments by which they are created that state their operational rules. For a corporation, the creating document is its articles of incorporation, the contents and form of which are usually dictated by state law. The corporation's operating rules are contained in its bylaws. For a partnership, the creating document is the partnership agreement, which usually includes the general operational rules, although a set of bylaws or other rules may be developed to guide its day-to-day management. Limited liability companies are created by articles of organization and governed by an operating agreement that is a combination of partnership agreement, limited partnership agreement, and corporate bylaws.

When forming a business entity, you must observe a number of organizational formalities. First among these is the organizational meeting, with its proceedings recorded in minutes. Depending on the rules in your state, a variety of actions may occur at this meeting, including selecting and approving the organizational structure, authorizing bank accounts, and retaining a lawyer and accountant (see Appendix D). Corporate rules also may require an initial meeting of the corporation at which directors other than those listed in the articles of incorporation may be elected, together with the corporation's officers.

Office-Sharing and Informal Group Practices

Throughout the country, many independent professional counselors share offices and overhead expenses. This type of arrangement may be reasonable and cost-effective; however, it can expose the counselor to increased liability risk based on the conduct of the other professionals in the informal group, conduct over which the counselor has no control or responsibility. The members of these loosely affiliated informal groups may assume there will be no liability for their colleagues but that is not always true. Here are some of the common indicators of a group practice, even if there is no formal legal entity:

- The members of the group use a group name, such as Counseling Associates.
- There is joint letterhead, billing, advertising, or an office sign.
- Client records of all practitioners are stored together.
- Group therapy sessions are conducted by more than one practitioner.
- The public perceives the operation to be a group practice.

If you are considered to be part of a group, whether or not you are an organized business entity, you may be held liable for the negligent acts of others in the group practice. You can minimize the risks by carefully checking out the references and licensing status of any other professionals who practice in your office and ensuring that all members of the group carry equivalent limits of liability insurance. If you operate as a group practice, you may wish to obtain a group liability insurance policy (see this chapter's discussion of insurance).

Alternatively, if you decide you want to maintain separate and independent practices but still share office space, be sure you and the other practitioners clearly identify yourselves as independent contractors and establish that by maintaining, for example, separate billing accounts and letterheads. Even if the therapists intend to operate as independent professionals, courts may give more weight to the public's perception. We are aware of a counselor who was sued on a theory of de facto partnership when an uninsured psychologist in her multidisciplinary office-sharing arrangement allegedly carried on a sexual relationship with his patient. In this case, the professionals used a joint name (such as XYZ Counseling Associates) on an office sign, letterhead, and phones, and it could have appeared to the public (clients) that the group was operating as a partnership. Other professionals have been sued in similar circumstances on a legal theory of ostensible agency.

Professional liability insurance should be purchased by all who share the office space, and copies of the policy face sheets or certificates of insurance should be maintained and updated annually. If the practices are truly independent, there should be no fee splitting. (In many states, splitting or sharing of fees between the referring professional and the professional who actually treats the client is illegal because the monetary incentive could cause the referral to be made based on the professional's financial interest rather than the client's best interest.) All clients should be apprised, in writing, of the fact that the group is comprised of individual, independent practitioners who are each responsible for their own acts and omissions as well as the fact that the arrangement is not a partnership, professional association, or other joint entity. This information should be communicated in the Informed Consent documents of all practitioners in the office. It is not enough for you to communicate this to your clients because that protects your office mates but doesn't protect you.

BUSINESS PROCEDURES

Once your professional practice has been established, it is vitally important that a variety of business procedures be implemented to ensure that your practice is conducted in a professional manner. Consideration must be given to tax recording and filing systems; business licensing; insurance (health, disability, premises liability, and content damage/theft); employment and related issues; billing and financial accounting; systems for filing claims for reimbursement with insurance companies; contracts for lease or purchase of property, office equipment, and furnishings; advertising; continuing education requirements and renewal of licensure; relationships with colleagues and supervisors; and myriad other issues. It is extremely important that you set up systems so that you don't let important items—such as your insurance policies or professional license—lapse.

Your financial and legal advisers will be able to assist with specific recommendations, but there are a variety of service organizations that offer general business advice. It is just as important to be prepared for the business aspects of your practice as it is to provide competent counseling services to the public.

Federal and State Taxes, Reporting, and Licensing

Federal, state, and some local governments require that businesses submit a variety of annual information and tax returns. Your local Internal Revenue Service office, state office of taxation, or a local government office should be able to provide you with the necessary information booklets and blank forms that must be filed for business licenses, state and local employee taxes, unemployment taxes, real and personal property taxes, and business income taxes, among others. Your lawyer and/or accountant can also help you to determine which reports and forms are required and when and where they must be filed.

Professional Liability Insurance

It should be evident by now that counselors can be prepared, competent, and licensed; learn about all the legal obligations and implications of counseling clients and operating a private business; and scrupulously tailor their professional actions to conform to the *ACA Code of Ethics*, and still become the target of ethical, administrative, or legal complaints. Clients may be dissatisfied with their progress in counseling or hear about a hot issue on television or radio, such as sexual abuse by therapists. They may have had unreasonable expectations about the results of counseling and blame the counselor when they see no measurable improvement. Consequently, even without any wrongdoing on the part of the counselor, an administrative or legal complaint may be filed against him or her.

A counselor must respond to any administrative, ethical, or legal complaint filed against him or her. Failure to respond to a complaint in court may result in a default judgment against the defendant counselor, with damages ordered as the court determines appropriate. Even at an early stage before trial in which the claim is found to be without merit, the costs to defend or negotiate that complaint may extend to thousands of dollars. Legal expenses for a trial can exceed $50,000, and without insurance, personal assets are at risk. Failure to respond to a licensure board complaint can lead to sanctions against the licensee, including loss of licensure.

Considerations When Purchasing Liability Insurance

Counselors should obtain professional liability insurance coverage at the outset of professional practice. The annual average premium for professional liability coverage for a full-time private practitioner in 2007 through the ACA Insurance Trust is less than $325. Exact premiums are dependent upon the state in which the counselor practices, as well as the type of practice specialty and number of hours worked per week. For students, the typical 2007 premiums range from $20 to $29. These amounts are well within the financial reach of most practicing counselors.

There are a number of factors to consider when purchasing professional liability coverage. Not all policies meet the needs of all counselors. Counselors may find coverage through individual policies, group plans, and plans sponsored by professional associations such as the ACA Insurance Trust. Regardless of where you obtain the policy, coverage is usually of two types:

- *Claims made*—covers claims actually made while the policy is in force.
- *Occurrence*—covers claims for alleged acts that occurred while the policy was in effect, even if the claim is made several years later after the policy is no longer in force.

Because claims can be, and often are, filed long after a client has terminated counseling, the occurrence type of policy affords greater protection to you as a practicing counselor. If your policy is of the claims-made type and you change to another insurance company, you will usually need to purchase a separate policy that extends your coverage, usually called *tail coverage*. You are advised to consult with a reputable liability insurance professional for a full explanation of policy features, benefits, and limitations.

It is important to secure coverage for all aspects of your professional practice, including supervision of students or interns, consulting with other professionals, service on accreditation or professional review boards, and actual counseling work with clients. However, be advised that most insurance contracts limit protection to situations in which the conduct complained of was unintentional. Most professional liability policies exclude coverage for claims based on sexual misconduct and other intentional wrongdoing such as fraud, dishonesty, or other criminal behavior. However, some policies will pay to defend the counselor in court against certain claims that are excluded, even though they will not pay damages if the counselor is held liable. This coverage can be important in the event an unsubstantiated claim is filed.

Other recommendations for purchasing professional liability insurance are as follows:

- Choose a carrier with an excellent or superior rating by an independent research company, such as A.M. Best or Standard & Poor's. Each company's rating scale is somewhat different, but the grade will signal whether the company is on sound financial footing and has adequate reserve funds.
- Choose an insurance company that is an admitted (licensed) carrier in your state so that your state's Guaranty Fund will stand behind your carrier in the event of a default.
- Consider how long the company has been in the field of providing professional malpractice coverage and whether their rates have been stable.
- Ask questions such as, Does the company have a good record of service? How long does it take to get your policy and any needed endorsements? Are they accessible by telephone?
- Find out whether the company provides assistance—such as training, publications, or online courses—in managing the risks associated with your practice.

Additionally, services such as the ACA Insurance Trust's Risk Management Helpline (see chapter 4) can often help to avert lawsuits and administrative complaints before they are filed. Not all insurance carriers provide the same level of assistance, so inquire about the details of services provided before signing up for coverage.

Do You Need Professional Liability Insurance?

It is obvious that professional counselors in private practice should obtain professional liability insurance. But what if you are employed by a school, agency, or organization? If you are an employed counselor and rely on your employer to provide coverage, you could be left with responsibility for unexpected expenses. For example, if you are a school or agency counselor, what happens to you if your employer claims that your actions fell outside the scope of your job duties? You may not be covered for these actions. If you do volunteer or pro bono work on the side, you may not be covered by your employer's policy.

Counselor educators should also make sure that the institution's policy covers them in their roles as supervisors of practicum students and interns. With the low cost of malpractice insurance for counselors, it usually makes sense for counselor educators to have their own policies. In one case, a counselor educator was sued, along with the university and counseling practicum student, as a result of the suicide attempt of the client of a student counselor. The client's parents claimed that the counseling was inadequate and caused them considerable expense for subsequent hospitalization and psychiatric care. The university's attorney advised the student and counselor educator to obtain their own legal counsel to protect their personal interests because the interests of the university were not necessarily consistent with the interests of the supervisor and student (P. L. Nelson, Executive Director, ACA Insurance Trust, personal communication, January 2006).

In another case, a student sought help from a counselor at a university counseling center and relayed that she had been the victim of date rape. The university was sued based on the date rape incident and the counselor was not involved. However, the administration demanded all client records to aid the university in defense of the lawsuit. Fortunately, the counselor had personal insurance and was able to obtain legal assistance to protect against the release of confidential records. If the counselor had not maintained an individual policy, the attorney's fees could have been quite expensive (P. L. Nelson, Executive Director, ACA Insurance Trust, personal communication, January 2006).

OTHER INSURANCE COVERAGE

Once you have established the location of your office and purchased or leased furnishings and equipment, it is important to consider a variety of insurance policies to minimize your risk of unprotected or insufficiently compensated losses. A competent insurance agent, broker, or your professional association insurance program director or administrator can help to demystify some of the complexities of policy contracts and coverage. However, it is important for you to read such documents thoroughly and be sure that both you and the agent or broker understand the nature of your professional practice and the scope of coverage and exclusions provided. Once established, insurance policies should be reviewed annually to confirm that conditions have not changed.

The descriptions of types of insurance coverage that follow are intentionally general, but they should give counselors an overview of the various policies available. Before you contract for any insurance coverage, be sure to investigate the rating, business reputation, and claims procedures of the underwriting company.

General Liability Insurance

General liability insurance is usually written as a comprehensive policy that protects your practice from legal liability for losses associated with the premises and operations, contracts, administrative errors, employees, fire, third-party medical expenses, personal injury, nonowned automobiles, and the like. The insurer's total liability to cover losses will be stated on the declarations page and will usually include a single limit for the majority of coverage. The comprehensive policy may also include workers' compensation and coverage for uninsured or underinsured motorists' protection. Policies vary widely, as do premiums for coverage, so counselors are advised to consult with several insurers to compare coverage and costs.

Property Insurance

Property insurance covers your practice's real or personal property, or interest in rental property from losses from multiple risks. These include fire, lightning, windstorm or other acts of God, smoke, vandalism, and malicious mischief. Coverage also is available for accounts receivable, office equipment, computers, electronic media, signs, fixtures, landscaping, fine arts, and the like that many practices may use in the course of business. It is recommended that a complete inventory of all real and personal property in which your practice has an interest be conducted annually to determine the level of protection required through the property insurance policy. Some items to consider when reviewing policies include whether coverage is provided for (1) replacement cost of items lost or damaged, including improvements you have made to the premises; (2) lost rents/income; (3) temporary quarters and equipment rental; and (4) lost earnings and extra expenses due to temporary relocation. Does the policy provide for automatic increases of property limits? Is coverage based on replacement rather than on actual cash value? Will the replacement cost be paid regardless of whether the property is actually replaced? Each of these can result in a substantial benefit to your practice in the event of a covered loss.

Directors' and Officers' (D&O) Liability Insurance

If you act as a clinical director or officer of a corporation or nonprofit entity other than your own professional corporation, you may need directors' and officers' (D&O) liability insurance. Check with your agent, broker, or administrator to see if this type of coverage is necessary for you.

Fidelity Bonds

Fidelity bonds generally cover the risks associated with the dishonesty and performance failure of employees, officers, and directors. For example, the bond could protect you in the event your office manager forged your signature on checks and pocketed the proceeds. The bonding or insurance company agrees to pay a third party for any losses that are the result of acts or negligence of their insured (i.e., your professional practice). These bonds will cover the acts of all employees, whether professional or non-professional, including fraud, dishonesty, disappearance, and destruction.

Such coverage may also be included in a comprehensive general liability policy or office package policy, so you should examine the terms carefully to avoid costly duplication.

Business Overhead Insurance

One risk associated with professional practice that many professionals overlook is business overhead expense coverage. If one or more of the key partners of a small counseling practice becomes disabled, the risk of financial ruin is great. If two counselors share all the overhead expenses of their practice and one becomes seriously ill or is injured, the expenses of continuing operations may force the closing or discontinuation of the practice because of the extent of financial commitments, such as salaries, rent, and utilities. Purchasing business overhead expense coverage can protect from this exposure by covering general overhead expenses for limited periods of time.

Employee Benefits Programs

Private practitioners with employees also should consider employee benefits programs. Group medical benefits, hospitalization, life, and income-replacement (disability) programs are designed to protect employees and their families from the expenses of illness or injury and can help to attract and retain good employees. However, the costs can be high, and numerous federal and state laws make providing medical benefits very complex. Your review of employee medical benefit programs should include a discussion of what benefits are to be provided, the amount the professional practice can afford to contribute, and whether employees will contribute to the amount paid by the firm, as well as the deductibles, basic benefit levels, limits of coverage, coinsurance percentages, and similar requirements of the policy. As the impact of managed care programs increases, providing medical benefits coverage is both complicated and expensive. Counselors need to examine a variety of programs and plans to determine what form will best meet the needs of their practice and employees.

Disability Income Protection

This insurance product is designed to replace the individual's income in the event of a long-term illness or accident that restricts his or her ability to continue to practice and earn a living. These policies are available for both long and short terms, although long-term policies are widely regarded as the most critical. Short-term illnesses can usually be covered by personal investments or other sources, but those sources are quickly exhausted by a long-term illness. Insurers will usually underwrite only a percentage of an individual's annual earnings from professional practice, and how the premiums are paid may affect the individual's tax situation, so it is wise to consult with both your employees (if you offer such coverage to your employees) and tax adviser at the time the policy is purchased. Additionally, long-term care insurance has become popular in recent years to cover nursing home care or in-home nursing care for someone who has suffered a disability.

Group Life Insurance

Most employee benefit programs contain group life insurance, frequently as part of a group medical plan. Term life insurance is the least costly to obtain on a group basis, and it may be convertible to permanent forms of insurance to provide security for employees who leave your employ. Providing a reasonable level of low-cost protection should be the primary goal of your program, but keep in mind that policy provisions may vary widely in benefits, conditions, eligibility, and exclusions and should be examined closely.

EMPLOYMENT LAW CONSIDERATIONS

Employment law has become complex in recent years, and counselor employers should gain some basic familiarity with civil rights and sexual harassment issues, as well as the legal ramifications of giving references for former employees. It is beyond the scope of this book to give a comprehensive discussion of the law in this area. This is an area of law that changes rapidly and can trap an unwary counselor faced with hiring or termination decisions. The information that follows in this section is a summary of the employment process, some of the proscriptions that may apply, and recommendations for your private practice. If you have employees, you should have a local attorney available who is well-versed in employment law. If you are an employed counselor, this discussion may also prove helpful to you.

Employment Discrimination

Before you consider hiring your first employee, be sure to learn all you can about employment discrimination laws that may affect your practice. These laws apply to all aspects of employment, from position announcements, applications, interviews, and testing to termination decisions.

Title VII of the Civil Rights Act of 1964 is the federal statute that forbids employment discrimination based on race, color, sex (including pregnancy), national origin, or religion. It applies to federal, state, and local government employers and to private employers with more than 15 employees if their business "affects interstate commerce." This has been broadly interpreted to include activities conducted in other states, such as consulting, speaking engagements, teaching, or conferences, so even a medium-sized private counseling service may find that its activities must comply with federal and state employment laws. Title VII applies to counselors working in state and federal agencies, colleges, and universities. Even though your small private agency may have fewer that 15 employees, and therefore is not technically subject to the federal statute, the policies embodied in the law are good guidelines to follow with employees and may help you to avoid other problems later. Furthermore, many states have similar employment discrimination laws that apply to all employers within the state, regardless of size.

Title VII provides U.S. Equal Employment Opportunity Commission (EEOC) enforcement, which is initiated by filing charges within 180 days of the alleged discriminatory act. In some areas, charges must be filed with a local civil rights agency within 300 days of the alleged discrimination (see U.S. Equal Employment Opportunity Commission, 1997). The EEOC has the power to investigate any such claims, to seek conciliation, or to bring suit against the employer. If the EEOC decides not to bring an action against the employer in court, notice is given that the original complainant has the right to sue the employer within 90 days. The remedies available to a successful complainant include back pay, injunctive relief (such as an order to rehire, reinstate, or promote the employee), and reasonable attorney's and expert fees as well as compensatory (for intentional discrimination) and punitive damages (upon a showing of malice or "reckless indifference").

Other federal laws also affect employment, including the Equal Pay Act of 1963, which requires men and women to be compensated equally for equal work. This applies to jobs that involve equal skill, effort, and responsibility and are performed under similar working conditions in the same establishment, although equal work need not be identical work (*Corning Glass Works v. Brennan*, 1974). Furthermore, the discrimination need not be intentional, and the Act covers most private employers and state and local governments.

The Age Discrimination in Employment Act of 1967 (ADEA) protects employees age 40 and older against employment discrimination based on age and includes mandatory retirement in most cases. The ADEA applies to employers with 20 or more employees, labor unions, employment agencies, and their agents. The ADEA is also enforced through the EEOC according to the enforcement scheme established for violations of Title VII.

The Family and Medical Leave Act of 1993 requires covered employers (with at least 50 employees within 75 miles) to provide up to 12 weeks of unpaid, job-protected leave to eligible employees (who have worked for at least 1 year or at least 1,250 hours over the previous 12 months) for certain family and medical reasons. (For more information see http://www.dol. gov/esa/whd/fmla; U.S. Department of Labor, 2007). The employer must maintain the employee's group health coverage for the duration of the leave, and using such leave cannot result in the loss of any employment benefit that had accrued prior to the start of the employee's leave.

The Immigration Reform and Control Act of 1986 prohibits discrimination on the basis of national origin or citizenship, except against unauthorized aliens.

The Americans With Disabilities Act of 1990, discussed in greater length later in this chapter, prohibits discrimination against qualified individuals who have a disability. It requires employers to make reasonable accommodations to the conditions of qualified individuals with disabilities and is enforced according to the administrative scheme set out in Title VII. However, if the employer can show he or she made a good faith effort to make reasonable accommodations, compensatory and punitive damages are not available.

State Nondiscrimination Statutes

Investigate state and local laws concerning discrimination that may be broader than the federal statutes. Even though your practice may fall outside the scope of the federal statutes, you may be subject to state regulations. Your local attorney may be able to help you understand your legal obligations to avoid charges of discrimination (see Appendix D).

Sexual Harassment

Establish a comprehensive antiharassment policy for your counseling practice and communicate it to all staff members, whether professional or nonprofessional employees. Make sure they understand that employers have a legal duty to provide a workplace that is free from sexual harassment. Additionally, employees must be protected from unwanted or unwelcome sexual overtures or invitations of a sexual nature. This applies whether the conduct originates with partners or owners of the firm, supervisors, other colleagues or employees, clients, or outsiders (U.S. Equal Employment Opportunity Commission, 2007). (For further information, consult http://www.eeoc.gov/types/sexual_harassment.html.)

Recruiting, Hiring, and Managing Employees

As you prepare to hire your first employees, whether they are administrative or professional, it is important that you take steps to make sure you are in compliance with federal, state, and local laws. The following are suggestions for new employers:

- Apply for an employer identification number (EIN) (online at http://www.irs.gov/businesses/small/article/0,,id=102767,00.html). This may be required for identification and tax-paying activities.

(Solo practitioners often use their Social Security number in lieu of an employer identification number.)

- Check with your state labor department to see if there are registration or other requirements.
- Consider creating job descriptions for prospective employees, including required skills and job performance standards. This may help at a later date if an employee does not live up to expectations and you must terminate employment.
- Consider developing an employee handbook with policies on compensation, hours, vacation, sick and other leave, discipline, and termination of employment. You should have all documents reviewed by local counsel to make sure that you are able to modify your policies and terminate problem employees in accordance with law.
- Apply for worker's compensation insurance; information is frequently available through your state's worker's compensation agency.
- Check into unemployment tax requirements, including IRS Form 940, available at http://www.irs.gov/formspubs/index.html (IRS, 2006).
- Set up a payroll system for withholding of taxes. There are many private firms to which you can outsource payroll functions. If you have few employees, consider getting initial payroll advice from your accountant (see Appendix D).
- When interviewing prospective employees, know what types of questions are allowed. You may be able to get information from the Equal Employment Opportunity Commission (http://www.eeoc.gov) or the Small Business Administration (SBA; http://www.sba.gov) or your own legal counsel.
- Establish employee personnel files. Compile resources for ongoing employment-related questions. Again, the SBA Web site just listed has information about many employment-related issues.

Employment Contracts

You may be in a situation—as employer or employee—in which a contract of employment is desirable in order to set forth the specific terms of employment, or a contract may be required to practice as part of the professional counseling firm or agency. Most states recognize and enforce reasonable clauses and covenants contained in employment contracts, even though they may follow the law of at-will termination of employment in other cases. There are two types of clauses that frequently are included in such contracts of which you should be aware.

The first is an indemnification or hold harmless clause, in which the employee counselor agrees to accept all liability from any and all lawsuits that may result from his or her professional actions. Two theories of law permit employers of counseling professionals to be held liable for the negligent acts of their employees. The first is the concept of *respondeat superior* (the Latin phrase means "let the master respond"), or *vicarious liability* (in other words, the employer is responsible for his or her subordinate). In a typical case, a dissatisfied client files a negligence or malpractice action against the counselor who failed to improve the client's condition and against the counseling agency or service that employs the counselor. The counseling service is presumed to have deeper pockets than the individual counselor, thus enhancing the chances of recovering on any award.

The second theory is that the counselor is acting as the agent for his or her supervisor or employer, who is the principal. The law of agency is far more complicated than this, but essentially the agent works on behalf of the principal, having a legal duty to do so, and can bind the principal through his or her actions. In both cases, the employer may be held responsible for the actions of the employee, even though he or she did not specifically consent to the act complained of or agree to accept liability.

The hold harmless clause changes the equation by shifting the financial responsibility for negligent acts of the employee back to the employee. Thus, although both the counselor and the counseling service in the negligence action described may be held legally liable for the counselor's breach of duty, the counselor may be required to reimburse the service for the costs of defending the lawsuit based on the provisions of the hold harmless clause in her or his employment contract. From the employee's standpoint, this type of clause may be troublesome because it shifts the burden of liability to the employee. Counselor employees (or independent contractors) should check with their professional liability insurance carriers to ascertain coverage before signing contracts that contain indemnification clauses.

The second type of clause that attorneys frequently add to employment contracts is the restrictive covenant, sometimes also called a covenant against competition, or covenant not to compete. Generally such clauses restrict employees from leaving a firm or practice and opening up a competing professional practice in the same geographic location for a set period of time. They are designed to protect the employer, who frequently invests much time and money in new employees, only to have the employees leave and take clients with them. As long as the clause is not broader than is reasonably necessary to protect the legitimate interests of the employer, and it relates directly to the specific duties of the former employee, courts will often uphold such agreements. In some states, such clauses in physician and psychologist contracts have been subject to scrutiny in recent years when they precluded a patient from exercising freedom of choice in selecting medical or psychological care (*Falmouth Ob-Gyn Associates v. Abisla*, 1994; *Comprehensive Psychology System, P.C. v. Prince*, 2005).

In the medical and mental health fields, we see that independent contractors are sometimes asked to sign contracts with restrictive covenants. It is doubtful that restrictive covenants in such contracts will be upheld because they are not incident to a valid employment contract. If a counselor is truly independent, it is difficult to make a case that he or she should not be able to practice elsewhere within the same vicinity.

Furthermore, you should check to see whether there is any prohibition against restrictive covenants in your licensure law or other state law. If you are the prospective employee, note that the time to negotiate modifications to a proposed restrictive covenant is before you sign the contract. It may pay to hire a local attorney at the beginning rather than risk a breach of contract action or payment of liquidated damages (i.e., damages agreed upon in advance by contract), which can often be in the range of $100,000 or more.

TRAINING AND SUPERVISING EMPLOYEES

As employers, counselors have a variety of responsibilities to their employees and to their clients that arise from the *respondeat superior* theory mentioned in the preceding section. To the extent they exercise control over employee conduct, employers may be held accountable for resulting actions, even though they did not intend for those acts to occur (*Doe v. Samaritan Counseling Center*, 1990). Following the negligence theory of *respondeat superior*, some courts have allowed recoveries against employers on the basis of negligent hiring, retention, supervision, and training of employees. In these cases, the negligence analysis (discussed in chapter 4) is used to determine whether employers should be held liable for damages caused by their employees. Was there a foreseeable risk that could have been avoided if the employer had not neglected his or her duty? Was the act complained of within the scope of the employment? Could reasonable training, whether preemployment or in-service, have averted or minimized the risk? For more information on the scope of these theories, counselors are advised to consult their own legal counsel. Note that employers are also responsible for the acts of volunteers, students, and supervisees working in a counseling service, and these individuals should be held to the same standards of conduct as employees. The material that follows in this section generally applies to volunteers, students, and supervisees as well as to employees.

There are ways to minimize employer exposure to liability for the acts of employees. Certainly, obtaining good liability insurance coverage is one possibility. Other ways that you can affirmatively diminish the risks of hiring employees include the following:

- Always check the references and backgrounds of applicants for employment for any position within your firm. If the applicant is a mental health professional, be sure to contact the state licensing board to ascertain his or her current licensure status. Require all applicants to provide certified original copies of transcripts and licenses. Call or write to previous employers to verify employment status and dates and ask about the applicant's job responsibilities while he or she was employed there.

- Be sure applicants for employment have the required professional degrees and preparation (including licensure, certification, or registration) to ensure competence. Discuss treatment theories and concepts with a professional applicant to determine for yourself that the applicant is competent to treat your clients. (The author is aware of a situation where transcripts and license were requested prior to the hiring of one therapist; unfortunately, the documents were not obtained until after many clients were seen. It turned out that the "therapist" was not only unlicensed but had never finished the master's degree requirements.)

- Require your employees (both professional and nonprofessional) to participate in training and professional development. Membership in professional associations and adherence to professional ethical standards should be encouraged.

- Discuss the internal policies and procedures of your agency or counseling service with your employees. Be sure that all employees understand the nature of the counselor–client relationship and the need for strict confidentiality of client information. Explain carefully that their continued employment depends on strict adherence to all employment policies, including rules concerning behavior and conduct with clients. If you are a HIPAA-covered entity, be certain training covers all privacy policies for the practice (see chapter 5).

- Be alert to changes in employee behavior or erratic performance. Are unusual noises coming from one office during counseling sessions? Is a counselor meeting a client after hours? Is that counselor's door locked during some appointments? Have other employees or clients commented on the strange behavior of an employee? Any of these may be signals that further investigation is needed immediately.

- If you are serving as a supervisor or consultant to another counselor, whether or not he or she is your employee, schedule regular meetings to discuss case management. Be sure to allow enough time to discuss adequately the case and treatment being provided. Remind the supervisee of the continuing need to protect client confidences, and ensure that the client is aware of the supervision or consultation through an appropriate informed consent process. Check back with the supervisee at regular intervals to ascertain whether progress is being made.

- If you become aware that an employee, particularly a mental health professional, needs additional training to become competent in a new specialty area or to manage a particularly difficult case (if referral is not appropriate), schedule in-service training, bring in an outside consultant, or find a training course or seminar that will satisfy the need.

HIRING WORKERS AS
INDEPENDENT CONTRACTORS VS. EMPLOYEES

In the mental health field, many therapists prefer the status of being independent rather than being under someone else's control as an employee. Likewise, the employer often prefers to hire professional counselors as independent contractors rather than pay benefits and file unemployment and social security taxes. The employer also often thinks that the independent contractor status will insulate him or her from liability for the therapist contractor. In reality, the courts, Internal Revenue Service (IRS), and various state agencies are not always bound by the parties' determination of whether the relationship is an employment or independent contractor arrangement. For many years, the following language of *U.S. v. Silk* (1947) (quoting then-current Treasury regulations) has been cited:

> If the relationship of employer and employee exists, the designation or description of the relationship by the parties as anything other than that of employer and employee is immaterial. Thus, if two individuals in fact stand in the relation of employer and employee to each other, it is of no consequence that the employee is designated as a partner, coadventurer, agent, or independent contractor.

Thus, a court in a malpractice case is free to decide whether a hired counselor is an employee or independent contractor. The professional who hires the counselor may be held vicariously liable for the negligent acts or omissions of the counselor even if the parties did not treat the worker as an employee. It is a big mistake in modern-day counseling practice not to obtain vicarious liability coverage for hired workers.

Additionally, there is the possibility of back taxes and other penalties for misclassifying a person as an independent contractor. No single factor determines whether a hired worker is an employee or independent contractor. The IRS looks at a number of factors to make this determination. For example, the agency looks at behavioral control issues such as whether the practice has the right to direct and control how the work is done. The IRS also looks at financial control factors, such as how the worker is paid and the extent to which the worker makes his or her services available to the rest of the relevant market. Yet another category addressed by the IRS is the type of relationship. This includes an analysis of written contracts, whether benefits are provided, and the duration of the relationship. (See IRS Topic 762—Independent Contractor vs. Employee at http://www.irs.gov/taxtopics/tc762.html. See also Wheeler, 2004.)

Because of the complexity of issues involved in the determination of whether a particular person is an employee or independent contractor, it is advisable to seek the advice of your local attorney and accountant before making the final determination and before entering into written contracts. This is complicated by the fact that such decisions could also invoke fee-splitting prohibitions under state law or the federal antikickback law for therapists who are seeing clients under federally funded programs.

BILLING AND COLLECTION PRACTICES

Do you ever find that your clients are behind in their payments or terminate counseling without paying their outstanding bills? If so, you are not alone. Keep in mind that collection actions frequently lead to malpractice counterclaims or complaints to licensure boards. This happens because clients may leave counseling with the belief that they were harmed or that nothing is better so they shouldn't have to pay for services; other clients may harbor resentment at the prospect of their credit being ruined by a collection action. Here are some suggestions to make this aspect of your counseling practice a bit easier for both you and your clients:

- Make your payment policies clear to clients at the very outset of the relationship. For example, if you charge for missed sessions, this should be a part of your written informed consent process.
- Whenever possible, collect fees (or applicable copayments) at the time of the session.
- Consider writing off the bill if a client leaves your practice feeling dissatisfied. In most cases, it isn't really worth insisting on collection of a $75 bill as a matter of principle.
- Consider accepting credit cards. For solo practitioners, the bank charges (usually 3 to 5%) may not be worth the hassle, but it may accelerate payment and reduce billing costs. Some small practices have reported success with electronic payment services.
- Educate your office staff not to discuss delinquent accounts outside the office or with other clients.
- If you must pursue collection, consider a collections attorney or reputable collection agency with experience in collecting mental health or medical payments. Only consider collection if you have specified this practice in your written informed consent and the client has signed the document to demonstrate acceptance of your practices. At the time of the problem with collection, notify the client in writing that the account will be turned over for collection before any action is actually taken.
- Obtain legal advice if you plan to charge interest or impose finance charges.
- Avoid calling clients before 9 a.m. or after 9 p.m. because this may be viewed as harassment.
- Do not allow your staff to misrepresent themselves as collection agents or attorneys; also do not allow them to contact a client's employer or third party to collect an overdue bill.

Third-Party Payments

The health insurance field has changed rapidly in this country over the past two decades with the spread of managed care. As medical costs rise and as the state and federal governments try to grapple with deficits, we will see further changes in the next several years. To provide the greatest assistance to clients, counselors must become as knowledgeable of health care issues as possible and must actively work to educate carriers and health care administrators about their competence and the scope of professional services they provide. Counselors also should learn about the statutes in the states in which they practice that apply to insurance reimbursement, including state-mandated benefits and antidiscrimination laws (see Appendix D for further suggestions).

Some insurance carriers limit their coverage to medical providers and are reluctant to provide reimbursement for the services of a counselor. In such cases, you may wish to educate the carrier that reimbursement for counseling sessions is appropriate based on the academic and clinical preparation and licensing of counselors and is in the best interest of the client. The American Counseling Association has included very useful templates on its Web site that can aid members who are seeking to be included on managed care panels (visit http://www.counseling.org/Counselors and go to Private Practice Pointers). As you prepare to submit claims for reimbursement on behalf of clients, there are several items to consider to make the claims process operate smoothly and to prevent potential legal problems:

- Establish procedures in your office for completing and filing claim forms promptly. Do not let claims pile up. Get complete insurance information from each client, including policy numbers, employer authorization numbers, and claim procedures. Be sure all claims filed are complete and accurate, including the signature of the provider. If you are a HIPAA-covered entity, you must comply with the HIPAA rules, including those pertinent to transactions and code sets (see chapter 5).
- Obtain the proper insurance claim forms, such as the HCFA-1500. These forms should be available from the applicable health insurance carrier. The majority of carriers are now accepting, or even requiring, electronic submission of health care claims (see the discussion of HIPAA in chapter 5).
- Know and use the appropriate *DSM-IV-TR* (American Psychiatric Association, 2000) diagnostic codes. Coding materials are updated periodically.
- Be sure to state all services you provide accurately and completely. The frequency and duration of sessions, as well as correct diagnosis codes, should be stated factually, not embellished for purposes of securing reimbursement.

- Keep accurate records of counseling sessions and of reimbursement requests submitted. Be sure your records support the claims you file in the event of a claims review or audit.
- Do not bill carriers for missed appointments; you may bill the client as long as this was covered as part of your informed consent. Avoid routinely charging lower fees to clients who do not have insurance coverage as this could result in a charge of fraud based upon a misstatement of your true billing rate. (This does not mean you can never make a billing allowance for someone who truly cannot pay for services.)
- Be sure clients know they are responsible for any charges that are not reimbursed by their insurance carriers, and bill clients regularly for any such charges. Be sure clients assign reimbursement to you if you are filing forms on their behalf.
- When payments are received, verify them against the claims submitted to be sure payment is in the correct amount. Refund any overpayments promptly, and request reconsideration of any underpayment.
- Review rejected claims promptly and prepare and submit written appeals for any processing errors. Request clarification for any rejected claim if the reason for rejection is not clear. Appeal that claim if you believe an error was made or if it was rejected because it was submitted by a counselor.
- Find out about claims and appeals procedures for any managed care, preferred provider organization, or health maintenance organization with which you may consider contracting. You could be held liable for failure to appeal an adverse utilization review decision that results in serious harm to your client.

ACCESS TO FACILITIES:
THE AMERICANS WITH DISABILITIES ACT

Who Is Covered?

The Americans With Disabilities Act of 1990 (ADA) protects "qualified individuals with a disability" from discrimination on the basis of disability. A person is considered disabled if he or she (1) has a physical or mental impairment that substantially limits one or more major life activity; (2) has a record of such an impairment; or (3) is regarded as having such an impairment. A number of conditions are specifically excluded from the definition of disability, including psychoactive substance use disorders resulting from current illegal use of drugs. Individuals who are currently using illegal drugs do not qualify for inclusion in programs offered by state and local government agencies either, with the exception of health and drug rehabilitation services.

Public Accommodations

Title III of the ADA prohibits discrimination based on disability in places of public accommodation, and one of the 12 categories of public accommodations is public services. These services include the offices of physicians, lawyers, and accountants as well as businesses such as pharmacies, laundries, banks, and gas stations. For our purposes, it is important to know that public services include privately owned and operated mental health counseling services, agencies, and practices.

Government entities must also comply with the law. Public agencies operated by state and local governments are covered by Title II of the ADA and have separate affirmative obligations. Federal government agencies are covered by the similar provisions of sections 501 and 504 of the Rehabilitation Act of 1973.

The U.S. Department of Justice is charged with enforcing the public accommodations sections of the ADA (EEOC handles employment matters). In practice, the Justice Department rules require that

- disabled persons must be served by, or admitted to, places of public accommodation;
- if the policies or practices of an establishment have the effect of excluding disabled people, reasonable modifications to those policies or practices must be made unless they would fundamentally alter the nature of the business;
- auxiliary aids and services must be provided to enable a person with a disability to use the goods or services of an establishment, as long as the provision of the auxiliary aids does not pose an undue burden or is not disruptive to business;
- barriers to accessibility (e.g., steps with no elevator or ramp to accommodate wheelchair-bound clients) in existing buildings must be removed if the removal is readily achievable. If a building is inaccessible to disabled people and removal of the barriers is not readily achievable, alternative methods must be used to serve disabled people if such methods would not impose an undue burden (ADA, 1990). See http://www.usdoj.gov/crt/ada/adahom1.htm for more information.

Because these rules apply to counselors in private practice, these counselors must take affirmative steps to comply with the regulations to the extent such steps are not "unduly burdensome," "would not fundamentally alter the nature of the services provided," or, in the case of barrier removal, are "readily achievable" (easily accomplished without much difficulty or expense).

Some of these requirements are relatively easy to meet. For example, written materials produced on word-processing programs can easily be reformatted to large text size to assist a client with vision problems. Some word-processing programs can even produce materials in Braille form through local service providers. Clearing furniture or potted plants that obstruct hallways, waiting rooms, and offices is a simple form of barrier removal. Installing ramps, grab bars, and raised toilets; widening doorways; and creating designated parking spaces are additional approaches recommended to address mobility impairments.

Many of the recommended measures are commonsense approaches to overcoming physical and mental limitations, but they are critically important to providing access to services for people with disabilities. It is important to ask the person with a disability what auxiliary aids and services he or she needs to benefit from your program. Not all blind people can read Braille. Not all people with hearing impairments can read lips. In fact, depending on the severity of the situation and the importance of the information to be communicated, a qualified sign language interpreter may be required. The counseling practice is probably required to pay for those services because it is unlawful to charge people with disabilities for auxiliary aids and services or reasonable accommodations. As already mentioned, the exception is in situations that impose an undue burden for the counselor. If you do need to provide an interpreter or other accommodations, it may be helpful to know that the IRS Code allows certain tax credits for small businesses that have total revenues of $1,000,000 or less in the prior year or 30 or fewer full-time employees (Small Business Administration, 2007). Also see http://www.usdoj.gov/crt/ada/smbustxt.htm for more information.

Individuals with disabilities can sue public accommodations for failing to comply with the provisions of the ADA, and the Justice Department is empowered to investigate complaints and litigate to compel compliance. At that stage, the courts may assess the full range of remedies, including damages, injunctive relief, civil penalties, and attorneys' fees. If you are not already familiar with your obligations under the ADA, it is important to formulate a plan for compliance now and to begin to implement it. Further information is available online at the already mentioned Web sites or through the toll-free ADA information line at 800–514–0301 (voice) or 800–514–0383 (TDD).

State and Local Government Entities

Title II of the ADA prohibits all state and local government entities from discriminating against any qualified individual with a disability in any program or activity they administer or operate. As in Title III, entities are required to provide reasonable accommodations, remove barriers, and provide auxiliary aids and services as required to permit full participation by individuals with disabilities, unless the agency can prove that "the action would result in a fundamental alteration in the nature of a service, program, or activity or in undue financial and administrative burdens" (Nondiscrimination on the Basis of Disability in State and Local Government Services Rule, 1992).

There are a variety of administrative requirements for compliance with Title II, including conducting a self-evaluation of programs and practices. In addition, if the entity employs 50 or more people, the self-evaluation, and its resulting modifications, must remain open to inspection for 3 years. Entities also are required to inform the public of the rights afforded by the ADA and the entity's efforts to make programs accessible. Further, entities with more than 50 employees are required to appoint an ADA coordinator to serve as the agency's contact person on ADA compliance and to establish grievance procedures.

New Counseling Approaches, Techniques, and Professional Expressions

Counselors and other mental health practitioners are creative people, always searching for better ways to serve clients and always on the lookout for new and challenging venues of professional expression. Recent decades have seen a parade of new counseling approaches, techniques, and professional expressions. Such new ideas can become very popular very quickly; a bandwagon phenomenon can occur. Weekend workshops, seminars, and conferences spring to life; there is great anticipation and hope that this new approach or technique will be the answer. Practitioners attend a weekend training course or read about the approach or technique in a professional journal or popular press and are eager to try the new approach or engage in the new activity. But ethical and legal risk may then be generated because of

- *premature acceptance:* Practitioners can fail to appropriately investigate the validity of the approach or technique; they may accept without question the claims made by the authors or proponents of the approach.
- *insufficient training:* Practitioners can attempt to utilize a new approach or technique when they have not received the requisite education, training, and supervision to safely and effectively utilize the technique.
- *overuse:* Practitioners can come to view all clinical work through the perspective of the new approach or technique, which may encourage its overapplication as well as its use in situations in which it is not appropriate.

Examples of new approaches and techniques that have burst into our professional awareness over the last several decades include hypnotherapy, new 12-Step applications, codependency, eye movement desensitization and reprocessing (EMDR), telephone and Internet counseling, forensic evaluation, and coaching. Currently the buzz seems to be centered on how neuroscience can help us understand the brain. There is great excitement and hope that neuroscience can scientifically validate many of our theories and approaches and help us develop new and more powerful therapies.

Many new approaches and techniques burn bright for a short period of time and then fade; others are embraced by mainstream practitioners and absorbed into the body of generally accepted approaches and techniques. For purposes of this book we simply want to remind you that when utilizing any approach, whether a tried and true mainstream approach or a new fringe technique, you must still meet the standard of care (see chapter 2). Probably nothing drives home this point more than the tragic case in Colorado in which two therapists were utilizing a rebirthing technique designed to address attachment disorder in an adopted child. In this case a counselor was charged with and found guilty of reckless child abuse.

> The rebirthing therapy session lasted for over an hour. During that time, the child repeatedly said that she could not breathe, that she needed air, that she was going to throw up, and that she was being squashed. She asked for help several times and also asked for directions about what she was supposed to do. Believing that the child was being manipulative, however, defendant and her associates ignored the pleas and continued with the procedure.
>
> The child eventually stopped moving or speaking. Defendant and her associates thought she was asleep. When they removed the blanket, however, they discovered that she was no longer breathing. She was then taken to a hospital, where she was declared brain dead. The cause of death was determined to be suffocation.
>
> Defendant was charged with and convicted of reckless child abuse resulting in death, § 18-6-401(1)(a) and (7)(a)(I), C.R.S. 2002, and other offenses not relevant here. She was sentenced to a mandatory minimum term of sixteen years and to concurrent lesser terms on the remaining counts. (*People v. Watkins*, 2003)

The trial courts judgment and sentence were affirmed by the Colorado Court of Appeals. Obviously, something went very wrong. Did the therapists prematurely accept the validity of this approach? Did they lack sufficient training? Or did they use the approach on a child for which it was not appropriate? The tragic result of this case reminds us of our primary ethical responsibility to do no harm, and it brings home the chilling reality that severe legal consequences await us if we allow the welfare of others to be abused.

Three New Counseling-Related Approaches

To make the point in a less dramatic way, we want to briefly mention three relatively new counseling-related approaches, techniques, and expressions. We think there are lessons to be learned from how each of these new concepts are in the process of moving from new and different to mainstream acceptance.

Coaching. In recent years, the practice of executive or personal coaching has become very popular. Many licensed mental health practitioners have come to see coaching as both an interesting professional expression and a potentially lucrative opportunity. The field of coaching is unlicensed and unregulated, and there is no recognized and enforced certification process. Although there are recognized coach training programs, many are not affiliated with accredited institutions of higher learning. As a result, anyone can establish a coaching practice. The danger to licensed counselors and other mental health professionals is that because the coaching field lacks certification/regulation, mental health professionals may assume that normal legal and ethical standards are not relevant. To our knowledge, there has not been a court case that has tested this assumption. However, because the boundary between counseling and coaching is blurred, we believe it is only a matter of time before a disgruntled or harmed coaching client brings a licensure complaint or malpractice lawsuit against a coach who is also a licensed mental health professional. If you are currently providing or considering establishing a coaching practice, we encourage you to

- remain mindful and observant of the ethical code and licensing requirements associated with your mental health credential;
- develop an informed consent document that clearly differentiates coaching services from clinical mental health services you may provide or be licensed to provide;
- participate in the evolving professional organizations within the coaching field, understand common practices, and be sure these practices are not in conflict with the ethical or legal requirements of your mental health license;
- avoid mixing mental health services with coaching (we understand there are some aspects of a counseling relationship that can legitimately involve coaching);
- never ignore the mental health needs of coaching clients (you can't pretend you don't recognize mental health issues) and make appropriate referrals;
- recognize that if you are a licensed counselor, you may still be held to the standards of the counseling profession even when calling yourself a coach;
- check with your liability insurance carrier to determine if coaching services will be covered.

Technology-Assisted Counseling. Not long after the Internet and related technology became accessible to the general public, the idea of utilizing this technology to deliver mental health services emerged. This new practice venue created a great deal of interest within the counseling profession. Proponents predicted that mental health services could be provided to clients who were geographically isolated and/or who might feel more comfortable without a face-to-face meeting with the counselor. However, it soon became apparent that because the Internet is largely unregulated, there was no way to prevent unlicensed and untrained persons from operating an Internet-based counseling practice. Critics raised a variety of serious concerns. These included

- how to secure accurate *client identities* especially when communication is restricted to e-mail or chat room contact;
- how to deal with *confidential information* when exchanged over the Internet or telephone;
- how to intervene and provide *appropriate support* if a client is at risk of harm to self or others;
- how to handle *licensing* given that counselors will be practicing across state and national borders. (Some state licensure boards have taken the position that the counselor must be licensed in the state where the client is physically located.)

Leadership was needed. Internet counseling (technology-assisted counseling) has been significantly influenced and guided by the National Board for Certified Counselors (NBCC). NBCC has carefully defined the terms of this new counseling activity and developed standards for the ethical practice of Internet counseling. These standards include the Internet counseling relationship; confidentiality in Internet counseling; and legal considerations, licensure, and certification (NBCC, 2007b). The 2005 *ACA Code of Ethics* also addresses technology-assisted services and the myriad of issues that have arisen and stresses the need for adequate informed consent (Standards A.12.a.–g.).

Unlike the evolving history of coaching, early Internet counseling was adopted by a respected credentialing organization that had the resources and expertise to guide this new counseling expression through a host of early developmental struggles. Although there are many unanswered legal questions and implications of technology-assisted counseling, early efforts to define standards and ethics can support practitioners in establishing productive counseling relationships that seek to serve the best interests of the client.

Forensic Evaluation. Forensic expertise involves a wide range of evaluation, consultation, and court testimony designed to assist courts to make determinations about complex mental health issues that affect both sides in a particular case. Forensic expertise has historically been the domain of psychologists and psychiatrists. Although mental health counselors have long provided evaluations and court testimony, they have not qualified for membership in the American Board of Forensic Psychology (membership is restricted to doctoral-level psychologists). For professional counselors, there was a gap in professional identity and credentialing, which led to the creation of the National Board of Forensic Evaluators (NBFE; http://www.nbfe.net). Established in 2003, NBFE was created to enhance the forensic skills of licensed mental health professionals. Recently, the American Counseling Association endorsed NBFE's workshop and home study program leading to status as a Certified Forensic Mental Health Evaluator (D. Kaplan, personal communication, October 10, 2006).

SUMMARY

The three examples of new professional expressions just described demonstrate different levels of clarity of professional identity and expected standards of practice. Forensic evaluators seem to have the most formalized support and clarity, followed by Internet counseling. Coaching remains the most vague and, therefore, the most open to interpretation.

As you consider utilizing these and other new counseling approaches or techniques or engaging in new professional endeavors, be mindful that when standards are vague there is increased risk. We do not intend to discourage creativity, risk-taking, or the advancement of the profession but rather to provide you with some perspectives that can assist in managing the inherent risks associated with practicing on the leading edge of a growing profession. Particularly important is to not go it alone. We encourage you to seek consultation and collaboration in any new endeavor, to look to your professional associations for guidance and assistance in establishing thoughtful standards for any new professional activities.

References

Acosta v. Byrum, 638 S.E.2d 246 (N.C. App. 2006).

Age Discrimination in Employment Act of 1967, 29 U.S.C. §§ 621–634, as amended. (Implementing regulations found at 29 C.F.R. § 1625.)

American Association of State Counseling Boards. (2006). *About AASCB.* Retrieved February 12, 2007, from http://www.aascb.org/about/index.htm

American Association of Suicidology. (2006). *AAS suicide fact sheets.* Retrieved October 10, 2006, from http://www.suicidology.org/displaycommon. cfm?an=1&subarticlenbr=185

American College Health Association. (2006). *NCHA—National college health assessment.* Retrieved August 25, 2006, from http://www.acha-ncha. org/index.html

American Counseling Association. (1995). Woman in false-memory case receives $2.6 million. *Counseling Today, 38*(3), 42.

American Counseling Association. (2005a). *ACA code of ethics.* Alexandria, VA: Author.

American Counseling Association. (2005b). *Policies and procedures for processing complaints of ethical violations.* Retrieved February 12, 2007, from http:// www.counseling.org/Resources/CodeOfEthics/TP/Home/CT2.aspx

American Counseling Association. (2007). *Licensure requirements for professional counselors.* Alexandria, VA: Author.

American Psychiatric Association. (1993, 2002). *The APA Board statement on memories of sexual abuse* (APA Reference Document No. 93003), December 1993 (retired); *Therapies focused on memories of childhood physical and sexual abuse* (APA Reference Document No. 200002), March 2002.

American Psychiatric Association. (2000). *Diagnostic and statistical manual of mental disorders* (4th ed., text rev.). Washington, DC: Author.

American Self-Harm Information Clearinghouse. (2006). *Awareness.* Retrieved October 10, 2006, from http://www.selfinjury.org

Americans With Disabilities Act of 1990, 42 U.S.C.A. §§ 12101–12213.

Applied Innovations, Inc. v. Regents of the University of Minnesota, 876 F.2d 626 (8th Cir. 1989).

Ariz. Rev. Stat. § 32-3251 (2006).

Arizona Board of Behavioral Health Examiners. (2006). *Complaints.* Retrieved October 9, 2006, from http://www.bbhe.state.az.us/complaints.htm

Association for Specialists in Group Work. (1998). *Best practice guidelines.* Retrieved November 12, 2006, from http://www.asgw.org/PDF/Best_Practices.pdf/

Bogust v. Iverson, 102 N.W.2d 228 (Wisc. 1960).

Boynton v. Burglass, 590 So. 2d 446 (Fla. Dist. Ct. App. 1991).

Bruff v. North Mississippi Heath Services, Inc., 244 F.3d 495 (5th Cir. 2001).

Centers for Disease Control and Prevention. (2005). *2005 Youth risk behavior surveillance system.* Retrieved January 3, 2007, from http://www.cdc.gov/HealthyYouth/yrbs

Child Welfare Information Gateway. (2007). Retrieved January 24, 2007, from http://www.childwelfare.gov

Colo. Rev. Stat. § 12-36-135 (2006).

Comprehensive Psychology System, P.C. v. Prince, 375 N.J. Super. 273, 867 A.2d 1187 (2005).

Contributing to Delinquency, *Mens Rea,* 31 A.L.R.3d 848.

Copyright Act of 1976, 17 U.S.C. §§ 101–810 (2006).

Corey, G., Corey, M., & Callanan, P. (2007). *Issues and ethics in the helping professions* (7th ed.). Belmont, CA: Thomson Brooks/Cole.

Corning Glass Works v. Brennan, 417 U.S. 188 (1974).

Council for Accreditation of Counseling and Related Educational Programs. (2001). *2001 standards.* Retrieved April 2, 2007, from http://www.cacrep.org/2001Standards.html

Council for Accreditation of Counseling and Related Educational Programs. (2007a). *Directory of accredited programs.* Retrieved April 2, 2007, from http://www.cacrep.org/directory-current.html

Council for Accreditation of Counseling and Related Educational Programs. (2007b). *What is CACREP?* Retrieved April 2, 2007, from http://www.cacrep.org/mission.html

Criminal Law, 21 Am. Jur. 2d § 174.

Darden, E. C. (2006). *Search and seizure, due process, and public schools.* Retrieved January 18, 2007, from http://www.centerforpubliceducation.org/site/c.kjJXJ5MPIwE/b.1537263/k.CB45/Search_and_seizure_due_process_and_public_schools.htm

Davis v. Lhim, 422 N.W.2d 688 (Mich. 1988).

D.C. Mental Health Information Act, D.C. Code § 7-1206.03 (2006).

Doe v. Samaritan Counseling Center, 791 P.2d 344 (Alaska 1990).

Doe v. Wood, King County Super. Ct. (Wash.), No.93-2-00985-2, Aug., 12, 1994.

Eckhardt v. Kirts, 534 N.E.2d 1339 (Ill. App. Ct. 1989).

Eisel v. Board of Education of Montgomery County, 597 A.2d 447 (Md. 1991).

Equal Pay Act of 1963, 29 U.S.C. § 206(d), as amended (2006).

Ewing v. Goldstein, 120 Cal. App. 4th 807 (2004).

Ewing v. Northridge Hosp. Med. Ctr., 120 Cal. App. 4th 1289 (2004).

Falmouth Ob-Gyn Associates v. Abisla, 417 Mass. 176, 629 N.E.2d 291 (1994).

Family and Medical Leave Act of 1993, 29 U.S.C. §§ 2601–2654 (2006).

Family Educational Rights and Privacy Act of 1974 (FERPA or Buckley Amendment), 20 U.S.C. § 1232g (2006).

Fla. Stat. § 491.003 (2006).

Fla. Stat. § 491.0112 (2006).

Fla. Stat. § 491.0147 (2006).

Gladding, S. T. (1996). *Counseling: A comprehensive profession* (3rd ed). Englewood Cliffs, NJ: Prentice Hall.

Grote v. J. S. Mayer & Co., 570 N.E.2d 1146 (Ohio Ct. App. 1990).

Hamman v. County of Maricopa, 161 Ariz. 58, 775 P.2d 1122 (1989).

Health Insurance Portability and Accountability Act of 1996 (HIPAA), Pub. L. No. 104-191. *See also* HIPAA Privacy Rule, 45 C.F.R. §§ 160.101–160.312 (2006), and 45 C.F.R. §§ 164.102–164.106 and §§ 164.500–164.534 (2006); and HIPAA Security Rule, 45 C.F.R. §§ 164.302–164.318 (2006).

Hedlund v. Superior Court, 34 Cal. 3d 695, 669 P.2d 41 (1983).

Herlihy, B., & Corey, G. (2006a). *ACA ethical standards casebook* (6th ed.). Alexandria, VA: American Counseling Association.

Herlihy, B., & Corey, G. (2006b). *Boundary issues in counseling* (2nd ed.). Alexandria, VA: American Counseling Association.

Hermann, M. A., & Herlihy, B. R. (2006). Legal and ethical implications of refusing to counsel homosexual clients. *Journal of Counseling & Development*, *84*(4), 414–418.

225 Ill. Comp. Stat. 107/10 (2006).

Immigration Reform and Control Act of 1986, 8 U.S.C. §§ 1324a–1324b (2006).

Interest of L. L., 90 Wis. 2d 585, 280 N.W.2d 343 (Wis. App. 1979).

Internal Revenue Code, 26 U.S.C. § 501(c)(3) and (4) (2006).

Internal Revenue Service. (2007). *Online Application—Forms SS-4*. Retrieved January 31, 2007, from http://www.irs.gov/business/small/article/0,,id=102767,00.html

Internal Revenue Service. (2006). *Forms and publications*. Retrieved January 31, 2007, from http://www.irs.gov/formspubs/index.html

Internal Revenue Service. *Topic 762—Independent contractor vs. employee*. Retrieved October 3, 2006, from http://www.irs.gov/taxtopics/tc762.html

Jablonski v. United States, 712 F.2d 391 (9th Cir. 1983).

Jaffee v. Redmond, 518 U.S. 1 (1996).

Jed Foundation. (2006). *Important facts about adolescent suicide*. Retrieved October 11, 2006, from http://www.jedfoundation.org/libraryNews_facts.php

Kottler, J. A. (2004). *Introduction to therapeutic counseling: Voices from the field* (5th ed.). Pacific Grove, CA: Thomson Brooks/Cole.

Kuehn v. Renton School Dist. No. 403, 694 P.2d 1078 (Wash. 1985).

Ky. Rev. Stat. § 209.020-.030 (2006).

Linke v. Northwestern School Corp., 734 N.E.2d 252 (Ind. App. 2000).

Mapp v. Ohio, 367 U.S. 643 (1961).

Maryland Board of Professional Counselors and Therapists. (2006). *Disciplinary matters*. Retrieved October 9, 2006, from http://www.dhmh. state.md.us/bopc/bopcweb/html/discipline_matters.htm

78 Md. Op. Att'y Gen. 189, 12/3/1993.

McIntosh v. Milano, 403 A.2d 500 (N.J. Super. 1979).

Minn. Stat. § 609.345 (2006).

Nally v. Grace Community Church, 204 Cal. Rptr. 303 (Cal. Ct. App. 1984); 253 Cal. Rptr. 97 (Cal. 1988), *rev'g* 240 Cal. Rptr. 215 (1987), *cert. denied*, 490 U.S. 1007 (1989).

National Board for Certified Counselors. (2007a). National counselor exam (NCE). Retrieved April 2, 2007, from http://www.nbcc.org/nce

National Board for Certified Counselors. (2007b). *The practice of Internet counseling*. Retrieved April 2, 2007, from http://www.nbcc.org/ webethics2

National Board for Certified Counselors. (2007c). *Statistics*. Retrieved April 2, 2007, from http://www.nbcc.org/stats

National Institute of Mental Health. (2006). *Older adults: Depression and suicide facts*. Retrieved October 10, 2006, from http://www.nimh.nih. gov/publicat/elderlydepsuicide.cfm

National Strategy for Suicide Prevention. (2006). *At a glance: Suicide among the elderly*. Retrieved October 10, 2006, from http://www.mentalhealth. samhsa.gov/suicideprevention/elderly.asp

Neukrug, M. S. (2007). *The world of the counselor: An introduction to the counseling profession* (3rd ed.). Pacific Grove, CA: Thomson Brooks/Cole.

New Jersey v. T. L. O., 469 U.S. 325 (1985).

N.Y. Educ. Law § 8402 (McKinney 2006).

N.Y. Pub. Health Law § 2803-P and Soc. Serv. Law § 5349-A (2006).

Nondiscrimination on the Basis of Disability in State and Local Government Services Rule, 28 C.F.R. Part 35 (1992).

Oleszko v. State Compensation Insurance Fund, 243 F.3d 1154 (9th Cir. 2001).

Peck v. Counseling Service of Addison County, Inc., 499 A.2d 422 (Vt. 1985).

Pennsylvania State Board of Psychology. (2000, July 17). *Special notice*. Retrieved January 17, 2007, from http://www.dos.state.pa.us/bpoa/ LIB/bpoa/20/10/psyspecialnotice.pdf

People v. Watkins, 83 P.3d 1182 (Colo. App. 2003).

Perreira v. Colorado, 768 P.2d 1198 (Colo. 1989).

Psychiatrists' Purchasing Group. (1994). Managing the risks involved in cases of recovered memories of abuse. *Rx for Risk, 5*(10), 1.

Public Health Service Act, 42 U.S.C.A. § 290dd-2 (2007). (Implementing regulations, Confidentiality of Alcohol and Drug Abuse Patient Records, at 42 C.F.R. Part 2, 2007.)

Ramona v. Ramona, No. 61898 (Napa County Superior Ct. July 11, 1994).

Rehabilitation Act of 1973 § 501, as amended, 29 U.S.C. § 791 and § 504, as amended, 29 U.S.C. § 794 (2006).

St. Paul Fire & Marine Ins. Co. v. Love, 459 N.W.2d 698 (Minn. Sup. Ct. 1990).

Searcy v. Auerbach, 980 F.2d 609 (9th Cir. 1992).

Simmons v. United States, 805 F.2d 1363 (9th Cir. 1986).

State v. Ohrtman, 466 N.W.2d 1 (Minn. Ct. App. 1991).

State v. Woods, 307 N.C. 213, 297 S.E.2d 574 (1982).

Stepakoff v. Kantar, 473 N.E.2d 1131 (Mass. 1985).

Sutherland v. Kroger Co., 110 S.E.2d 716 (W.Va. 1959).

Tarasoff v. Regents of the University of California, 551 P.2d 334 (Cal. 1976).

Texas Board of Examiners of Professional Counselors. (2007). *Enforcement actions.* Retrieved April 4, 2007, from http://www.dshs.state.tx.us/counselor/lpc_enforce.shtm

Tex. Health & Safety Code § 611.004 (2006).

Thapar v. Zezulka, 994 S.W.2d 635 (Tex. 1999).

Title VII of the Civil Rights Act of 1964, as amended by the Civil Rights Act of 1991, 42 U.S.C. § 2000e. (Implementing regulations found at 29 C.F.R. §§ 1601–1614.)

Uniting and Strengthening America by Providing Appropriate Tools Required to Intercept and Obstruct Terrorism (USA Patroit Act) Act of 2001, Pub. L. No. 107–56, 115 Stat. 272 (2001).

U.S. v. Silk, 331 U.S. 704 (1947).

28 U.S.C. § 1331 (2006).

28 U.S.C. § 1332 (2006).

U.S. Department of Labor, Employment Standards Administration. (2007). *Compliance assistance—Family and Medical Leave Act (FMLA).* Retrieved April 7, 2007, from http://www.dol.gov/esa/whd/fmla

U.S. Equal Employment Opportunity Commission. (1997, June 10). *Filing a charge.* Retrieved September 28, 2006, from http://www.eeoc.gov/facts/howtofil.html

U.S. Equal Employment Opportunity Commission. (2007, May 17). *Sexual harassment.* Retrieved September 28, 2006, from http://www.eeoc.gov/types/sexual_harassment.html

Vernonia School Dist. 47J v. Acton, 515 U.S. 646 (1995).

Va. Code Ann., § 54.1-2400.1 (2006).

Va. Code Ann. § 54.1-3500 (2006).

Wheeler, A. M. (2004, December). Independent contractor or employee. *Legal and Regulatory Compliance: Updates for Counselors, Mental Health Professionals, and Counselor Educators, 1*(3), 1–6.

Whitlock, J. L., Eckenrode, J. E., & Silverman, D. (2006). The epidemiology of self-injurious behavior in a college population. *Pediatrics, 117*(6), 1943–1945.

Appendix A

ACA CODE OF ETHICS

ACA CODE OF ETHICS PREAMBLE

The American Counseling Association is an educational, scientific, and professional organization whose members work in a variety of settings and serve in multiple capacities. ACA members are dedicated to the enhancement of human development throughout the life span. Association members recognize diversity and embrace a cross-cultural approach in support of the worth, dignity, potential, and uniqueness of people within their social and cultural contexts.

Professional values are an important way of living out an ethical commitment. Values inform principles. Inherently held values that guide our behaviors or exceed prescribed behaviors are deeply ingrained in the counselor and developed out of personal dedication, rather than the mandatory requirement of an external organization.

ACA CODE OF ETHICS PURPOSE

The *ACA Code of Ethics* serves five main purposes:

1. The *Code* enables the association to clarify to current and future members, and to those served by members, the nature of the ethical responsibilities held in common by its members.
2. The *Code* helps support the mission of the association.
3. The *Code* establishes principles that define ethical behavior and best practices of association members.
4. The *Code* serves as an ethical guide designed to assist members in constructing a professional course of action that best serves those utilizing counseling services and best promotes the values of the counseling profession.
5. The *Code* serves as the basis for processing of ethical complaints and inquiries initiated against members of the association.

The *ACA Code of Ethics* contains eight main sections that address the following areas:

Section A: The Counseling Relationship   166
Section B: Confidentiality, Privileged Communication,
     and Privacy   174
Section C: Professional Responsibility   179
Section D: Relationships With Other Professionals   183
Section E: Evaluation, Assessment, and Interpretation   184
Section F: Supervision, Training, and Teaching   189
Section G: Research and Publication   196
Section H: Resolving Ethical Issues   200

Each section of the *ACA Code of Ethics* begins with an Introduction. The introductions to each section discuss what counselors should aspire to with regard to ethical behavior and responsibility. The Introduction helps set the tone for that particular section and provides a starting point that invites reflection on the ethical mandates contained in each part of the *ACA Code of Ethics*.

When counselors are faced with ethical dilemmas that are difficult to resolve, they are expected to engage in a carefully considered ethical decision-making process. Reasonable differences of opinion can and do exist among counselors with respect to the ways in which values, ethical principles, and ethical standards would be applied when they conflict. While there is no specific ethical decision-making model that is most effective, counselors are expected to be familiar with a credible model of decision making that can bear public scrutiny and its application.

Through a chosen ethical decision-making process and evaluation of the context of the situation, counselors are empowered to make decisions that help expand the capacity of people to grow and develop.

A brief glossary (see pp. 202–203) is given to provide readers with a concise description of some of the terms used in the *ACA Code of Ethics*.

SECTION A
THE COUNSELING RELATIONSHIP

Introduction

Counselors encourage client growth and development in ways that foster the interest and welfare of clients and promote formation of healthy relationships. Counselors actively attempt to understand the diverse cultural backgrounds of the clients they serve. Counselors also explore their own cultural identities and how these affect their values and beliefs about the counseling process.

Counselors are encouraged to contribute to society by devoting a portion of their professional activity to services for which there is little or no financial return (pro bono publico).

A.1. Welfare of Those Served by Counselors

A.1.a. Primary Responsibility

The primary responsibility of counselors is to respect the dignity and to promote the welfare of clients.

A.1.b. Records

Counselors maintain records necessary for rendering professional services to their clients and as required by laws, regulations, or agency or institution procedures. Counselors include sufficient and timely documentation in their client records to facilitate the delivery and continuity of needed services. Counselors take reasonable steps to ensure that documentation in records accurately reflects client progress and services provided. If errors are made in client records, counselors take steps to properly note the correction of such errors according to agency or institutional policies. *(See A.12.g.7., B.6., B.6.g., G.2.j.)*

A.1.c. Counseling Plans

Counselors and their clients work jointly in devising integrated counseling plans that offer reasonable promise of success and are consistent with abilities and circumstances of clients. Counselors and clients regularly review counseling plans to assess their continued viability and effectiveness, respecting the freedom of choice of clients. *(See A.2.a., A.2.d., A.12.g.)*

A.1.d. Support Network Involvement

Counselors recognize that support networks hold various meanings in the lives of clients and consider enlisting the support, understanding, and involvement of others (e.g., religious/spiritual/community leaders, family members, friends) as positive resources, when appropriate, with client consent.

A.1.e. Employment Needs

Counselors work with their clients considering employment in jobs that are consistent with the overall abilities, vocational limitations, physical restrictions, general temperament, interest and aptitude patterns, social skills, education, general qualifications, and other relevant characteristics and needs of clients. When appropriate, counselors appropriately trained in career development will assist in the placement of clients in positions that are consistent with the interest, culture, and the welfare of clients, employers, and/or the public.

A.2. Informed Consent in the Counseling Relationship
(See A.12.g., B.5., B.6.b., E.3., E.13.b., F.1.c., G.2.a.)

A.2.a. Informed Consent

Clients have the freedom to choose whether to enter into or remain in a counseling relationship and need adequate information about the counseling process and the counselor. Counselors have an obligation to review in writing and verbally with clients the rights and responsibilities of both the counselor and the client. Informed consent is an ongoing part of the counseling process, and counselors appropriately document discussions of informed consent throughout the counseling relationship.

A.2.b. Types of Information Needed

Counselors explicitly explain to clients the nature of all services provided. They inform clients about issues such as, but not limited to, the following: the purposes, goals, techniques, procedures, limitations, potential risks, and benefits of services; the counselor's qualifications, credentials, and relevant experience; continuation of services upon the incapacitation or death of a counselor; and other pertinent information. Counselors take steps to ensure that clients understand the implications of diagnosis, the intended use of tests and reports, fees, and billing arrangements. Clients have the right to confidentiality and to be provided with an explanation of its limitations (including how supervisors and/or treatment team professionals are involved); to obtain clear information about their records to participate in the ongoing counseling plans; and to refuse any services or modality change and to be advised of the consequences of such refusal.

A.2.c. Developmental and Cultural Sensitivity

Counselors communicate information in ways that are both developmentally and culturally appropriate. Counselors use clear and understandable language when discussing issues related to informed consent. When clients have difficulty understanding the language used

by counselors, they provide necessary services (e.g., arranging for a qualified interpreter or translator) to ensure comprehension by clients. In collaboration with clients, counselors consider cultural implications of informed consent procedures and, where possible, counselors adjust their practices accordingly.

A.2.d. Inability to Give Consent

When counseling minors or persons unable to give voluntary consent, counselors seek the assent of clients to services, and include them in decision making as appropriate. Counselors recognize the need to balance the ethical rights of clients to make choices, their capacity to give consent or assent to receive services, and parental or familial legal rights and responsibilities to protect these clients and make decisions on their behalf.

A.3. Clients Served by Others

When counselors learn that their clients are in a professional relationship with another mental health professional, they request release from clients to inform the other professionals and strive to establish positive and collaborative professional relationships.

A.4. Avoiding Harm and Imposing Values

A.4.a. Avoiding Harm

Counselors act to avoid harming their clients, trainees, and research participants and to minimize or to remedy unavoidable or unanticipated harm.

A.4.b. Personal Values

Counselors are aware of their own values, attitudes, beliefs, and behaviors and avoid imposing values that are inconsistent with counseling goals. Counselors respect the diversity of clients, trainees, and research participants.

A.5. Roles and Relationships With Clients
(See F.3., F.10., G.3.)

A.5.a. Current Clients

Sexual or romantic counselor–client interactions or relationships with current clients, their romantic partners, or their family members are prohibited.

A.5.b. Former Clients

Sexual or romantic counselor–client interactions or relationships with former clients, their romantic partners, or their family members are prohibited for a period of 5 years following the last professional contact. Counselors, before engaging in sexual or romantic interactions or relationships with clients, their romantic partners, or client family members after 5 years following the last professional contact, demonstrate forethought and document (in written form) whether the interactions or relationship can be viewed as exploitive in some way and/or whether there is still potential to harm the former client; in cases of potential exploitation and/or harm, the counselor avoids entering such an interaction or relationship.

A.5.c. Nonprofessional Interactions or Relationships (Other Than Sexual or Romantic Interactions or Relationships)

Counselor–client nonprofessional relationships with clients, former clients, their romantic partners, or their family members should be avoided, except when the interaction is potentially beneficial to the client. *(See A.5.d.)*

A.5.d. Potentially Beneficial Interactions

When a counselor–client nonprofessional interaction with a client or former client may be potentially beneficial to the client or former client, the counselor must document in case records, prior to the interaction (when feasible), the rationale for such an interaction, the potential benefit, and anticipated consequences for the client or former client and other individuals significantly involved with the client or former client. Such interactions should be initiated with appropriate client consent. Where unintentional harm occurs to the client or former client, or to an individual significantly involved with the client or former client, due to the nonprofessional interaction, the counselor must show evidence of an attempt to remedy such harm. Examples of potentially beneficial interactions include, but are not limited to, attending a formal ceremony (e.g., a wedding/commitment ceremony or graduation); purchasing a service or product provided by a client or former client (excepting unrestricted bartering); hospital visits to an ill family member; mutual membership in a professional association, organization, or community. *(See A.5.c.)*

A.5.e. Role Changes in the Professional Relationship

When a counselor changes a role from the original or most recent contracted relationship, he or she obtains informed consent from the client and explains the right of the client to refuse services related to the change. Examples of role changes include

1. changing from individual to relationship or family counseling, or vice versa;
2. changing from a nonforensic evaluative role to a therapeutic role, or vice versa;
3. changing from a counselor to a researcher role (i.e., enlisting clients as research participants), or vice versa; and
4. changing from a counselor to a mediator role, or vice versa.

Clients must be fully informed of any anticipated consequences (e.g., financial, legal, personal, or therapeutic) of counselor role changes.

A.6. Roles and Relationships at Individual, Group, Institutional, and Societal Levels

A.6.a. Advocacy

When appropriate, counselors advocate at individual, group, institutional, and societal levels to examine potential barriers and obstacles that inhibit access and/or the growth and development of clients.

A.6.b. Confidentiality and Advocacy

Counselors obtain client consent prior to engaging in advocacy efforts on behalf of an identifiable client to improve the provision of services and to work toward removal of systemic barriers or obstacles that inhibit client access, growth, and development.

A.7. Multiple Clients

When a counselor agrees to provide counseling services to two or more persons who have a relationship, the counselor clarifies at the outset which person or persons are clients and the nature of the relationships the counselor will have with each involved person. If it becomes apparent that the counselor may be called upon to perform potentially conflicting roles, the counselor will clarify, adjust, or withdraw from roles appropriately. *(See A.8.a., B.4.)*

A.8. Group Work
(See B.4.a.)

A.8.a. Screening

Counselors screen prospective group counseling/therapy participants. To the extent possible, counselors select members whose needs and goals are compatible with goals of the group, who will not impede the group process, and whose well-being will not be jeopardized by the group experience.

A.8.b. Protecting Clients

In a group setting, counselors take reasonable precautions to protect clients from physical, emotional, or psychological trauma.

A.9. End-of-Life Care for Terminally Ill Clients

A.9.a. Quality of Care

Counselors strive to take measures that enable clients

1. to obtain high-quality end-of-life care for their physical, emotional, social, and spiritual needs;
2. to exercise the highest degree of self-determination possible;
3. to be given every opportunity possible to engage in informed decision making regarding their end-of-life care; and
4. to receive complete and adequate assessment regarding their ability to make competent, rational decisions on their own behalf from a mental health professional who is experienced in end-of-life care practice.

A.9.b. Counselor Competence, Choice, and Referral

Recognizing the personal, moral, and competence issues related to end-of-life decisions, counselors may choose to work or not work with terminally ill clients who wish to explore their end-of-life options. Counselors provide appropriate referral information to ensure that clients receive the necessary help.

A.9.c. Confidentiality

Counselors who provide services to terminally ill individuals who are considering hastening their own deaths have the option of breaking or not breaking confidentiality, depending on applicable laws and the specific circumstances of the situation and after seeking consultation or supervision from appropriate professional and legal parties. *(See B.5.c., B.7.c.)*

A.10. Fees and Bartering

A.10.a. Accepting Fees From Agency Clients

Counselors refuse a private fee or other remuneration for rendering services to persons who are entitled to such services through the counselor's employing agency or institution. The policies of a particular agency may make explicit provisions for agency clients to receive counseling services from members of its staff in private practice. In such instances, the clients must be informed of other options open to them should they seek private counseling services.

A.10.b. Establishing Fees

In establishing fees for professional counseling services, counselors consider the financial status of clients and locality. In the event that the established fee structure is inappropriate for a client, counselors assist clients in attempting to find comparable services of acceptable cost.

A.10.c. Nonpayment of Fees

If counselors intend to use collection agencies or take legal measures to collect fees from clients who do not pay for services as agreed upon, they first inform clients of intended actions and offer clients the opportunity to make payment.

A.10.d. Bartering

Counselors may barter only if the relationship is not exploitive or harmful and does not place the counselor in an unfair advantage, if the client requests it, and if such arrangements are an accepted practice among professionals in the community. Counselors consider the cultural implications of bartering and discuss relevant concerns with clients and document such agreements in a clear written contract.

A.10.e. Receiving Gifts

Counselors understand the challenges of accepting gifts from clients and recognize that in some cultures, small gifts are a token of respect and showing gratitude. When determining whether or not to accept a gift from clients, counselors take into account the therapeutic relationship, the monetary value of the gift, a client's motivation for giving the gift, and the counselor's motivation for wanting or declining the gift.

A.11. Termination and Referral

A.11.a. Abandonment Prohibited

Counselors do not abandon or neglect clients in counseling. Counselors assist in making appropriate arrangements for the continuation of treatment, when necessary, during interruptions such as vacations, illness, and following termination.

A.11.b. Inability to Assist Clients

If counselors determine an inability to be of professional assistance to clients, they avoid entering or continuing counseling relationships. Counselors are knowledgeable about culturally and clinically appropriate referral resources and suggest these alternatives. If clients decline the suggested referrals, counselors should discontinue the relationship.

A.11.c. Appropriate Termination

Counselors terminate a counseling relationship when it becomes reasonably apparent that the client no longer needs assistance, is not likely to benefit, or is being harmed by continued counseling. Counselors may terminate counseling when in jeopardy of harm by the client, or another person with whom the client has a relationship, or when clients do not pay fees as agreed upon. Counselors provide pretermination counseling and recommend other service providers when necessary.

A.11.d. Appropriate Transfer of Services

When counselors transfer or refer clients to other practitioners, they ensure that appropriate clinical and administrative processes are completed and open communication is maintained with both clients and practitioners.

A.12. Technology Applications

A.12.a. Benefits and Limitations

Counselors inform clients of the benefits and limitations of using information technology applications in the counseling process and in business/billing procedures. Such technologies include but are not limited to computer hardware and software, telephones, the World Wide Web, the Internet, online assessment instruments, and other communication devices.

A.12.b. Technology-Assisted Services

When providing technology-assisted distance counseling services, counselors determine that clients are intellectually, emotionally, and physically capable of using the application and that the application is appropriate for the needs of clients.

A.12.c. Inappropriate Services

When technology-assisted distance counseling services are deemed inappropriate by the counselor or client, counselors consider delivering services face to face.

A.12.d. Access

Counselors provide reasonable access to computer applications when providing technology-assisted distance counseling services.

A.12.e. Laws and Statutes

Counselors ensure that the use of technology does not violate the laws of any local, state, national, or international entity and observe all relevant statutes.

A.12.f. Assistance

Counselors seek business, legal, and technical assistance when using technology applications, particularly when the use of such applications crosses state or national boundaries.

A.12.g. Technology and Informed Consent

As part of the process of establishing informed consent, counselors do the following:

1. Address issues related to the difficulty of maintaining the confidentiality of electronically transmitted communications.
2. Inform clients of all colleagues, supervisors, and employees, such as Informational Technology (IT) administrators, who might have authorized or unauthorized access to electronic transmissions.
3. Urge clients to be aware of all authorized or unauthorized users including family members and fellow employees who have access to any technology clients may use in the counseling process.
4. Inform clients of pertinent legal rights and limitations governing the practice of a profession over state lines or international boundaries.
5. Use encrypted Web sites and e-mail communications to help ensure confidentiality when possible.
6. When the use of encryption is not possible, counselors notify clients of this fact and limit electronic transmissions to general communications that are not client specific.
7. Inform clients if and for how long archival storage of transaction records are maintained.
8. Discuss the possibility of technology failure and alternate methods of service delivery.
9. Inform clients of emergency procedures, such as calling 911 or a local crisis hotline, when the counselor is not available.
10. Discuss time zone differences, local customs, and cultural or language differences that might impact service delivery.
11. Inform clients when technology-assisted distance counseling services are not covered by insurance. *(See A.2.)*

A.12.h. Sites on the World Wide Web

Counselors maintaining sites on the World Wide Web (the Internet) do the following:

1. Regularly check that electronic links are working and professionally appropriate.
2. Establish ways clients can contact the counselor in case of technology failure.
3. Provide electronic links to relevant state licensure and professional certification boards to protect consumer rights and facilitate addressing ethical concerns.
4. Establish a method for verifying client identity.
5. Obtain the written consent of the legal guardian or other authorized legal representative prior to rendering services in the event the client is a minor child, an adult who is legally incompetent, or an adult incapable of giving informed consent.
6. Strive to provide a site that is accessible to persons with disabilities.
7. Strive to provide translation capabilities for clients who have a different primary language while also addressing the imperfect nature of such translations.
8. Assist clients in determining the validity and reliability of information found on the World Wide Web and other technology applications.

SECTION B

CONFIDENTIALITY, PRIVILEGED COMMUNICATION, AND PRIVACY

Introduction

Counselors recognize that trust is a cornerstone of the counseling relationship. Counselors aspire to earn the trust of clients by creating an ongoing partnership, establishing and upholding appropriate boundaries, and maintaining confidentiality. Counselors communicate the parameters of confidentiality in a culturally competent manner.

B.1. Respecting Client Rights

B.1.a. Multicultural/Diversity Considerations

Counselors maintain awareness and sensitivity regarding cultural meanings of confidentiality and privacy. Counselors respect differing views toward disclosure of information. Counselors hold ongoing discussions with clients as to how, when, and with whom information is to be shared.

B.1.b. Respect for Privacy

Counselors respect client rights to privacy. Counselors solicit private information from clients only when it is beneficial to the counseling process.

B.1.c. Respect for Confidentiality

Counselors do not share confidential information without client consent or without sound legal or ethical justification.

B.1.d. Explanation of Limitations

At initiation and throughout the counseling process, counselors inform clients of the limitations of confidentiality and seek to identify foreseeable situations in which confidentiality must be breached. *(See A.2.b.)*

B.2. Exceptions

B.2.a. Danger and Legal Requirements

The general requirement that counselors keep information confidential does not apply when disclosure is required to protect clients or identified others from serious and foreseeable harm or when legal requirements demand that confidential information must be revealed. Counselors consult with other professionals when in doubt as to the validity of an exception. Additional considerations apply when addressing end-of-life issues. *(See A.9.c.)*

B.2.b. Contagious, Life-Threatening Diseases

When clients disclose that they have a disease commonly known to be both communicable and life threatening, counselors may be justified in disclosing information to identifiable third parties, if they are known to be at demonstrable and high risk of contracting the disease. Prior to making a disclosure, counselors confirm that there is such a diagnosis and assess the intent of clients to inform the third parties about their disease or to engage in any behaviors that may be harmful to an identifiable third party.

B.2.c. Court-Ordered Disclosure

When subpoenaed to release confidential or privileged information without a client's permission, counselors obtain written, informed consent from the client or take steps to prohibit the disclosure or have it limited as narrowly as possible due to potential harm to the client or counseling relationship.

B.2.d. Minimal Disclosure

To the extent possible, clients are informed before confidential information is disclosed and are involved in the disclosure decision-making process. When circumstances require the disclosure of confidential information, only essential information is revealed.

B.3. Information Shared With Others

B.3.a. Subordinates

Counselors make every effort to ensure that privacy and confidentiality of clients are maintained by subordinates, including employees, supervisees, students, clerical assistants, and volunteers. *(See F.1.c.)*

B.3.b. Treatment Teams

When client treatment involves a continued review or participation by a treatment team, the client will be informed of the team's existence and composition, information being shared, and the purposes of sharing such information.

B.3.c. Confidential Settings

Counselors discuss confidential information only in settings in which they can reasonably ensure client privacy.

B.3.d. Third-Party Payers

Counselors disclose information to third-party payers only when clients have authorized such disclosure.

B.3.e. Transmitting Confidential Information

Counselors take precautions to ensure the confidentiality of information transmitted through the use of computers, electronic mail, facsimile machines, telephones, voicemail, answering machines, and other electronic or computer technology. *(See A.12.g.)*

B.3.f. Deceased Clients

Counselors protect the confidentiality of deceased clients, consistent with legal requirements and agency or setting policies.

B.4. Groups and Families

B.4.a. Group Work

In group work, counselors clearly explain the importance and parameters of confidentiality for the specific group being entered.

B.4.b. Couples and Family Counseling

In couples and family counseling, counselors clearly define who is considered "the client" and discuss expectations and limitations of confidentiality. Counselors seek agreement and document in writing such agreement among all involved parties having capacity to give consent concerning each individual's right to confidentiality and any obliga-

tion to preserve the confidentiality of information known.

B.5. Clients Lacking Capacity to Give Informed Consent

B.5.a. Responsibility to Clients

When counseling minor clients or adult clients who lack the capacity to give voluntary, informed consent, counselors protect the confidentiality of information received in the counseling relationship as specified by federal and state laws, written policies, and applicable ethical standards.

B.5.b. Responsibility to Parents and Legal Guardians

Counselors inform parents and legal guardians about the role of counselors and the confidential nature of the counseling relationship. Counselors are sensitive to the cultural diversity of families and respect the inherent rights and responsibilities of parents/guardians over the welfare of their children/charges according to law. Counselors work to establish, as appropriate, collaborative relationships with parents/guardians to best serve clients.

B.5.c. Release of Confidential Information

When counseling minor clients or adult clients who lack the capacity to give voluntary consent to release confidential information, counselors seek permission from an appropriate third party to disclose information. In such instances, counselors inform clients consistent with their level of understanding and take culturally appropriate measures to safeguard client confidentiality.

B.6. Records

B.6.a. Confidentiality of Records

Counselors ensure that records are kept in a secure location and that only authorized persons have access to records.

B.6.b. Permission to Record

Counselors obtain permission from clients prior to recording sessions through electronic or other means.

B.6.c. Permission to Observe

Counselors obtain permission from clients prior to observing counseling sessions, reviewing session transcripts, or viewing recordings of sessions with supervisors, faculty, peers, or others within the training environment.

B.6.d. Client Access

Counselors provide reasonable access to records and copies of records when requested by competent clients. Counselors limit the access of clients to their records, or portions of their records, only when there is compelling evidence that such access would cause harm to the client. Counselors document the request of clients and the rationale for withholding some or all of the record in the files of clients. In situations involving multiple clients, counselors provide individual clients with only those parts of records that relate directly to them and do not include confidential information related to any other client.

B.6.e. Assistance With Records

When clients request access to their records, counselors provide assistance and consultation in interpreting counseling records.

B.6.f. Disclosure or Transfer

Unless exceptions to confidentiality exist, counselors obtain written permission from clients to disclose or transfer records to legitimate third parties. Steps are taken to ensure that receivers of counseling records are sensitive to their confidential nature. *(See A.3., E.4.)*

B.6.g. Storage and Disposal After Termination

Counselors store records following termination of services to ensure reasonable future access, maintain records in accordance with state and federal statutes governing records, and dispose of client records and other sensitive materials in a manner that protects client confidentiality. When records are of an artistic nature, counselors obtain client (or guardian) consent with regard to handling of such records or documents. *(See A.1.b.)*

B.6.h. Reasonable Precautions

Counselors take reasonable precautions to protect client confidentiality in the event of the counselor's termination of practice, incapacity, or death. *(See C.2.h.)*

B.7. Research and Training

B.7.a. Institutional Approval

When institutional approval is required, counselors provide accurate information about their research proposals and obtain approval prior to conducting their research. They conduct research in accordance with the approved research protocol.

B.7.b. Adherence to Guidelines

Counselors are responsible for understanding and adhering to state, federal, agency, or institutional policies or applicable guidelines regarding confidentiality in their research practices.

B.7.c. Confidentiality of Information Obtained in Research

Violations of participant privacy and confidentiality are risks of participation in research involving human participants. Investigators maintain all research records in a secure manner. They explain to participants the risks of violations of privacy and confidentiality and disclose to participants any limits of confidentiality that reasonably can be expected. Regardless of the degree to which confidentiality will be maintained, investigators must disclose to participants any limits of confidentiality that reasonably can be expected. *(See G.2.e.)*

B.7.d. Disclosure of Research Information

Counselors do not disclose confidential information that reasonably could lead to the identification of a research participant unless they have obtained the prior consent of the person. Use of data derived from counseling relationships for purposes of training, research, or publication is confined to content that is disguised to ensure the anonymity of the individuals involved. *(See G.2.a., G.2.d.)*

B.7.e. Agreement for Identification

Identification of clients, students, or supervisees in a presentation or publication is permissible only when they have reviewed the material and agreed to its presentation or publication. *(See G.4.d.)*

B.8. Consultation

B.8.a. Agreements

When acting as consultants, counselors seek agreements among all parties involved concerning each individual's rights to confidentiality, the obligation of each individual to preserve confidential information, and the limits of confidentiality of information shared by others.

B.8.b. Respect for Privacy

Information obtained in a consulting relationship is discussed for professional purposes only with persons directly involved with the case. Written and oral reports present only data germane to the purposes of the consultation, and every effort is made to protect client identity and to avoid undue invasion of privacy.

B.8.c. Disclosure of Confidential Information

When consulting with colleagues, counselors do not disclose confidential information that reasonably could lead to the identification of a client or other person or organization with whom they have a confidential relationship unless they have obtained the prior consent of the person or organization or the disclosure cannot be avoided. They disclose information only to the extent necessary to achieve the purposes of the consultation. *(See D.2.d.)*

Section C

Professional Responsibility

Introduction

Counselors aspire to open, honest, and accurate communication in dealing with the public and other professionals. They practice in a non-discriminatory manner within the boundaries of professional and personal competence and have a responsibility to abide by the *ACA Code of Ethics*. Counselors actively participate in local, state, and national associations that foster the development and improvement of counseling. Counselors advocate to promote change at the individual, group, institutional, and societal levels that improves the quality of life for individuals and groups and removes potential barriers to the provision or access of appropriate services being offered. Counselors have a responsibility to the public to engage in counseling practices that are based on rigorous research methodologies. In addition, counselors engage in self-care activities to maintain and promote their emotional, physical, mental, and spiritual well-being to best meet their professional responsibilities.

C.1. Knowledge of Standards

Counselors have a responsibility to read, understand, and follow the *ACA Code of Ethics* and adhere to applicable laws and regulations.

C.2. Professional Competence

C.2.a. Boundaries of Competence

Counselors practice only within the boundaries of their competence, based on their education, training, supervised experience, state and national professional credentials, and appropriate professional experience. Counselors gain knowledge, personal awareness, sensitivity, and skills pertinent to working with a diverse client population. *(See A.9.b., C.4.e., E.2., F.2., F.11.b.)*

C.2.b. New Specialty Areas of Practice

Counselors practice in specialty areas new to them only after appropriate education, training, and supervised experience. While developing skills in new specialty areas, counselors take steps to ensure the competence of their work and to protect others from possible harm. *(See F.6.f.)*

C.2.c. Qualified for Employment

Counselors accept employment only for positions for which they are qualified by education, training, supervised experience, state and national professional credentials, and appropriate professional experience. Counselors hire for professional counseling positions only individuals who are qualified and competent for those positions.

C.2.d. Monitor Effectiveness

Counselors continually monitor their effectiveness as professionals and take steps to improve when necessary. Counselors in private practice take reasonable steps to seek peer supervision as needed to evaluate their efficacy as counselors.

C.2.e. Consultation on Ethical Obligations

Counselors take reasonable steps to consult with other counselors or related professionals when they have questions regarding their ethical obligations or professional practice.

C.2.f. Continuing Education

Counselors recognize the need for continuing education to acquire and maintain a reasonable level of awareness of current scientific and professional information in their fields of activity. They take steps to maintain competence in the skills they use, are open to new procedures, and keep current with the diverse populations and specific populations with whom they work.

C.2.g. Impairment

Counselors are alert to the signs of impairment from their own physical, mental, or emotional problems and refrain from offering or providing professional services when such impairment is likely to harm a client or others. They seek assistance for problems that reach the level of professional impairment, and, if necessary, they limit, suspend, or terminate their professional responsibilities until such time it is determined that they may safely resume their work. Counselors assist colleagues or supervisors in recognizing their own professional impairment and provide consultation and assistance when warranted with colleagues or supervisors showing signs of impairment and intervene as appropriate to prevent imminent harm to clients. *(See A.11.b., F.8.b.)*

C.2.h. Counselor Incapacitation or Termination of Practice

When counselors leave a practice, they follow a prepared plan for transfer of clients and files. Counselors prepare and disseminate to an identified colleague or "records custodian" a plan for the transfer of clients and files in the case of their incapacitation, death, or termination of practice.

C.3. Advertising and Soliciting Clients

C.3.a. Accurate Advertising

When advertising or otherwise representing their services to the public, counselors identify their credentials in an accurate manner that is not false, misleading, deceptive, or fraudulent.

C.3.b. Testimonials

Counselors who use testimonials do not solicit them from current clients nor former clients nor any other persons who may be vulnerable to undue influence.

C.3.c. Statements by Others

Counselors make reasonable efforts to ensure that statements made by others about them or the profession of counseling are accurate.

C.3.d. Recruiting Through Employment

Counselors do not use their places of employment or institutional affiliation to recruit or gain clients, supervisees, or consultees for their private practices.

C.3.e. Products and Training Advertisements

Counselors who develop products related to their profession or conduct workshops or training events ensure that the advertisements concerning these products or events are accurate and disclose adequate information for consumers to make informed choices. *(See C.6.d.)*

C.3.f. Promoting to Those Served

Counselors do not use counseling, teaching, training, or supervisory relationships to promote their products or training events in a manner that is deceptive or would exert undue influence on individuals who may be vulnerable. However, counselor educators may adopt textbooks they have authored for instructional purposes.

C.4. Professional Qualifications

C.4.a. Accurate Representation

Counselors claim or imply only professional qualifications actually completed and correct any known misrepresentations of their qualifications by others. Counselors truthfully represent the qualifications of their professional colleagues. Counselors clearly distinguish between paid and volunteer work experience and accurately describe their continuing education and specialized training. *(See C.2.a.)*

C.4.b. Credentials

Counselors claim only licenses or certifications that are current and in good standing.

C.4.c. Educational Degrees

Counselors clearly differentiate between earned and honorary degrees.

C.4.d. Implying Doctoral-Level Competence

Counselors clearly state their highest earned degree in counseling or closely related field. Counselors do not imply doctoral-level competence when only possessing a master's degree in counseling or a related field by referring to themselves as "Dr." in a counseling context when their doctorate is not in counseling or a related field.

C.4.e. Program Accreditation Status

Counselors clearly state the accreditation status of their degree programs at the time the degree was earned.

C.4.f. Professional Membership

Counselors clearly differentiate between current, active memberships and former memberships in associations. Members of the American Counseling Association must clearly differentiate between professional membership, which implies the possession of at least a master's degree in counseling, and regular membership, which is open to individuals whose interests and activities are consistent with those of ACA but are not qualified for professional membership.

C.5. Nondiscrimination

Counselors do not condone or engage in discrimination based on age, culture, disability, ethnicity, race, religion/spirituality, gender, gender identity, sexual orientation, marital status/partnership, language preference, socioeconomic status, or any basis proscribed by law. Counselors do not discriminate against clients, students, employees, supervisees, or research participants in a manner that has a negative impact on these persons.

C.6. Public Responsibility

C.6.a. Sexual Harassment

Counselors do not engage in or condone sexual harassment. Sexual harassment is defined as sexual solicitation, physical advances, or verbal or nonverbal conduct that is sexual in nature, that occurs in connection with professional activities or roles, and that either

1. is unwelcome, is offensive, or creates a hostile workplace or learning environment, and counselors know or are told this; or
2. is sufficiently severe or intense to be perceived as harassment to a reasonable person in the context in which the behavior occurred.

Sexual harassment can consist of a single intense or severe act or multiple persistent or pervasive acts.

C.6.b. Reports to Third Parties

Counselors are accurate, honest, and objective in reporting their professional activities and judgments to appropriate third parties, including courts, health insurance companies, and those who are the recipients of evaluation reports. *(See B.3., E.4.)*

C.6.c. Media Presentations

When counselors provide advice or comment by means of public lectures, demonstrations, radio or television programs, prerecorded tapes, technology-based applications, printed articles, mailed material, or other media, they take reasonable precautions to ensure that

1. the statements are based on appropriate professional counseling literature and practice,
2. the statements are otherwise consistent with the *ACA Code of Ethics,* and
3. the recipients of the information are not encouraged to infer that a professional counseling relationship has been established.

C.6.d. Exploitation of Others

Counselors do not exploit others in their professional relationships. *(See C.3.e.)*

C.6.e. Scientific Bases for Treatment Modalities

Counselors use techniques/procedures/modalities that are grounded in theory and/or have an empirical or scientific foundation. Counselors who do not must define the techniques/procedures as "unproven" or "developing" and explain the potential risks and ethical considerations of using such techniques/procedures and take steps to protect clients from possible harm. *(See A.4.a., E.5.c., E.5.d.)*

C.7. Responsibility to Other Professionals

C.7.a. Personal Public Statements

When making personal statements in a public context, counselors clarify that they are speaking from their personal perspectives and that they are not speaking on behalf of all counselors or the profession.

SECTION D
RELATIONSHIPS WITH OTHER PROFESSIONALS

Introduction

Professional counselors recognize that the quality of their interactions with colleagues can influence the quality of services provided to clients. They work to become knowledgeable about colleagues within and outside the field of counseling. Counselors develop positive working relationships and systems of communication with colleagues to enhance services to clients.

D.1. Relationships With Colleagues, Employers, and Employees

D.1.a. Different Approaches

Counselors are respectful of approaches to counseling services that differ from their own. Counselors are respectful of traditions and practices of other professional groups with which they work.

D.1.b. Forming Relationships

Counselors work to develop and strengthen interdisciplinary relations with colleagues from other disciplines to best serve clients.

D.1.c. Interdisciplinary Teamwork

Counselors who are members of interdisciplinary teams delivering multifaceted services to clients keep the focus on how to best serve the clients. They participate in and contribute to decisions that affect the well-being of clients by drawing on the perspectives, values, and experiences of the counseling profession and those of colleagues from other disciplines. *(See A.1.a.)*

D.1.d. Confidentiality

When counselors are required by law, institutional policy, or extraordinary circumstances to serve in more than one role in judicial or administrative proceedings, they clarify role expectations and the parameters of confidentiality with their colleagues. *(See B.1.c., B.1.d., B.2.c., B.2.d., B.3.b.)*

D.1.e. Establishing Professional and Ethical Obligations

Counselors who are members of interdisciplinary teams clarify professional and ethical obligations of the team as a whole and of its individual members. When a team decision raises ethical concerns, counselors first attempt to resolve the concern within the team. If they cannot reach resolution among team members, counselors pursue other avenues to address their concerns consistent with client well-being.

D.1.f. Personnel Selection and Assignment

Counselors select competent staff and assign responsibilities compatible with their skills and experiences.

D.1.g. Employer Policies

The acceptance of employment in an agency or institution implies that counselors are in agreement with its general policies and principles. Counselors strive to reach agreement with employers as to acceptable standards of conduct that allow for changes in institutional policy conducive to the growth and development of clients.

D.1.h. Negative Conditions

Counselors alert their employers of inappropriate policies and practices. They attempt to effect changes in such policies or procedures through constructive action within the organization. When such policies are potentially disruptive or damaging to clients or may limit the effectiveness of services provided and change cannot be effected, counselors take appropriate further action. Such action may include referral to appropriate certification, accreditation, or state licensure organizations, or voluntary termination of employment.

D.1.i. Protection From Punitive Action

Counselors take care not to harass or dismiss an employee who has acted in a responsible and ethical manner to expose inappropriate employer policies or practices.

D.2. Consultation

D.2.a. Consultant Competency

Counselors take reasonable steps to ensure that they have the appropriate resources and competencies when providing consultation services. Counselors provide appropriate referral resources when requested or needed. *(See C.2.a.)*

D.2.b. Understanding Consultees

When providing consultation, counselors attempt to develop with their consultees a clear understanding of problem definition, goals for change, and predicted consequences of interventions selected.

D.2.c. Consultant Goals

The consulting relationship is one in which consultee adaptability and growth toward self-direction are consistently encouraged and cultivated.

D.2.d. Informed Consent in Consultation

When providing consultation, counselors have an obligation to review, in writing and verbally, the rights and responsibilities of both counselors and consultees. Counselors use clear and understandable language to inform all parties involved about the purpose of the services to be provided, relevant costs, potential risks and benefits, and the limits of confidentiality. Working in conjunction with the consultee, counselors attempt to develop a clear definition of the problem, goals for change, and predicted consequences of interventions that are culturally responsive and appropriate to the needs of consultees. *(See A.2.a., A.2.b.)*

<u>SECTION E</u>

EVALUATION, ASSESSMENT, AND INTERPRETATION

Introduction

Counselors use assessment instruments as one component of the counseling process, taking into account the client personal and cultural context. Counselors promote the well-being of individual clients or groups of clients by developing and using appropriate educational, psychological, and career assessment instruments.

E.1. General

E.1.a. Assessment

The primary purpose of educational, psychological, and career assessment is to provide measurements that are valid and reliable in either comparative or absolute terms. These include, but are not limited to, measurements of ability, personality, interest, intelligence, achievement, and performance. Counselors recognize the need to interpret the statements in this section as applying to both quantitative and qualitative assessments.

E.1.b. Client Welfare

Counselors do not misuse assessment results and interpretations, and they take reasonable steps to prevent others from misusing the information these techniques provide. They respect the client's right to know the results, the interpretations made, and the bases for counselors' conclusions and recommendations.

E.2. Competence to Use and Interpret Assessment Instruments

E.2.a. Limits of Competence

Counselors utilize only those testing and assessment services for which they have been trained and are competent. Counselors using technology-assisted test interpretations are trained in the construct being measured and the specific instrument being used prior to using its technology-based application. Counselors take reasonable measures to ensure the proper use of psychological and career assessment techniques by persons under their supervision. (See A.12.)

E.2.b. Appropriate Use

Counselors are responsible for the appropriate application, scoring, interpretation, and use of assessment instruments relevant to the needs of the client, whether they score and interpret such assessments themselves or use technology or other services.

E.2.c. Decisions Based on Results

Counselors responsible for decisions involving individuals or policies that are based on assessment results have a thorough understanding of educational, psychological, and career measurement, including validation criteria, assessment research, and guidelines for assessment development and use.

E.3. Informed Consent in Assessment

E.3.a. Explanation to Clients

Prior to assessment, counselors explain the nature and purposes of assessment and the specific use of results by potential recipients. The explanation will be given in the language of the client (or other legally authorized person on behalf of the client), unless an explicit exception has been agreed upon in advance. Counselors consider the client's personal or cultural context, the level of the client's understanding of the results, and the impact of the results on the client. (See A.2., A.12.g., F.1.c.)

E.3.b. Recipients of Results

Counselors consider the examinee's welfare, explicit understandings, and prior agreements in determining who receives the assessment results. Counselors include accurate and appropriate interpretations with any release of individual or group assessment results. *(See B.2.c., B.5.)*

E.4. Release of Data to Qualified Professionals

Counselors release assessment data in which the client is identified only with the consent of the client or the client's legal representative. Such data are released only to persons recognized by counselors as qualified to interpret the data. *(See B.1., B.3., B.6.b.)*

E.5. Diagnosis of Mental Disorders

E.5.a. Proper Diagnosis

Counselors take special care to provide proper diagnosis of mental disorders. Assessment techniques (including personal interview) used to determine client care (e.g., locus of treatment, type of treatment, or recommended follow-up) are carefully selected and appropriately used.

E.5.b. Cultural Sensitivity

Counselors recognize that culture affects the manner in which clients' problems are defined. Clients' socioeconomic and cultural experiences are considered when diagnosing mental disorders. *(See A.2.c.)*

E.5.c. Historical and Social Prejudices in the Diagnosis of Pathology

Counselors recognize historical and social prejudices in the misdiagnosis and pathologizing of certain individuals and groups and the role of mental health professionals in perpetuating these prejudices through diagnosis and treatment.

E.5.d. Refraining From Diagnosis

Counselors may refrain from making and/or reporting a diagnosis if they believe it would cause harm to the client or others.

E.6. Instrument Selection

E.6.a. Appropriateness of Instruments

Counselors carefully consider the validity, reliability, psychometric limitations, and appropriateness of instruments when selecting assessments.

E.6.b. Referral Information

If a client is referred to a third party for assessment, the counselor provides specific referral questions and sufficient objective data about the client to ensure that appropriate assessment instruments are utilized. *(See A.9.b., B.3.)*

E.6.c. Culturally Diverse Populations

Counselors are cautious when selecting assessments for culturally diverse populations to avoid the use of instruments that lack appropriate psychometric properties for the client population. *(See A.2.c., E.5.b.)*

E.7. Conditions of Assessment Administration
(See A.12.b, A.12.d.)

E.7.a. Administration Conditions

Counselors administer assessments under the same conditions that were established in their standardization.

When assessments are not administered under standard conditions, as may be necessary to accommodate clients with disabilities, or when unusual behavior or irregularities occur during the administration, those conditions are noted in interpretation, and the results may be designated as invalid or of questionable validity.

E.7.b. Technological Administration

Counselors ensure that administration programs function properly and provide clients with accurate results when technological or other electronic methods are used for assessment administration.

E.7.c. Unsupervised Assessments

Unless the assessment instrument is designed, intended, and validated for self-administration and/or scoring, counselors do not permit inadequately supervised use.

E.7.d. Disclosure of Favorable Conditions

Prior to administration of assessments, conditions that produce most favorable assessment results are made known to the examinee.

E.8. Multicultural Issues/ Diversity in Assessment

Counselors use with caution assessment techniques that were normed on populations other than that of the client. Counselors recognize the effects of age, color, culture, disability, ethnic group, gender, race, language preference, religion, spirituality, sexual orientation, and socioeconomic status on test administration and interpretation, and place test results in proper perspective with other relevant factors. *(See A.2.c., E.5.b.)*

E.9. Scoring and Interpretation of Assessments

E.9.a. Reporting

In reporting assessment results, counselors indicate reservations that exist regarding validity or reliability due to circumstances of the assessment or the inappropriateness of the norms for the person tested.

E.9.b. Research Instruments

Counselors exercise caution when interpreting the results of research instruments not having sufficient technical data to support respondent results. The specific purposes for the use of such instruments are stated explicitly to the examinee.

E.9.c. Assessment Services

Counselors who provide assessment scoring and interpretation services to support the assessment process confirm the validity of such interpretations. They accurately describe the purpose, norms, validity, reliability, and applications of the procedures and any special qualifications applicable to their use. The public offering of an automated test interpretations service is considered a professional-to-professional consultation. The formal responsibility of the consultant is to the consultee, but the ultimate and overriding responsibility is to the client. *(See D.2.)*

E.10. Assessment Security

Counselors maintain the integrity and security of tests and other assessment techniques consistent with legal and contractual obligations. Counselors do not appropriate, reproduce, or modify published assessments or parts thereof without acknowledgment and permission from the publisher.

E.11. Obsolete Assessments and Outdated Results

Counselors do not use data or results from assessments that are obsolete or outdated for the current purpose. Counselors make every effort to prevent the misuse of obsolete measures and assessment data by others.

E.12. Assessment Construction

Counselors use established scientific procedures, relevant standards, and current professional knowledge for assessment design in the development, publication, and utilization of educational and psychological assessment techniques.

E.13. Forensic Evaluation: Evaluation for Legal Proceedings

E.13.a. Primary Obligations

When providing forensic evaluations, the primary obligation of counselors is to produce objective findings that can be substantiated based on information and techniques appropriate to the evaluation, which may include examination of the individual and/or review of records. Counselors are entitled to form professional opinions based on their professional knowledge and expertise that can be supported by the data gathered in evaluations. Counselors will define the limits of their reports or testimony, especially when an examination of the individual has not been conducted.

E.13.b. Consent for Evaluation

Individuals being evaluated are informed in writing that the relationship is for the purposes of an evaluation and is not counseling in nature, and entities or individuals who will receive the evaluation report are identified. Written consent to be evaluated is obtained from those being evaluated unless a court orders evaluations to be conducted without the written consent of individuals being evaluated. When children or vulnerable adults are being evaluated, informed written consent is obtained from a parent or guardian.

E.13.c. Client Evaluation Prohibited

Counselors do not evaluate individuals for forensic purposes they currently counsel or individuals they have counseled in the past. Counselors do not accept as counseling clients individuals they are evaluating or individuals they have evaluated in the past for forensic purposes.

E.13.d. Avoid Potentially Harmful Relationships

Counselors who provide forensic evaluations avoid potentially harmful professional or personal relationships with family members, romantic partners, and close friends of individuals they are evaluating or have evaluated in the past.

SECTION F

SUPERVISION, TRAINING, AND TEACHING

Introduction

Counselors aspire to foster meaningful and respectful professional relationships and to maintain appropriate boundaries with supervisees and students. Counselors have theoretical and pedagogical foundations for their work and aim to be fair, accurate, and honest in their assessments of counselors-in-training.

F.1. Counselor Supervision and Client Welfare

F.1.a. Client Welfare

A primary obligation of counseling supervisors is to monitor the services provided by other counselors or counselors-in-training. Counseling supervisors monitor client welfare and supervisee clinical performance and professional development. To fulfill these obligations, supervisors meet regularly with supervisees to review case notes, samples of clinical work, or live observations. Supervisees have a responsibility to understand and follow the *ACA Code of Ethics*.

F.1.b. Counselor Credentials

Counseling supervisors work to ensure that clients are aware of the qualifications of the supervisees who render services to the clients. *(See A.2.b.)*

F.1.c. Informed Consent and Client Rights

Supervisors make supervisees aware of client rights including the protection of client privacy and confidentiality in the counseling relationship. Supervisees provide clients with professional disclosure information and inform them of how the supervision process influences the limits of confidentiality. Supervisees make clients aware of who will have access to records of the counseling relationship and how these records will be used. *(See A.2.b., B.1.d.)*

F.2. Counselor Supervision Competence

F.2.a. Supervisor Preparation

Prior to offering clinical supervision services, counselors are trained in supervision methods and techniques. Counselors who offer clinical supervision services regularly pursue continuing education activities including both counseling and supervision topics and skills. *(See C.2.a., C.2.f.)*

F.2.b. Multicultural Issues/ Diversity in Supervision

Counseling supervisors are aware of and address the role of multiculturalism/diversity in the supervisory relationship.

F.3. Supervisory Relationships

F.3.a. Relationship Boundaries With Supervisees

Counseling supervisors clearly define and maintain ethical professional, personal, and social relationships with their supervisees. Counseling supervisors avoid nonprofessional relationships with current supervisees. If supervisors must assume other professional roles (e.g., clinical and administrative supervisor, instructor) with supervisees, they work to minimize potential conflicts and explain to supervisees the expectations and responsibilities associated with each role. They do not engage in any form of nonprofessional interaction that may compromise the supervisory relationship.

F.3.b. Sexual Relationships

Sexual or romantic interactions or relationships with current supervisees are prohibited.

F.3.c. Sexual Harassment

Counseling supervisors do not condone or subject supervisees to sexual harassment. *(See C.6.a.)*

F.3.d. Close Relatives and Friends

Counseling supervisors avoid accepting close relatives, romantic partners, or friends as supervisees.

F.3.e. Potentially Beneficial Relationships

Counseling supervisors are aware of the power differential in their relationships with supervisees. If they believe nonprofessional relationships with a supervisee may be potentially beneficial to the supervisee, they take precautions similar to those taken by counselors when working with clients. Examples of potentially beneficial interactions or relationships include attending a formal ceremony; hospital visits; providing support during a stressful event; or mutual membership in a professional association, organization, or community. Counseling supervisors engage in open discussions with supervisees when they consider entering into relationships with them outside of their roles as clinical and/or administrative supervisors. Before engaging in nonprofessional relationships, supervisors discuss with supervisees and document the rationale for such interactions, potential benefits or drawbacks, and anticipated consequences for the supervisee. Supervisors clarify the specific nature and limitations of the additional role(s) they will have with the supervisee.

F.4. Supervisor Responsibilities

F.4.a. Informed Consent for Supervision

Supervisors are responsible for incorporating into their supervision the principles of informed consent and participation. Supervisors inform supervisees of the policies and procedures to which they are to adhere and the mechanisms for due process appeal of individual supervisory actions.

F.4.b. Emergencies and Absences

Supervisors establish and communicate to supervisees procedures for contacting them or, in their absence, alternative on-call supervisors to assist in handling crises.

F.4.c. Standards for Supervisees

Supervisors make their supervisees aware of professional and ethical standards and legal responsibilities.

Supervisors of postdegree counselors encourage these counselors to adhere to professional standards of practice. *(See C.1.)*

F.4.d. Termination of the Supervisory Relationship

Supervisors or supervisees have the right to terminate the supervisory relationship with adequate notice. Reasons for withdrawal are provided to the other party. When cultural, clinical, or professional issues are crucial to the viability of the supervisory relationship, both parties make efforts to resolve differences. When termination is warranted, supervisors make appropriate referrals to possible alternative supervisors.

F.5. Counseling Supervision Evaluation, Remediation, and Endorsement

F.5.a. Evaluation

Supervisors document and provide supervisees with ongoing performance appraisal and evaluation feedback and schedule periodic formal evaluative sessions throughout the supervisory relationship.

F.5.b. Limitations

Through ongoing evaluation and appraisal, supervisors are aware of the limitations of supervisees that might impede performance. Supervisors assist supervisees in securing remedial assistance when needed. They recommend dismissal from training programs, applied counseling settings, or state or voluntary professional credentialing processes when those supervisees are unable to provide competent professional services. Supervisors seek consultation and document their decisions to dismiss or refer supervisees for assistance. They ensure that supervisees are aware of options available to them to address such decisions. *(See C.2.g.)*

F.5.c. Counseling for Supervisees

If supervisees request counseling, supervisors provide them with acceptable referrals. Counselors do not provide counseling services to supervisees. Supervisors address interpersonal competencies in terms of the impact of these issues on clients, the supervisory relationship, and professional functioning. *(See F.3.a.)*

F.5.d. Endorsement

Supervisors endorse supervisees for certification, licensure, employment, or completion of an academic or training program only when they believe supervisees are qualified for the endorsement. Regardless of qualifications, supervisors do not endorse supervisees whom they believe to be impaired in any way that would interfere with the performance of the duties associated with the endorsement.

F.6. Responsibilities of Counselor Educators

F.6.a. Counselor Educators

Counselor educators who are responsible for developing, implementing, and supervising educational programs are skilled as teachers and practitioners. They are knowledgeable regarding the ethical, legal, and regulatory aspects of the profession, are skilled in applying that knowledge, and make students and supervisees aware of their responsibilities. Counselor educators conduct counselor education and training programs in an ethical manner and serve as role models for professional behavior. *(See C.1., C.2.a., C.2.c.)*

F.6.b. Infusing Multicultural Issues/Diversity

Counselor educators infuse material related to multiculturalism/diversity into all courses and workshops for the development of professional counselors.

F.6.c. Integration of Study and Practice

Counselor educators establish education and training programs that integrate academic study and supervised practice.

F.6.d. Teaching Ethics

Counselor educators make students and supervisees aware of the ethical responsibilities and standards of the profession and the ethical responsibilities of students to the profession. Counselor educators infuse ethical considerations throughout the curriculum. *(See C.1.)*

F.6.e. Peer Relationships

Counselor educators make every effort to ensure that the rights of peers are not compromised when students or supervisees lead counseling groups or provide clinical supervision. Counselor educators take steps to ensure that students and supervisees understand they have the same ethical obligations as counselor educators, trainers, and supervisors.

F.6.f. Innovative Theories and Techniques

When counselor educators teach counseling techniques/procedures that are innovative, without an empirical foundation, or without a well-grounded theoretical foundation, they define the counseling techniques/procedures as "unproven" or "developing" and explain to students the potential risks and ethical considerations of using such techniques/procedures.

F.6.g. Field Placements

Counselor educators develop clear policies within their training programs regarding field placement and other clinical experiences. Counselor educators provide clearly stated roles and responsibilities for the student or supervisee, the site supervisor, and the program supervisor. They confirm that site supervisors are qualified to provide supervision and inform site supervisors of their professional and ethical responsibilities in this role.

F.6.h. Professional Disclosure

Before initiating counseling services, counselors-in-training disclose their status as students and explain how this status affects the limits of confidentiality. Counselor educators ensure that the clients at field placements are aware of the services rendered and the qualifications of the students and supervisees rendering those services. Students and supervisees obtain client permission before they use any information concerning the counseling relationship in the training process. *(See A.2.b.)*

F.7. Student Welfare

F.7.a. Orientation

Counselor educators recognize that orientation is a developmental process that continues throughout the educational and clinical training of students. Counseling faculty provide prospective students with information about the counselor education program's expectations:

1. the type and level of skill and knowledge acquisition required for successful completion of the training;
2. program training goals, objectives, and mission, and subject matter to be covered;
3. bases for evaluation;
4. training components that encourage self-growth or self-disclosure as part of the training process;
5. the type of supervision settings and requirements of the sites for required clinical field experiences;
6. student and supervisee evaluation and dismissal policies and procedures; and
7. up-to-date employment prospects for graduates.

F.7.b. Self-Growth Experiences

Counselor education programs delineate requirements for self-disclosure or self-growth experiences in their admission and program materials. Counselor educators use professional judgment when designing training experiences they conduct that require student and supervisee self-growth or self-disclosure. Students and supervisees are made aware of the ramifications their self-disclosure may have when counselors whose primary role as teacher, trainer, or supervisor requires acting on ethical obligations to the profession. Evaluative components of experiential training experiences explicitly delineate predetermined academic standards that are separate and do not depend on the student's level of self-disclosure. Counselor educators may require trainees to seek professional help to address any personal concerns that may be affecting their competency.

F.8. Student Responsibilities

F.8.a. Standards for Students

Counselors-in-training have a responsibility to understand and follow the *ACA Code of Ethics* and adhere to applicable laws, regulatory policies, and rules and policies governing professional staff behavior at the agency or placement setting. Students have the same obligation to clients as those required of professional counselors. *(See C.1., H.1.)*

F.8.b. Impairment

Counselors-in-training refrain from offering or providing counseling services when their physical, mental, or emotional problems are likely to harm a client or others. They are alert to the signs of impairment, seek assistance for problems, and notify their program supervisors when they are aware that they are unable to effectively provide services. In addition, they seek appropriate professional services for themselves to remediate the problems that are interfering with their ability to provide services to others. *(See A.1., C.2.d., C.2.g.)*

F.9. Evaluation and Remediation of Students

F.9.a. Evaluation

Counselors clearly state to students, prior to and throughout the training program, the levels of competency expected, appraisal methods, and timing of evaluations for both didactic and clinical competencies. Counselor educators provide students with ongoing performance appraisal and evaluation feedback throughout the training program.

F.9.b. Limitations

Counselor educators, throughout ongoing evaluation and appraisal, are aware of and address the inability of some students to achieve counseling competencies that might impede performance. Counselor educators

1. assist students in securing remedial assistance when needed,
2. seek professional consultation and document their decision to dismiss or refer students for assistance, and
3. ensure that students have recourse in a timely manner to address decisions to require them to seek assistance or to dismiss them and provide students with due process according to institutional policies and procedures. *(See C.2.g.)*

F.9.c. Counseling for Students

If students request counseling or if counseling services are required as part of a remediation process, counselor educators provide acceptable referrals.

F.10. Roles and Relationships Between Counselor Educators and Students

F.10.a. Sexual or Romantic Relationships

Sexual or romantic interactions or relationships with current students are prohibited.

F.10.b. Sexual Harassment

Counselor educators do not condone or subject students to sexual harassment. *(See C.6.a.)*

F.10.c. Relationships With Former Students

Counselor educators are aware of the power differential in the relationship between faculty and students. Faculty members foster open discussions with former students when considering engaging in a social, sexual, or other intimate relationship. Faculty members discuss with the former student how their former relationship may affect the change in relationship.

F.10.d. Nonprofessional Relationships

Counselor educators avoid nonprofessional or ongoing professional relationships with students in which there is a risk of potential harm to the student or that may compromise the training experience or grades assigned. In addition, counselor educators do not accept any form of professional services, fees, commissions, reimbursement, or remuneration from a site for student or supervisee placement.

F.10.e. Counseling Services

Counselor educators do not serve as counselors to current students unless this is a brief role associated with a training experience.

F.10.f. Potentially Beneficial Relationships

Counselor educators are aware of the power differential in the relationship between faculty and students. If they believe a nonprofessional relationship with a student may be potentially beneficial to the student, they take precautions similar to those taken by counselors when working with clients. Examples of potentially beneficial interactions or relationships include, but are not limited to, attending a formal ceremony; hospital visits; providing support during a stressful event; or mutual membership in a professional association, organization, or community. Counselor educators engage in open discussions with students when they consider entering into relationships with students outside of their roles as teachers and supervisors. They discuss with students the rationale for such interactions, the potential benefits and drawbacks, and the anticipated consequences for the student. Educators clarify the specific nature and limitations of the additional role(s) they will have with the student prior to engaging

in a nonprofessional relationship. Nonprofessional relationships with students should be time-limited and initiated with student consent.

F.11. Multicultural/ Diversity Competence in Counselor Education and Training Programs

F.11.a. Faculty Diversity

Counselor educators are committed to recruiting and retaining a diverse faculty.

F.11.b. Student Diversity

Counselor educators actively attempt to recruit and retain a diverse student body. Counselor educators demonstrate commitment to multicultural/ diversity competence by recognizing and valuing diverse cultures and types of abilities students bring to the training experience. Counselor educators provide appropriate accommodations that enhance and support diverse student well-being and academic performance.

F.11.c. Multicultural/Diversity Competence

Counselor educators actively infuse multicultural/diversity competency in their training and supervision practices. They actively train students to gain awareness, knowledge, and skills in the competencies of multicultural practice. Counselor educators include case examples, role-plays, discussion questions, and other classroom activities that promote and represent various cultural perspectives.

SECTION G
RESEARCH AND PUBLICATION

Introduction

Counselors who conduct research are encouraged to contribute to the knowledge base of the profession and promote a clearer understanding of the conditions that lead to a healthy and more just society. Counselors support efforts of researchers by participating fully and willingly whenever possible. Counselors minimize bias and respect diversity in designing and implementing research programs.

G.1. Research Responsibilities

G.1.a. Use of Human Research Participants

Counselors plan, design, conduct, and report research in a manner that is consistent with pertinent ethical principles, federal and state laws, host institutional regulations, and scientific standards governing research with human research participants.

G.1.b. Deviation From Standard Practice

Counselors seek consultation and observe stringent safeguards to protect the rights of research participants when a research problem suggests a deviation from standard or acceptable practices.

G.1.c. Independent Researchers

When independent researchers do not have access to an Institutional Review Board (IRB), they should consult with researchers who are familiar with IRB procedures to provide appropriate safeguards.

G.1.d. Precautions to Avoid Injury

Counselors who conduct research with human participants are responsible for the welfare of participants throughout the research process and should take reasonable precautions to avoid causing injurious psychological, emotional, physical, or social effects to participants.

G.1.e. Principal Researcher Responsibility

The ultimate responsibility for ethical research practice lies with the principal researcher. All others involved in the research activities share ethical obligations and responsibility for their own actions.

G.1.f. Minimal Interference

Counselors take reasonable precautions to avoid causing disruptions in the lives of research participants that could be caused by their involvement in research.

G.1.g. Multicultural/Diversity Considerations in Research

When appropriate to research goals, counselors are sensitive to incorporating research procedures that take into account cultural considerations. They seek consultation when appropriate.

G.2. Rights of Research Participants
(See A.2., A.7.)

G.2.a. Informed Consent in Research

Individuals have the right to consent to become research participants. In seeking consent, counselors use language that

1. accurately explains the purpose and procedures to be followed,
2. identifies any procedures that are experimental or relatively untried,
3. describes any attendant discomforts and risks,
4. describes any benefits or changes in individuals or organizations that might be reasonably expected,
5. discloses appropriate alternative procedures that would be advantageous for participants,
6. offers to answer any inquiries concerning the procedures,
7. describes any limitations on confidentiality,
8. describes the format and potential target audiences for the dissemination of research findings, and
9. instructs participants that they are free to withdraw their consent and to discontinue participation in the project at any time without penalty.

G.2.b. Deception

Counselors do not conduct research involving deception unless alternative procedures are not feasible and the prospective value of the research justifies the deception. If such deception has the potential to cause physical or emotional harm to research participants, the research is not conducted, regardless of prospective value. When the methodological requirements of a study necessitate concealment or deception, the investigator explains the reasons for this action as soon as possible during the debriefing.

G.2.c. Student/Supervisee Participation

Researchers who involve students or supervisees in research make clear to them that the decision regarding whether or not to participate in research activities does not affect one's academic standing or supervisory relationship. Students or supervisees who choose not to participate in educational research are provided with an appropriate alternative to fulfill their academic or clinical requirements.

G.2.d. Client Participation

Counselors conducting research involving clients make clear in the informed consent process that clients are free to choose whether or not to participate in research activities. Counselors take necessary precautions to protect clients from adverse consequences of declining or withdrawing from participation.

G.2.e. Confidentiality of Information

Information obtained about research participants during the course of an investigation is confidential. When the possibility exists that others may obtain access to such information, ethical research practice requires that the possibility, together with the plans for protecting confidentiality, be explained to participants as a part of the procedure for obtaining informed consent.

G.2.f. Persons Not Capable of Giving Informed Consent

When a person is not capable of giving informed consent, counselors provide an appropriate explanation to, obtain agreement for participation from, and obtain the appropriate consent of a legally authorized person.

G.2.g. Commitments to Participants

Counselors take reasonable measures to honor all commitments to research participants. *(See A.2.c.)*

G.2.h. Explanations After Data Collection

After data are collected, counselors provide participants with full clarification of the nature of the study to remove any misconceptions participants might have regarding the research. Where scientific or human values justify delaying or withholding information, counselors take reasonable measures to avoid causing harm.

G.2.i. Informing Sponsors

Counselors inform sponsors, institutions, and publication channels regarding research procedures and outcomes. Counselors ensure that appropriate bodies and authorities are given pertinent information and acknowledgment.

G.2.j. Disposal of Research Documents and Records

Within a reasonable period of time following the completion of a research project or study, counselors take steps to destroy records or documents (audio, video, digital, and written) containing confidential data or information that identifies research participants. When records are of an artistic nature, researchers obtain participant consent with regard to handling of such records or documents. *(See B.4.a., B.6g.)*

G.3. Relationships With Research Participants (When Research Involves Intensive or Extended Interactions)

G.3.a. Nonprofessional Relationships

Nonprofessional relationships with research participants should be avoided.

G.3.b. Relationships With Research Participants

Sexual or romantic counselor–research participant interactions or relationships with current research participants are prohibited.

G.3.c. Sexual Harassment and Research Participants

Researchers do not condone or subject research participants to sexual harassment.

G.3.d. Potentially Beneficial Interactions

When a nonprofessional interaction between the researcher and the research participant may be potentially beneficial, the researcher must document, prior to the interaction (when feasible), the rationale for such an interaction, the potential benefit, and anticipated consequences for the research participant. Such interactions should be initiated with appropriate consent of the research participant. Where unintentional harm occurs to the research participant due to the nonprofessional interaction, the researcher must show evidence of an attempt to remedy such harm.

G.4. Reporting Results

G.4.a. Accurate Results

Counselors plan, conduct, and report research accurately. They provide thorough discussions of the limitations of their data and alternative hypotheses. Counselors do not engage in misleading or fraudulent research, distort data, misrepresent data, or deliberately bias their results. They explicitly mention all variables and conditions known to the investigator that may have affected the outcome of a study or the interpretation of data. They describe the extent to which results are applicable for diverse populations.

G.4.b. Obligation to Report Unfavorable Results

Counselors report the results of any research of professional value. Results that reflect unfavorably on institutions, programs, services, prevailing opinions, or vested interests are not withheld.

G.4.c. Reporting Errors

If counselors discover significant errors in their published research, they take reasonable steps to correct such errors in a correction erratum, or through other appropriate publication means.

G.4.d. Identity of Participants

Counselors who supply data, aid in the research of another person, report research results, or make original data available take due care to disguise the identity of respective participants in the absence of specific authorization from the participants to do otherwise. In situations where participants self-identify their involvement in research studies, researchers take active steps to ensure that data is adapted/changed to protect the identity and welfare of all parties and that discussion of results does not cause harm to participants.

G.4.e. Replication Studies

Counselors are obligated to make available sufficient original research data to qualified professionals who may wish to replicate the study.

G.5. Publication

G.5.a. Recognizing Contributions

When conducting and reporting research, counselors are familiar with and give recognition to previous work on the topic, observe copyright laws, and give full credit to those to whom credit is due.

G.5.b. Plagiarism

Counselors do not plagiarize; that is, they do not present another person's work as their own work.

G.5.c. Review/Republication of Data or Ideas

Counselors fully acknowledge and make editorial reviewers aware of prior publication of ideas or data where such ideas or data are submitted for review or publication.

G.5.d. Contributors

Counselors give credit through joint authorship, acknowledgment, footnote statements, or other appropriate means to those who have contributed significantly to research or concept development in accordance with such contributions. The principal contributor is listed first, and minor technical or professional contributions are acknowledged in notes or introductory statements.

G.5.e. Agreement of Contributors

Counselors who conduct joint research with colleagues or students/supervisees establish agreements in advance regarding allocation of tasks, publication credit, and types of acknowledgment that will be received.

G.5.f. Student Research

For articles that are substantially based on students' course papers, projects, dissertations or theses, and on which students have been the primary contributors, they are listed as principal authors.

G.5.g. Duplicate Submission

Counselors submit manuscripts for consideration to only one journal at a time. Manuscripts that are published in whole or in substantial part in another journal or published work are not submitted for publication without acknowledgment and permission from the previous publication.

G.5.h. Professional Review

Counselors who review material submitted for publication, research, or other scholarly purposes respect the confidentiality and proprietary rights of those who submitted it. Counselors use care to make publication decisions based on valid and defensible standards. Counselors review article submissions in a timely manner and based on their scope and competency in research methodologies. Counselors who serve as reviewers at the request of editors or publishers make every effort to only review materials that are within their scope of competency and use care to avoid personal biases.

Section H

Resolving Ethical Issues

Introduction

Counselors behave in a legal, ethical, and moral manner in the conduct of their professional work. They are aware that client protection and trust in the profession depend on a high level of professional conduct. They hold other counselors to the same standards and are willing to take appropriate action to ensure that these standards are upheld.

Counselors strive to resolve ethical dilemmas with direct and open communication among all parties involved and seek consultation with colleagues and supervisors when necessary. Counselors incorporate ethical practice into their daily professional work. They engage in ongoing professional development regarding current topics in ethical and legal issues in counseling.

H.1. Standards and the Law
(See F.9.a.)

H.1.a. Knowledge

Counselors understand the *ACA Code of Ethics* and other applicable ethics codes from other professional organizations or from certification and licensure bodies of which they are members. Lack of knowledge or misunderstanding of an ethical responsibility is not a defense against a charge of unethical conduct.

H.1.b. Conflicts Between Ethics and Laws

If ethical responsibilities conflict with law, regulations, or other governing legal authority, counselors make known their commitment to the *ACA Code of Ethics* and take steps to resolve the conflict. If the conflict cannot be resolved by such means, counselors may adhere to the requirements of law, regulations, or other governing legal authority.

H.2. Suspected Violations

H.2.a. Ethical Behavior Expected

Counselors expect colleagues to adhere to the *ACA Code of Ethics.* When counselors possess knowledge that raises doubts as to whether another counselor is acting in an ethical manner, they take appropriate action. *(See H.2.b., H.2.c.)*

H.2.b. Informal Resolution

When counselors have reason to believe that another counselor is violating or has violated an ethical standard, they attempt first to resolve the issue informally with the other counselor if feasible, provided such action does not violate confidentiality rights that may be involved.

H.2.c. Reporting Ethical Violations

If an apparent violation has substantially harmed or is likely to substantially harm a person or organization and is not appropriate for informal resolution or is not resolved properly, counselors take further action appropriate to the situation. Such action might include referral to state or national committees on professional ethics, voluntary national certification bodies, state licensing boards, or to the appropriate institutional authorities. This standard does not apply when an intervention would violate confidentiality rights or when counselors have been retained to review the work of another counselor whose professional conduct is in question.

H.2.d. Consultation

When uncertain as to whether a particular situation or course of action may be in violation of the *ACA Code of Ethics,* counselors consult with other counselors who are knowledgeable about ethics and the *ACA Code of Ethics,* with colleagues, or with appropriate authorities

H.2.e. Organizational Conflicts

If the demands of an organization with which counselors are affiliated pose a conflict with the *ACA Code of*

Ethics, counselors specify the nature of such conflicts and express to their supervisors or other responsible officials their commitment to the *ACA Code of Ethics*. When possible, counselors work toward change within the organization to allow full adherence to the *ACA Code of Ethics*. In doing so, they address any confidentiality issues.

H.2.f. Unwarranted Complaints

Counselors do not initiate, participate in, or encourage the filing of ethics complaints that are made with reckless disregard or willful ignorance of facts that would disprove the allegation.

H.2.g. Unfair Discrimination Against Complainants and Respondents

Counselors do not deny persons employment, advancement, admission to academic or other programs, ten-ure, or promotion based solely upon their having made or their being the subject of an ethics complaint. This does not preclude taking action based upon the outcome of such proceedings or considering other appropriate information.

H.3. Cooperation With Ethics Committees

Counselors assist in the process of enforcing the *ACA Code of Ethics*. Counselors cooperate with investigations, proceedings, and requirements of the ACA Ethics Committee or ethics committees of other duly constituted associations or boards having jurisdiction over those charged with a violation. Counselors are familiar with the *ACA Policies and Procedures for Processing Complaints of Ethical Violations* and use it as a reference for assisting in the enforcement of the *ACA Code of Ethics*.

GLOSSARY OF TERMS

Advocacy – promotion of the well-being of individuals and groups, and the counseling profession within systems and organizations. Advocacy seeks to remove barriers and obstacles that inhibit access, growth, and development.

Assent – to demonstrate agreement, when a person is otherwise not capable or competent to give formal consent (e.g., informed consent) to a counseling service or plan.

Client – an individual seeking or referred to the professional services of a counselor for help with problem resolution or decision making.

Counselor – a professional (or a student who is a counselor-in-training) engaged in a counseling practice or other counseling-related services. Counselors fulfill many roles and responsibilities such as counselor educators, researchers, supervisors, practitioners, and consultants.

Counselor Educator – a professional counselor engaged primarily in developing, implementing, and supervising the educational preparation of counselors-in-training.

Counselor Supervisor – a professional counselor who engages in a formal relationship with a practicing counselor or counselor-in-training for the purpose of overseeing that individual's counseling work or clinical skill development.

Culture – membership in a socially constructed way of living, which incorporates collective values, beliefs, norms, boundaries, and lifestyles that are cocreated with others who share similar worldviews comprising biological, psychosocial, historical, psychological, and other factors.

Diversity – the similarities and differences that occur within and across cultures, and the intersection of cultural and social identities.

Documents – any written, digital, audio, visual, or artistic recording of the work within the counseling relationship between counselor and client.

Examinee – a recipient of any professional counseling service that includes educational, psychological, and career appraisal utilizing qualitative or quantitative techniques.

Forensic Evaluation – any formal assessment conducted for court or other legal proceedings.

Multicultural/Diversity Competence – a capacity whereby counselors possess cultural and diversity awareness and knowledge about self and others, and how this awareness and knowledge is applied effectively in practice with clients and client groups.

Multicultural/Diversity Counseling – counseling that recognizes diversity and embraces approaches that support the worth, dignity, potential, and uniqueness of individuals within their historical, cultural, economic, political, and psychosocial contexts.

Student – an individual engaged in formal educational preparation as a counselor-in-training.

Supervisee – a professional counselor or counselor-in-training whose counseling work or clinical skill development is being overseen in a formal supervisory relationship by a qualified trained professional.

Supervisor – counselors who are trained to oversee the professional clinical work of counselors and counselors-in-training.

Teaching – all activities engaged in as part of a formal educational program designed to lead to a graduate degree in counseling.

Training – the instruction and practice of skills related to the counseling profession. Training contributes to the ongoing proficiency of students and professional counselors.

BUILDING AND MAINTAINING A SUCCESSFUL SUPERVISION RELATIONSHIP

Burt Bertram, EdD, LMFT, LMHC (Florida Qualified Supervisor)

CHECKLIST OF SUGGESTIONS

The foundation of a successful clinical supervision relationship is built on the creation of a safe and respectful relationship in which the supervisor models transparency and in so doing encourages the supervisee to be open and honest in the presentation of his or her clinical questions and countertransference concerns. This checklist offers suggestions for creating this type of supervision relationship.

1. Introductions
   a. Supervisor provides
      - professional experience and interests;
      - theoretical orientation;
      - supervision style;
      - relevant personal/familial/cultural background.
   b. Supervisee provides
      - professional interests;
      - prior experience in counseling and/or human services;
      - theoretical orientation;
      - relevant personal/familial/cultural background.
2. Goals
   a. Supervisor
      - makes explicit goals or learning the supervisor believes is developmentally appropriate for the supervisee.
   b. Supervisee
      - defines the goals of his or her practicum, internship, or post-degree supervision requirements.

3. Supervision style
    a. Learning style
        - How does the supervisee learn?
        - How can the supervisor support the learning of the supervisee?
    b. Temperament
        - What is the temperament of the supervisee?
        - What are the implications for communication and learning?
    c. Feedback preferences
        - How does the supervisee prefer to receive feedback (general feedback as well as critical feedback)?
4. Process of supervision
    a. Expectations
        - Supervisor should describe the process of supervision in terms of how time will be structured and what will be expected of the supervisee. (Examples: come to supervison with questions, bring clinical files.)
        - Supervisors should keep in mind information about the supervisee's learning style and feedback preferences.
    b. Role clarification
        - Supervisor should define the activities of supervision (teacher, consultant, expert, etc.) and differentiate supervision from personal counseling.
        - Supervisors should describe the delicate balance of clinical collaboration (between supervisor and supervisee) vs. the responsibility of the supervisor to act as evaluator, gatekeeper, and definer of clinical direction.
5. Regular supervision
    a. Time and place
        - Define the day, time, and place of weekly supervision.
        - Include a process for rescheduling should that be necessary.
6. Emergency/urgent clinical situations
    a. Criteria for immediate supervision
        - Provide direction about the circumstances under which the supervisee should immediately inform the supervisor of clinical developments rather than waiting until the next scheduled supervision session. Examples could include:
            - harm to self or others;
            - manditory reporting issues (abuse);
            - legal concerns;
            - ethical conflicts.
    b. How to interrupt
        - Provide the process for interrupting the supervisior with an urgent concern as well as contact information (phone numbers) in the event the supervisor is not physically available.

    c. Alternate supervision
- Provide name/contact information for an alternative supervisor in the event the primary supervisor is completely unavailable.

7. Supervisee strengths
    a. Remain alert to perceiving, commenting on, and helping the supervisee to more fully utilize emerging clinical strengths and administrative/writing competence as well as existing life experience or character strengths.

8. Agency functioning
    a. Overview
- Provide an overview of the "big picture" of the clinical process of the agency for
  - initial contact of new client;
  - intake and/or assessment;
  - development of treatment approach/plan;
  - treatment approach/process;
  - definition of successful treatment;
  - termination or closure process;
  - follow-up.

    b. Protocols
- Provide agency protocols for
  - client threat of harm to self;
  - threat of harm to others;
  - abuse reporting;
  - legal or ethical concerns;
  - record keeping/documentation;
  - administrative/staff meetings.

9. Make explicit
    a. Make a commitment to make explicit any issue or concern that has a bearing on supervisee learning and clinical effectiveness, and invite the supervisee to do the same.
    b. Describe the checking-in process, in which periodically the supervisor will check in with the supervisee to solicit feedback on the supervision process and the supervision relationship.

10. Working with clients
    a. Client selection
- Describe the process by which the supervisee will have direct access to clients (observation, cotherapy, supervised caseload). Help the supervisee understand what is expected of him or her in order to be ready for a supervised caseload.

    b. Record keeping
- Describe the record-keeping/documentation requirements of the agency and assure the supervisee that he or she will receive adequate coaching.

c. Taping (if appropriate)
  • Discuss the process for securing written authorization for taping of client counseling sessions.
11. Preventing and/or responding to inevitable bumps in the road
  a. Inevitably most supervisees will encounter some bump in the road during their training experience. Most of these obstacles (lack of knowledge, lack of skill, lack of confidence, countertransference, interpersonal tension with other staff members, exhaustion/burn-out, and others) are developmentally inevitable.
  b. One of the most important dimensions of good supervision is to assist the supervisee through these inevitable bumps in the road—without slipping into becoming the supervisee's therapist. Walking this line is challenging but critical.
12. Faculty consultation (appropriate for post-degree practicum or internship)
  a. Supervisors are invited and encouraged at any time to consult with the supervisee's faculty contact person (assuming the supervisee is a student). If there is a concern, don't wait until the situation has escalated to a crisis. Please contact the faculty member so collaborative problem-solving discussions can be initiated. In the interest of transparency and trust (except in the rarest of circumstances), supervisors are encouraged to tell each supervisee of their intention to consult with faculty.

TOP TEN
RISK MANAGEMENT STRATEGIES

1. *Risk Management Tool Kit*
   Create a file or binder in which you keep copies of all relevant risk management materials, including
   a. *ethical codes*
      - relevant code(s) of ethics: ACA, ASCA, AMHCA, AAMFT, etc.
      - ethical decision-making model (Corey, Corey, & Callanan, 2007)
   b. *laws/statutes*
      - counselor licensure statute and rules
      - abuse reporting laws
      - civil commitment (mental health and/or substance abuse)
      - HIPAA
   c. *articles/checklist*
      - subpoena checklist (see chapter 5)
   d. *attorney*
      - list of local attorneys who have expertise in mental health and health law
   Annually review these documents to ensure current familiarity, and update when/as appropriate.

2. *Colleague Consultation*
   Two heads are better than one. Obtain colleague consultation when confronted with difficult counseling situations. To that end, identify colleagues for whom you have professional regard and establish in advance of the need a reciprocal consultation relationship.

3. *Informed Consent*
   Develop an informed consent process (written document, verbal explanation, and commitment to reviewing consent as circumstances change); be sure the process clearly defines confidentiality, privilege, and privacy guidelines as well as limits and exceptions to confidentiality, privilege, and privacy (see chapters 2, 3, and 4).

4. *Institution Policies*
   Know the internal policies that regulate the practice of counseling in your school or agency. Adhere to these policies. If there are policies that are at odds with legal or ethical requirements, bring these to the attention of appropriate officers within the institution.

5. *Termination and Abandonment*
   Avoid terminating a client who is in a crisis. Otherwise, termination should be accomplished, when appropriate, after giving adequate notice and referrals (see chapter 2).

6. *Document Clinical Decision Making*
   Properly and fully document the circumstances surrounding difficult or dangerous client situations (abuse, threats of harm to self or others, etc.), decisions made, action taken, and follow-up (see chapter 9).

7. *Manage Co-occurring Relationships*
   Co-occurring relationship (dual roles) must be effectively managed in order to prevent harm to clients. This is true regardless of whether the co-occurring relationship is a regular part of your job responsibilities (school counselors who counsel students and also have other relationships), or evolve from unforeseeable circumstances, or are an intentional/conscious choice. Be mindful of your state licensure board's position on boundary issues, as well as updated guidance in the 2005 *ACA Code of Ethics* on roles and relationships with clients, supervisees, and others (see chapter 8).

8. *Practice Within Your Scope of Competence*
   Recognize and respect the limitations of your competence; expand competence by securing the appropriate education, training, or supervision (see chapter 2).

9. *Supervision*
   Supervisors and supervisees are at risk if supervision is not properly administered. Supervisors and supervisees should be mindful in the selection process to ensure a good fit (theoretical approach, supervision style, availability of supervisor, etc.), clearly define the mutual expectations of both supervisor and supervisee, and monitor to ensure fulfillment of the expectations. If required, engage in regular supervision as defined by statute or policy.

10. *Professional Liability Insurance*
    Obtain and maintain professional liability insurance, preferably coverage that will provide attorney representation if a complaint is brought against you by the state licensure board as well as attorney fees and settlement/damages resulting from a civil lawsuit.

Appendix D

HOW TO ACCESS LAWS AND
FIND A LOCAL ATTORNEY

1. *Know Your Limits*
   Recognize that, as a counselor, you are not a lawyer and that you should not try to solve all legal and ethical dilemmas by yourself.

2. *How to Find Laws Online*
   If you have a citation to a law and want to look up a current version, you may be able to access it on http://www.findlaw.com or http://www.law.cornell.edu, or your state's home Web page. Recognize that the most up-to-date versions of the law may not be available on such Web sites that are of no cost to you. For important issues, contact your local attorney who is likely to have access to paid subscription services such as Westlaw or Lexis. Many state counselor licensure laws and regulations are available on the applicable state's Web site. ACA's *Licensure Requirements for Professional Counselors* (ACA, 2007) is a useful resource on state regulatory requirements; it contains licensure board Web sites and other contact information.

3. *How to Find an Attorney*
   To find an attorney experienced in counselor licensure issues, you should ask other counselors, psychologists, social workers, and psychiatrists in your community who they recommend. Personal referrals are often very helpful in this process. Other attorneys, even the attorney who drafted your will, might be able to recommend a colleague with the expertise you require. You might also look up the attorney in a legal directory (such as http://www.martindale.com or http://www.findlaw.com). You can then pick a state, city, and practice area such as "health care" or "medical malpractice," which may help you to narrow your search. Realize that not all attorneys choose to be listed in such directories. Also, if you are insured through the ACA Insurance Trust, you may call the Trust's helpline to obtain names of local attorneys. You may reach the Trust at 800–347–6647.